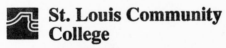

THE AGE OF

EXTREMISM

Also by James Gardner

Culture or Trash?

THE AGE OF

EXTREMISM

THE ENEMIES OF COMPROMISE IN AMERICAN POLITICS, CULTURE, AND RACE RELATIONS

JAMES GARDNER

A BIRCH LANE PRESS BOOK
PUBLISHED BY CAROL PUBLISHING GROUP

A Birch Lane Press Book
Published by Carol Publishing Group
Birch Lane Press is a registered trademark of Carol Communications, Inc.

In Canada: Canadian Manda Group, One Atlantic Avenue, Suite 105, Toronto,
Ontario M6K 3E7

Carol Publishing Group books may be purchased in bulk at special discounts for
sales promotion, fund-raising, or educational purposes. Special editions can be
created to specifications. For details, contact Special Sales Department, Carol
Publishing Group, 120 Enterprise Avenue, Secaucus, N.J. 07094.

Manufactured in the United States of America
10 9 8 7 6 5 4 3 2 1

Library of Congress Cataloging-in-Publication Data

Gardner, James, 1960–
    The age of extremism : the enemies of compromise in American politics,
culture, and race relations / James Gardner.
        p.   cm.
    ISBN 1-55972-388-2 (hc)
    1. United States—Civilization—1970–   2. Radicalism—United
States.   3. United States—Politics and government—1989–   4. United
States—Race relations.   I. Title.
    E169.12.G364   1997
    973.929—dc21   96–51725
                                                                        CIP

FOR KATHRYN MARIS

CONTENTS

AUTHOR TO READER

The middle of humanity thou never knowest,
but the extremity of both ends.
—Shakespeare, *Timon of Athens*, 4.3

This book is an essay in cultural criticism rather than sociology or history. As such it is a subjective evaluation of phenomena that are themselves highly subjective. It deals with the vast proliferation of extremist discourse in contemporary society, as manifested in religion and politics, in civil rights and academia, in popular culture and high culture.

Surely extremism has been present in human societies almost from the beginning of recorded history. Furthermore, some ages invariably have tended more toward extremism than others have. And yet, as this book will try to demonstrate, never before have examples of extreme behavior presented themselves with such formulaic regularity as we encounter today. Indeed, so prevalent has extremist discourse become, compared with earlier periods of human history, and so varied is its assault on the center of society, that it is no exaggeration to characterize the present period as an *age* of extremism.

Now, the backdrop against which this extremism is set seems to be marked by a peculiar malaise—to which the book's first chapter is devoted—that haunts society at the present time. The connection between this malaise and the extremism at the core of the book is twofold. On the one hand, both phenomena can be seen to derive from a single cause that precedes both. I refer to that convulsive change that we have been experiencing for the past generation, a change from an industrial to a postindustrial society. At every level and in every province of society, one feels the effects of this change. The sense that society is changing too quickly, that it is out of control, creates a great and general malaise in society at large.

At the same time, this change itself shocks the extreme right with the specter of a society in which traditional values and traditional privileges are called into question. Furthermore, society's ever-increasing powers of assimilation and cooptation harrow many on the left with the threat of an oppressive, monolithic state that will crush their cherished difference and impose strict conformity on the world. From such fears as these come many of the manifestations of extremist behavior discussed in this book. These in turn only corroborate the vague sense of many people in the center that they are losing control of their lives, that "the world is going crazy." And this sentiment, in turn, confirms the malaise from which many of them suffer in the first place.

In the course of this book, I often invoke terms like *center* and *circumference*. The former is conceived not as a point but as a zone defined and contained by the circumference, that is, by those on the outside of society. This model, which I have found merely convenient, does not pretend to account for all of humanity at the present time. By the "center" I mean roughly the industrialized, or post-industrialized world, rather than agrarian societies. And by the circumference, by the extremes, I mean those who actively reject the center, whatever the nature of their rejection, rather than those who never belonged to the center in the first place, namely immigrants from the third world, the homeless, the insane, and those who admittedly live on the margins of society.

At no time in history, it would seem, have center and circumference been so violently at odds. That conflict, both in its present state and in its likely evolution, is the subject of this book.

THE AGE OF

EXTREMISM

1

THE DISMAY OF AMERICAN SOCIETY

Without quite realizing how it happened, we have become a sad society. We have been troubled before this, but in different ways. Until recently we have been so energetic in our collective happiness that, even when faced with the greatest economic blight in our nation's history, even in the heart of the Great Depression, our citizens felt an innocent, spontaneous camaraderie such as we can only imagine today. There have been tragic nations throughout history: the Jews weeping beside the waters of Babylon, the eternally outraged and exiled Armenians, the perennially oppressed peoples of Russia. But we Americans have not been a party to that sadness. It has been our nature to be happy and hopeful, as befits the citizens of a government which, in principle, is the most liberal and enlightened in human history.

But now that mood appears to be changing. Part of the cause is economic. Though past economic downturns have seemed, at worst, like protracted slumps, what terrifies us about our present circumstances is the prevalent belief that we are witnessing a massive, revolutionary reordering of everything we know, a change that will catastrophically diminish our prospects and deprive us of the benefits we now enjoy. What makes this sadness so strange and incalculable is that it arises amid prosperity. The stock market hit 81 record highs in 1996, and the president said, and we can well believe, that the economy is "the healthiest it's been in three decades."

Indeed, one would be hard put to find a time when the population as a whole was so affluent. Usually it has been far worse off. Our employment rate, close to 95 percent, is the envy of the industrialized world. While the economy grows, according to the figures for 1996, at almost 4 percent a year, the rate of violent crime in major cities has dropped eight percentage points, to the lowest overall rate since 1989. And in New York, traditionally one of the most violent cities, it has dropped 12 percent, to its lowest level in almost thirty years. Meanwhile we are living longer, healthier lives, and we are going to college in record numbers. Our citizens have more television sets, Walkmans, and laptops than ever before—a point that will seem superficial only to superficial minds. One hears such things, and yet the sadness is undiminished.

Little things bring this sadness to the front and center of our consciousness. Here in New York we had a difficult winter in 1996. Record amounts of snow fell on the city, accompanied by temperatures far below normal. The cold, sluggish weather persevered far into the spring, bringing snow in April and chilly weather in May. Then, suddenly, the temperature leapt to 96° F. How did New Yorkers, that famously doughty breed, respond to this atmospheric inclemency? In an article in the *New York Times*, one elderly woman commented, "We had a cold winter. We should have a warm spring. That would be justice. We did not have a warm spring. Now we have this, whatever this is. I say that the weather is like the world: crazy."[1]

A thirty-one-year-old man, a mover, had this to say: "God said, when it comes near the end, you wouldn't know the difference in the weather. You wouldn't be able to tell between summer and winter. You may have noticed that there have been a lot of planes crashing lately. That's in the Bible, too. It says when we're near the end there will be signs in the sky. So I think that's it. We're near the end."[2]

What makes these two reactions significant, however comical they may appear, is that they underscore a pervasive gloom that has settled on a large part of our society. Collectively our society is like a sick man for whom every movement, every sound, and every smell serve as irritants, bringing home to him the sad condition of his life. That bravely resilient and strenuous joy that inspired our forebears, during the Depression, to sing "Happy Days Are Here Again," despite crushing evidence to the contrary, has evaporated utterly. "I was less depressed during the Depression," Ruth K. Goldberg, eighty-four years old, told the *New York Times*. "There was hope then. We were marching and organizing. There seemed to be a future, that life would get better for everyone. Nowadays, you have to be a moron or a right-winger not to be depressed." She proceeded to give an itemized list of grievances which, though specific to her, could have been supplied in one form or another by people from all walks of our society. "The mayor depresses me. Imus [a New York radio personality] depresses me. No respect for the office of president. This culture of violence. The people living on the street. And the fact that we are not making anything anymore, just shoving paper around for mergers and downsizing to make a few people richer."[3]

Even the Unabomber, in the manifesto published in the *Washington Post*, expressed similar sentiments. "The world today seems to be going crazy," he wrote, and he would seem to be in a position to know.

It is easy to find confirmation of such meditations in the culture at large. Toward the end of his novel *American Psycho*, Bret Easton Ellis writes, "Walking down Fifth Avenue around four o'clock in the afternoon, everyone on the street looks sad, the air is full of decay, bodies lie on the cold pavement, miles of it, some are moving, most are not. History is sinking and only a very few seem dimly aware that things are getting bad."[4] In the smugly cynical futuristic film *Strange Days*, we see a man in a Santa Claus suit being mugged as a voice-over comments, "The economy sucks; gas is over a few bucks a gallon, literally kids are shooting each other over recess; the whole thing sucks." Add to this the rasping, anguished melodies of Nirvana's suicidal Kurt Cobain, which are accepted by many as the despairing anthems of the terminally undeceived Generation X, as well as the sadomasochistic chants of

Nine Inch Nails, and you have, from every conceivable direction, the makings of a culture of despair.

Surely this is not the first time anyone has felt this way. Many writers from the beginning of the century, like Spengler in *The Decline of the West*, were moved by a similar spirit. In his notes to *The Waste Land*, T. S. Eliot quotes Hermann Hesse as saying, "Already half of Europe . . . is on the road to Chaos. Drunk and reeling in a state of divine madness, it sings, like Dimitri Karamazoff, its drunken hymns. The bourgeois merely laughs, but the saint and seer listens in tears." The difference between then and now is that this opinion used to be shared by a few members of an overeducated elite; now it has become the common property of men and women of all walks of life. In 1800 the aristocracy said such things about the emerging middle class. In 1900 the middle class shuddered in much the same way at the rise of the working class. In the sixties the older generation felt a similar revulsion in the face of rebellious youth. But nowadays everyone is saying this about everyone else, and some people are even saying it about themselves.

The strength of this conviction is something of a mystery, but several reasons for its pervasiveness come to mind. First, there is a nervous sense that things are changing too drastically, that we are on the brink of something incalculably big, which will alter everything and which we cannot understand. The fact that we are approaching the millennium doesn't help, either. It is amazing how a society that is as unreligious and rationalistic as ours should yet be unable to free itself, in the presence of a new millennium, from its oldest and most primitive fears. Our rationalism will not permit most of us to believe that the end of the world is at hand. But in the silence of our own thought, many of us can spook ourselves into believing that there is some new order on the horizon.

It is the giddy speed of the change, combined with our inability to predict its course with any precision, that causes our greatest dismay. Every six months or so the computer industry reinvents itself, holding out further promises to alter our life for the better, but beyond recognition. The Internet offers a form of communication more revolutionary, we are told, than the invention of movable type. We have created babies in a test tube, and already genetic engineering is altering the way we look and the food we eat. Some scientists believe it may be possible to live for several hundred years, while others believe that exotic new diseases like the Ebola virus may soon wipe out mankind as we know it.

Of course there is a deeper cause, which may be the main cause, of our sadness. But it is one that few people acknowledge and that the politician and television commentator never acknowledge at all: life is hard. "Man is born to suffering as sparks fly upwards," writes the author of the Book of Job. There was a time when this was generally believed. Now we do not believe it anymore. Our life may be hard, but the reason for this, we firmly believe, is some unfortunate accident rather than anything as preindustrial, as outdated, as the human condition. And yet life remains hard for all the old reasons. We grow old and we die. Every game we play results as surely in the loss of one party as in the victory of another. Every time someone profits it is at the expense of someone else, usually, we like to think, ourselves. Though we are no better at changing these things than we ever were, we have lost the philosophical resignation that inured earlier generations to much of their sting.

These are problems to which the general absence of religion in our society has made us vulnerable, almost as though our spirit's immune system had broken down, leaving us prey to spiritual crisis in the face of even the slightest inclemency. Into our voided souls rushes an overwhelming sense of meaninglessness, combined with its radical corollary, an almost incontinent willingness to believe in anything at all.

One difference, the crucial difference, between us and earlier generations is that we have been bred on the belief, though it is never stated in so many words, that we are headed toward some ultimate perfection to which, for entirely obscure reasons, we imagine we are fully entitled. Since the Enlightenment, there has been the presumption of steady amelioration. So implicit is this opinion that, even to those who now reject the Enlightenment for three or four fashionable reasons, it seems that, when things do not steadily improve, we are being somehow cheated out of what had been promised to us. Nowhere has this been more true than with the

Baby Boomers. In the vibrant aftermath of the Second World War, millions of Americans emerged from the working class into the middle class. Our citizens became better educated and better traveled. The mood of the country suggested that this new model of progress, this endless ascent, was as inexorable as the law of gravity itself. Thus, when the trend began to reverse itself, it provoked immediate despair. For people are less likely to see how far they have come than how far they are receding, even when, in absolute terms, they have advanced considerably.

Our collective irritability in the face of any adversity recalls Tocqueville's famous account of the French Revolution. Why, he asked, did the revolution that abolished feudalism occur in 1789, when the injustices of the old order had been reduced almost to nothing, rather than in 1689, when they were in full force? He argued that it was the very power of their earlier application that had made them seem to be not only unshakable but so pervasive as to be a force of nature. And it was the very weakness of their survival, one hundred years later, that made the retention of any part of the older system seem intolerable.

At this time, progress has materially improved our lives so much that all but our very poorest citizens enjoy creature comforts unknown in earlier generations. In former times, a father expected that many of his children would not survive infancy, that his wife might well die in childbirth. There was ample reason to fear that a common cold might suddenly and mysteriously end one's life. Those who lived long were usually in a condition of economic servility for which our society affords little parallel, and the drudgery of their lives was further galled by the immedicable assault of headaches and toothaches. In short there was the reasonable expectation of misery, a context in which happiness came as a pleasant surprise. Life was hard.

Now life is still hard, but, at least in America, it is hard more for spiritual reasons and less for economic or social ones. More important, we live our lives in the implicit expectation of happiness, a context in which any moment of misery comes as a disruptive surprise that suggests to us that everything we expected, everything we have been promised, has been a fake. "We had a vision [during the postwar years] that life was good, and a conviction you could make it even better," asserts Michael Piore, an economist at MIT. "Now that conviction is gone."[5]

One direct cause of our nervousness is corporate downsizing. According to the New York Times, forty-three million jobs have been lost in the United States since 1979. And although the total number of jobs created during that period is seventy million, only relatively few of those laid off find jobs as well-paying as the ones they left behind. Now job loss and job creation are part of the continual restructuring of the economy. What makes the present cycle scarier than those of the past is that jobs lost in the white-collar sector are replaced by new jobs in the blue-collar sector. "In a reversal from the early eighties," write the authors of the New York Times's report on downsizing, "workers with at least some college education make up the majority of people whose jobs were eliminated, outnumbering those with no more than high school educations. And better-paid workers—those earning at least $50,000—account for twice the share of the lost jobs that they did in the 1980s."[6] The upshot is that, in a process precisely symmetrical to that of forty years ago, people are descending for the first time from the middle to the working class just as they used to ascend from the working class into the middle class. "Whereas those with no more than high school educations used to be hardest hit," the Times continues, "now it is frequently people with college degrees, even advanced degrees." They go on to report, "whereas twenty-five years ago the vast majority of the people who were laid off found jobs that paid as well as their old ones, Labor Department numbers show that now only about 35 percent of laid-off, full-time workers end up in equally remunerative or better-paid jobs."[7]

The ramifications of this change extend not only to those whose jobs have been lost but also to their family and friends and all who know them. The Times reports that as many as three-quarters of all households have had "a close encounter" with layoffs since 1980. In one third of all families there has been an actual layoff, and one adult in ten "acknowledged that a lost job in their household had precipitated a major crisis in their lives." The Times writers concluded that "the result is the most acute job insecurity since the Depression. And this in turn has produced an unrelenting angst that is shattering people's notions of work and self and the very promise of tomorrow. . . . And many economists and chief executives think the job shuffling may be a permanent fixture, always with us, as if the nation had caught a chronic, rasping cough."[8]

There are several direct causes for the sea change that has befallen our economy. Capitalism, in its mechanical and impersonal way, has grown more efficient than ever before, paring itself down and divesting itself of all surplusage to become as competitive as its shareholders require and as competitors here and abroad have made necessary. Because of improvements in management and technology, General Motors, for example, can make as many cars with 315,000 employees today as with half a million two decades ago. Equally suggestive of this trend is the fact that, while the great cinematic epics of the past, those of deMille and Lean and Attenborough, required thousands upon thousands of extras, now only a hundred are necessary, together with one computer that can "spit out clones for the rest." Even the federal government, traditionally an employer of the poorer sectors of society, scaled down its workforce, between 1979 and 1993, by almost half a million jobs.

But the main reason for the commotion in contemporary society, and for the sadness that accompanies it, is a still greater upheaval in human events that increasingly foists upon us an entirely new model of economics and of human conduct. We are speaking of a revolution so massive that it has left no province of human activity unaltered. There have been three great revolutions in human history. All three have been technological, and all the political, economic, and intellectual upheavals that have boisterously claimed our attention these past six thousand years have been in fact mere aftershocks of these three quieter and more shattering revolutions that have underscored them.

The first was the Neolithic revolution, which began roughly ten thousand years ago in Europe and six thousand years ago in Africa and the New World. This revolution in agriculture made possible the development of cities and empires, and from it stemmed everything from the Pyramids of Egypt to the art, poetry, and laws of Greece and Rome, not to mention the court of Versailles, the Great Wall of China, and Machu Picchu.

Surely agricultural society changed drastically over the millennia, but it was not until the second stage of the Industrial Revolution, about 150 years ago, that mankind entered the next phase of its social evolution. The heavy industrialization that resulted made possible mass communications and the exponential acceleration of transport. It scarred our planet with all manner of heavy machinery such as the face of the earth had never seen before. It took us to the moon, recorded the human voice, and memorialized the human countenance through the miracle of photography. In under 125 years, from about 1850 to 1975, it also brought us advanced capitalism, smog, and two world wars.

Now that era is over. In its place we have the postindustrial world and the clamorous aftershock known as postmodern culture. Much of our confusion about the present stems from our not appreciating just how massive a cataclysm this is. The very look of our physical artifacts, from cars to buildings and packaging, has become lighter and more efficient by disowning the heaviness of the industrial age, a heaviness no longer adequate to our changed circumstances. Meanwhile the Internet has vastly increased the avenues of communication, and already technology has altered our eating habits and our appearance.

Not the least effect of this technological transformation is a major shift in class consciousness that has been under way for the past decade. Marxists, for once, might help us to understand this phenomenon, but thus far they have largely ignored it. They insist on invoking the old categories that were relevant during the Industrial Revolution—the conflict between capital and labor—but that are less relevant in the postindustrial world. They have not understood that the very ideas of a middle class and a working class are moribund. More precisely, the distinction between them is far less significant than it once was. As long as living men and women can remember, the manifest destiny of the working class was to lift itself up into the middle class. It is not so much that this goal is unattainable as that it has ceased to matter, since, one tends to have more benefits and more leisure than in the past even if one has less real income. As more people sit behind desks rather than stand at assembly lines, the distinction between white collar and blue collar fades into oblivion. A perfect example of the blurring of earlier boundaries is the computer industry, in which even the highest-paid executives often wear shorts and running shoes rather than a jacket and tie. In such circumstances, one can imagine the confusion, not to mention the despair, of the Generation Xers, who were promised that if they went to college, and especially if they went to graduate school, there would be a high-paying career waiting for them. Increasingly that correlation turns out to have been a reality of the industrial age that is less characteristic of the postindustrial age.

But the shift from industrial to postindustrial society has occasioned spiritual and cultural changes at least as great as its economic changes. Most tellingly, one encounters everywhere a sense that the world has grown infinitely older than it was, that everything has been seen and done before. Of course this view itself is not unique to our time and is itself subject to recurrence. "*Mundus senescit*," Gregory of Tours wrote in the closing years of the sixth century. "The world grows old." This world-weariness characterized European culture at the end of the sixteenth century, as well as at the beginning of the twentieth, during the Edwardian age. But now, it seems, it has become more pervasive than ever before, the shared heritage of people from all classes and walks of life.

This feeling is everywhere in evidence, yet few appreciate its importance. It is the *idée maîtresse* of Jean Baudrillard, the major French philosopher of the moment. Though M. Baudrillard is surely guilty of much exaggeration, his importance consists in his being one of very few contemporary writers fully to appreciate this particular aspect of postmodern culture. As he writes in his essay "Simulacra and Simulations," "When the real is no longer what it used to be, nostalgia assumes its full meaning. There is a proliferation of myths of origin and signs of reality, of secondhand truth, objectivity, and authenticity. There is an escalation of the true, of the lived experience; a resurrection of the figurative where the object and substance have disappeared."[9] Once one gets past the jargon, the slender kernel of truth in this statement is that we as a civilization feel as though we have seen everything twice or more.

In former times, of course, people were acutely aware of the past, but they lived in the present, implicitly appreciating the uniqueness and the "nowness" of each act. Today, by contrast, whenever we say or do anything, we are overwhelmingly aware that it has been said or done before. The Valley Girl idiom that crops up so often in the speech of our nation's young people affects the intonations of quotation rather than of direct utterance. Every young film star is the next Tom Cruise or the next Julia Roberts. Each aspiring novelist is billed as the new Salinger, the new Pynchon, the new Didion. In their commercials, major corporations resurrect for Baby Boomers the jingles they grew up with but haven't heard in years. Coca-Cola revives in plastic the distinctively shaped glass bottles of fifty years ago (and one could not ask for a more perfect metaphor to represent the shift from industrial heaviness to postindustrial lightness). A postmodern simulacrum of Times Square in the twenties, during its glory days, is even now emerging from the rotting squalor that Forty-second Street became during the final stages of the Industrial Revolution. Fashion designers are resurrecting the twenties, the fifties, the sixties, the seventies. In these circumstances, is it so unreasonable to conclude that we have seen too much and lived too long?

The artistic and literary community is prey to a different kind of anguish from that of the population at large, though one that is, if anything, far more acute. It is a centennial anguish, as opposed to a millennial anguish—a fin de siècle mood that reprises, with rather less brilliance, a similar attitude among the dissolute absinthe drinkers of Paris in the Belle Epoque. The twentieth century is drawing to a close, and, as Eugen Weber remarks in his book *Fin de Siècle*, "the notion of end, somehow, goes with thoughts of diminution and decay."[10]

In their obsessive concern with this fin de siècle, certain members of the culturati persuade themselves that they are pioneers marching toward some new watershed in art history. In this scenario, the very real affliction of AIDS replays the ravages of tertiary syphilis on the artistic community of the last century. Though AIDS is less menacing now than when it first entered public awareness in the early eighties, the arts community has, in the wake of this devastation, become saturated with a morbidity very different from the general optimism that characterized the art world only ten years ago. Whether in the freakish images of Joel-Peter Witkin, the corpse photo-graphs of Andres Serrano, or the necrophiliac novels of Dennis Cooper, a darkness, a *delectatio morbosa*, falls across the artistic community. Disseminated through the spooky music of Nine Inch Nails and the youth movement known as the Goths and such films as *Seven* and *The Usual Suspects*, this mood has entered into the thinking of the population at large. It reflects, even as it fortifies, the general sense that things are out of control, that the world, as the good woman said apropos of the weather, is going mad. And this appearance of madness is most often experienced as the assault upon the center of society by a battalion of extreme convictions, against which the center is too weak and too morally dispirited to defend itself.

In a sense the present book is an examination, without necessarily being an endorsement, of this view that the world is going mad. Everywhere we look we seem to witness the revolt of the fringe against the center. By contrast, it seems, the center is so riven with self-doubt that it lacks the spiritual resources to counter the raging certitude of the extremes. "The best lack all conviction," Yeats wrote in the days of Spengler, "while the worst / Are full of passionate intensity." Gradually the ineluctable awareness of these extremes so saturates our culture as to begin to define it. Though most people do not belong to extremist movements, the extremes have never been as visible or as strident as they are today. Just as in America the fifties was generally an age of remorseless conformity in which the center exerted an almost tyrannous pull on all who tried to resist it, so today, for a variety of social and intellectual reasons, the extremes appear to have overwhelmed the center.

Extremism surely has existed in one form or another for most of modern history. But in our age, for the first time, it has become the first rather than the last resort. We have seen extremism emerge, with almost formulaic, mechanical regularity, in every part of society: religion and politics, art and music, philosophy and science. In logic there is an operation known as the reductio ad absurdum, the act of taking things to their logical conclusion. Ours is the age in which the reductio ad absurdum, the desire to go as far as one can go, was finally made flesh and translated into action. Because homosexuals should not be discriminated against, there are some in their movement—a tiny minority, to be sure—who publicly assert their right to sodomize seven-year-old boys. Because this should not be their right, there are those on the extreme right who would illegalize homosexuality altogether. Because some men have raped some women, there are feminists who question the moral validity of any form of heterosexuality other than artificial insemination; and there are right-wingers who, antagonized by such opinions, agitate for the continuing suppression of women.

Ours is also an age in which a dizzying proliferation of religious movements challenges the secular foundations of the free state. The secular state that is the logical consequence of the Enlightenment is assailed by the religious right on one side and by the likes of Scientology and Satanism on the other. Ours, too, is an age in which, in the visual arts, politics has increasingly gained the ascendancy of form and promiscuity has supplanted modesty. In literature profanity often banishes grammar, and a morbid, sexualized violence, admired both for its own sake and for its direct contravention of the most cherished principles of the center, suffuses our films and music. To call these cultural products extreme is not to pass judgment on them but merely to describe their more or less stated aims.

To all appearances, ours is the age of infinite fracturing and polarizing of society. We see black against white and white against black; we see black and white separatists united only in their hatred of Jews; we see some Jews responding in kind. We have seen Arabs willing to blow themselves up to hurt Israel and the United States of America. We have seen, in Italy, France, Germany and Russia, the reemergence of the forces of fascism, which we thought had been relegated long ago to the trash heap of history. Above all there has arisen in the United States a radical right so extreme that it seeks to bring down the federal government.

And yet an irony becomes apparent. The constant presence of these extremists inspires many of us to feel that society is drifting out of control. As such it is in part a cause of the malaise that hangs over our society. And yet these extremists are the only ones who remain largely unaltered by the economic and social upheavals that have jolted the rest of us. For the turmoil of our transition to a postindustrial society is like an earthquake whose epicenter is in the midmost point of industrial society: the further removed one is from that center, the less one is affected. What concerns us in this book is all that is outside of that center insofar as it impinges, however painfully, upon the center; all that will not be assimilated to the center; all that, precisely for this reason, frightens and discommodes the great mass of the population that inhabits the center.

By temperament the people who figure in this book are the survivors of an earlier age—like militia members or Islamic fundamentalists. Or they are members of some underclass or political outcasts who, for the most part, never enjoyed the fruits of industrialized society in the first place and thus had no high-paying jobs to lose. Similarly, fifteen years ago, when blue-collar workers were being laid off, it was not these people who suffered, for they, whether as intellectuals or as outcasts, were not part of that segment of the population, either.

In another sense these extremists perform an essential function in our society. Only by their inhabiting the circumference can we define our center. Such definition is important work for any society, but especially for one undergoing as revolutionary a transition as ours. Anyone who doubts the urgency of this task need go no further than the recent controversy surrounding the assertion, in Bob Woodward's book *The Choice*, that first lady Hillary Rodham Clinton had held séances in the White House. In these "séances" Mrs. Clinton was supposed to have had conversations with Eleanor Roosevelt, among other long-dead worthies. In order to do damage control, not only did her press officers issue statements mocking the idea of such séances, but Mrs. Clinton herself explained, "While I had a number of conversations with Jean Houston [the woman conducting the "séances"], it is simply not true that she is my spiritual adviser. . . . The bottom line is: I have no spiritual advisers or any other alternative to my deeply held Methodist faith and traditions upon which I have relied since childhood."[11]

Whether or not the séance story was true, and it probably was not, both sides understood what was at stake. Most Americans do not believe in séances or in supernaturalism, at least not of that sort. Thus, if it could be proved that Mrs. Clinton had actually held the séances, it would strongly suggest that she was different from the population as a whole, that she was "out there," that she was not of the center. That Mrs. Clinton should believe in nothing at all is acceptable in our generally secular, not to say atheistic, society. That she should express her abiding belief in the principles of Methodism is also allowed: a little religion is not a bad thing, especially when it sounds a conventional note in a woman as unconventional as Mrs. Clinton. But the holding of séances, implying a belief in the ability to contact the dead, is defined by the center as outside of the center. And since it is the foremost duty of the politician literally to incarnate the center in word and deed, even as he or she is altering the center, so any action that challenges that centrality calls into question the politician's entire career.

These days, however, the center that Mrs. Clinton aspires to occupy appears, for the reasons outlined, to be undergoing the most strenuous challenge in its history. The present book, unapologetically written from the perspective of the center, assesses that challenge while examining its origins and its likely outcome. From the perspective of the center this book looks out toward that circumference where, at this moment, a proliferation of conflicts clamors for our attention and consumes our strength, all the while threatening the very future of our civil society.

2

CENTER AND CIRCUMFERENCE

Most of us are inside the center looking out. Some of us are outside the center looking in. This book, as has been stated already, is written from the perspective of the center and is intended for those who are in the center. From this vantage point, it looks out in all directions toward the circumference, to those people who choose not to be assimilated into the larger collectivity of our society.

Contemporary philosophy, which delights in "deconstructing" those mental models that shape the beliefs and presuppositions of *sensus communis*, would doubtless have much to say about this notion of the center. Obviously, it is used in the present context as a kind of shorthand, to define a felt reality that influences people's thinking and behavior. For our present purposes the center is conceived not as a point but as a circle, a zone in which most of the citizens of our industrialized society find relative happiness. It is the behavioral equivalent of the biosphere, that is, the zone where a certain kind of life can exist.

Since this notion of the center is a manner of speaking, it is entitled, I hope, to a certain measure of indeterminacy. It is not in my interest to establish with any precision the degrees of centrality, nor to deny that, given the infinite variety of the human soul, we will never find any one being who can be considered entirely

centralized, entirely typical of anything. I think that Kant somewhere defines the lunatic as a waking dreamer and the dreamer as
a sleeping lunatic, or words to that effect. To put it another way,
we are all to some degree extremists in our dreams, in that part of
our private lives that, in virtue of its being private, is somehow at
variance with the public realm that is the center. Indeed, as Blaise
Pascal usefully reminds us, no two human beings are more different from one another than each of us is different from himself at
different moments or periods of his life.

Nor do I deny that most of the five billion people who now
inhabit the earth do not yet fall within the zone that I have defined
as the center. Rather I am speaking of industrialized society of the
First World, increasingly the Second World, China and the former
Soviet bloc, and even parts of the so-called Third World, in India,
South America, and Africa, where islands of industry, and even of
postindustrialism, emerge from the sea of agrarian society. Nor do
I deny that at present there are whole communities in the First
World that have a center unto themselves and as such are at variance with the industrialized society that concerns us here. The le-
gion of homeless people in our midst can be seen as so many
emissaries, whether temporary or permanent, from a culture radically different from our own.

All of these considerations make it impossible to chart with
unerring precision the exact extent of what we call the center.
Under the light of such concentrated scrutiny, the center seems to
vanish. But when we stand back, it suddenly reappears, and it is
this perpetual resiliency, despite our best efforts to deny its reality,
that gives greatest strength to the notion of a common center.

But there is still another reason for asserting the reality of the
center: many of those people who oppose the center, and all of
those who are discussed as doing so in the present book, would
admit, if they were candid, that this opposition was precisely the
point of their activity. Thus although it may seem arrogant of this
book, by talking of the center and the circumference, literally to
"marginalize" the "Other," as contemporary philosophy would
have it, nevertheless, the "Other" in question is usually inclined to
"marginalize" itself. That is to say that those people who will be

discussed in the present book have brought their behavior to a certain level of consciousness. And it is this articulated revolt against the center, which implies possessing and acting on an idea of the center, that enables us, by defining their eccentricity, also to define our centrality. Such a consideration has nothing to do with the bushmen, the Eskimos, or the homeless in our midst, in other words, those who do not reject the center but are simply not part of it. But it has everything to do with those people who consciously reject the consensus of the center: those who assert that the earth is flat, not on the basis of traditional belief but on pseudoscientific grounds; those who assert their right to sexual intimacy with children; those who deny the existence of the Holocaust. This book examines those who reject the center rather than those who were never assimilated to it in the first place.

It is important, as a point of intellectual honesty, to acknowledge from the beginning this position of centrality, since the present book is about nothing if not perspective. In one sense the center, seen from the circumference, looks like the extreme and the extreme looks like the center. The true extremist will declare that you and I are the extremes. To the extremist, the most radical and sanguinary doctrines we can name make perfect sense, and our refusal to embrace them appears to be a mark of perverse obstinacy.

What constitutes this center and extreme is highly susceptible to change and evolution. It is likely that you and everyone you know will accept that all people are created equal and that no race should have more privileges than any other. This is the opinion of the center, though it has surely not been so at all times. It was a radical, revolutionary opinion as recently as two hundred years ago when it was introduced into the Constitution of the United States. One hundred years ago it was not obvious to everyone that this ideal comprised anyone other than whites. Thirty years ago it was not obvious to every Southerner that it comprised blacks as well as whites. Today it is the bedrock of our society, and anyone asserting otherwise places himself outside the pale of centrist society.

It is at this point that we come up against what might be called the epistemology of extremism, an approach to knowledge that informs many of the arguments that the extremes mount against the center. In the case of the inalienable rights of all humans, for example, there are those who, either through perversity or through ignorance, will not acquiesce in this opinion of the center. To the white supremacist, the idea that blacks should enjoy the same rights as white people is hardly self-evident, and he can probably cite some scriptural passage that he has taken out of context, or some biological datum that he has misinterpreted, to prove his point. In vain will you explain to him that blacks are human beings. Either he will dispute that status or he will fail to see what it has to do with the equitable apportionment of rights.

And herein consists the main strength of the extremist's argument: like a Stealth bomber working under the level of radar, it attacks the center at its point of greatest vulnerability, not so much by arguing facts and figures, a debate the extremist knows he cannot win, as by calling into question the most universal axioms upon which our thoughts are based. But these axioms have been so implicit in our thinking, and for so long, that when we are questioned about them we are at once thrown back on that most vulnerable position of all, the article of faith. Why, after all, should a black man's status as a human being—even if the supremacist does not dispute this—entitle him to our respect? The question is not easy to answer in any logical way, since axioms in general cannot be proved by reason but must be accepted upon faith. At that point we will be reduced to asserting that we simply "hold these truths to be self-evident." And the racist holds them not to be self-evident. Though he can never persuade us in this way, in a sense his point is not to persuade us at all but merely to be seen to parry successfully our efforts to sway him. For whenever the center confronts the extremes, anything less than its complete victory spells defeat.

Another ploy in the extremist's arsenal is the assertion of what might be called the "global" duping of his opponent. Once we fail to subscribe to the theory that the United States government and the United Nations are mere fronts for the international Zionist conspiracy, the extremist will assert that we ourselves have been brainwashed and that everything we say and believe can be under-

stood only within the context of this brainwashing. Now you cannot very well prove that you have not been brainwashed, since,
once the premise of your being brainwashed has been entertained,
everything you say is understood within that context and appears
to be only further proof of your having been deceived.

Yet another advantage of the extremist is that, in many cases,
he cares more about his subject than you do and thus knows far
more about it. Though we are confident that extremist prejudice is
the result of ignorance—which in one sense, the Socratic sense, it
is indeed—nevertheless we quickly learn that the extremist probably has at his disposal a great deal of information that the mass of
centrist society either never knew or has completely forgotten.
Thus most of us do not doubt that the Holocaust happened, but
we have necessarily had to take other people's word for it. Few of
us, on the spur of the moment and in the heat of argument, could
provide facts, figures, and diagrams to prove, contrary to the assertions of those who deny the Holocaust, that the showers used
in Auschwitz, because of the width of their nozzles or some other
criterion, were suitable only to the emission of gas and not to the
emission of water.

Similarly, when a Freeman or Tax Protest fanatic cites some
obscure point of law, most of us, not being lawyers, are in no position to counter his claims. And so, when one Larry Martz was
indicted for illegal possession of firearms, according to the *New
York Times*, "At the start of the trial in Common Pleas Court, Mr.
Martz, who chose to defend himself, stood defiantly in the court's
spectator section. He said he would not cross into the main part of
the courtroom because the judge had no jurisdiction over him. He
argued that the courtroom's United States flag had fringes and that
a fringed flag was a military flag, meaning that he would be sub-
jecting himself to a military tribunal and losing his full constitutional rights."[1] His challenge of the federal government's right to
arraign him, when he asserts that he does not acknowledge the authority or jurisdiction of that government, is precisely the sort of
axiomatic attack that calls into question so much that is so fundamental: this claim, if seriously addressed, would incapacitate any
judicial inquiry for years. And as for the claim about the fringed

flag, it is unlikely that either the judge or anyone else in the court-room had any knowledge of its truth or falsehood.

Naturally the extremist will not persuade you, as Mr. Martz persuaded neither the judge nor the jury, and just as naturally you will never persuade him. His argumentation exists for only two reasons, first in hopes of confounding the center, which numerically and morally has the advantage, and second in hopes that a third party will simply throw up his hands and, in a perverse parody of open-mindedness, exclaim that he doesn't know one way or the other and thus will suspend judgment. At that point, once again, the center has lost and the extreme has won.

As the case made by Mr. Martz also reveals, symbolism is fundamental to the thinking of extremists, especially those on the right. Reality, as it presents itself to common sense, is mechanically and regularly stood on its head. In this way what is real, in the present case the United States government, is, so to speak, dematerialized, transformed into a symbolic projection of corrupt special interests; and what is purely symbolic, like the fringed flag, is reinvested with lethal and immediate consequence.

The incident of the fringed flag points up something else at the very heart of the extremist theory of knowledge: the primacy of metaphor. In essence, a metaphor asserts that x is not x but y; or that x, in addition to being x, is y. This metaphorical conception of the world comes most powerfully into play in the case of prejudice, whereby the individual object of the extremist's attention ceases to be an individual and becomes the incarnation of a class, a race, or a religion. Without this ability to universalize particulars, the extremist and the bigot are, so to speak, out of a job. They have lost their stock in trade.

Now it could be argued with some justice that society and indeed civilization itself are compounded of metaphors and abstractions of this very sort. Both the marketing department of a corporation and the election strategists of the Democratic and Republican parties derive their existence from the confidence that, economically or politically, women, blacks, and senior citizens will behave in a certain way. The amorous young man whose "type" is the blond ballerina is apt to project onto each individual example of this preference the characteristics of a class. The novelist, when writing his books, conceives at each moment a typical reader who will respond to his words in one way and not another. But the crucial difference between the mainstream and extremists is that there is a point beyond which the mainstream refuses to pass, a point at which the extremist lurches into life, and that is the point at which generalities become specifics and abstractions are made flesh.

By the same token, we of the center must not make a similar mistake in assessing the clamorous voices of the extreme. In many if not most cases, the extremist will claim to speak for a whole class of people, and we, for our part, will feel an almost overwhelming temptation to believe him. Thus, when Louis Farrakhan claims to speak for all blacks, or when Larry Kramer appears to speak for all homosexuals, we must remind ourselves that these claims are so far from being true that neither man can accurately be said to speak even for the organization with which he is associated, whether the Nation of Islam or ACT UP. It is necessary to state, as axiomatic, that it is impossible for one person, except in a certain specific legal sense, truly to speak for another, let alone for a whole group of people. Two people can be substantially in agreement on a subject, but one has only to examine that subject in any detail to see the minute disparities of opinion emerging between them. Now this fact is easy enough to accept as an axiom, and so stated it seems self-evidently true. But it is rather harder, faced with some aggressive and outlandish claim, to have the presence of mind to put the axiom into consistent practice. The temptation to become indignant is so strong that it requires even greater presence of mind to remember that each racist and extremist is in essence a monad, even when there is legitimate reason to believe that there are others substantially in agreement with him.

Thus far we have used the term "extremist" without defining it precisely. It is not enough to say that the extremist is outside of the center. Not every person who acts at variance with the center of society is an extremist, however odd or menacing he may seem. In this book a distinction is made between extremists, on the one hand, and what we might call misfits and eccentrics, on the other. As regards the misfit it is enough to say that lack of an articulated and often public consciousness of his act distinguishes him from the extremist. A man who molests little children is not an extremist, though we are apt to define him as a misfit, a pervert, or some other term of our choosing. But the members of NAMBLA (North American Man-Boy Love Association) have gone to the lengths of articulating an entire philosophy around this predilection and of publicly advocating it. Thus they have elevated to a high degree of public consciousness the selfsame impulse upon which the misfit happens to act. Furthermore, the extremist believes in, and often publicly professes, not only the justice but even the moral superiority of his cause, whereas the misfit, more often than not, is content to hide his actions from the world.

As for the distinction between the eccentric and the extremist, the former is usually motivated by personal taste, whereas the latter is moved to action by some intellectual doctrine. As such, the difference between extremist and eccentric is the difference between the collectivity and the individual. The extremist either is part of a larger organization, as are militia members and members of the Jewish Defense League, or, like the Unabomber, he sees himself as acting in the service of a cause, even a movement, larger than himself.

And yet there is one more thing that needs to be said about this collective mentality, which is at the heart of extremism and forms an important part of its perennial appeal. Traditionally we distinguish between the individual and the collectivity. But there is a third thing, something in the order of a collective individualism, that inspires people to join cults, militias, clans, gangs, and sects. Though the members of these groups are often alienated from the mass of society, as is the individual loner, perhaps they lack the spiritual wherewithal to go it entirely alone. The group they join affords them that collective opposition to the whole that their vanity or their anger craves, without the added burden of radical individualism. It is easy to see how perfect a resolution this is: one preserves one's sense of apartness, and one has camaraderie as well. There is, after all, a pleasure to belonging and a pleasure (for some) to being alienated, and nothing answers these twin urges quite as well as the radicalized sect.

Of course, there are many groups, such as sports teams or Ki-wanis clubs, that bear some structural similarity to the groups I am describing. The key difference, in this context, is that a sports team is by its nature a temporary association—it ceases to be in force the moment one removes the numbered jersey—whereas identification with an extremist organization saturates the person-hood of the individual and implicitly remains in force even after the members have left one another's presence. These latter associations are thus existential rather than merely recreational. This is the idea behind their wearing hidden tattoos or swearing oaths: even when they move about in the center of society, there is al-ways that part of them that cannot be assimilated, that remains alienated.

Just as earth scientists tell us that the biosphere, to which we have already compared the center, required many millions of years to evolve, so the center as we know it today is a fragile structure that has developed over several thousand years. And extremism it-self, which we tend to see as an ingrained and ineradicable part of the human condition, has also had its history and its evolution.

Historically, at the risk of our sounding paradoxical, the cen-ter preceded the circumference. This is because extremism is char-acterized by a collective and determined antagonism to the center, and as such it owes its existence to a preceding consensus that it opposes. To indulge in still another paradox, in the beginning the world was all center and all circumference. The human race com-prised thousands if not millions of atomized communities, each with its own center, each defined in opposition to all the others. Yet within each of those atomized communities—with the excep-tion, we may imagine, of certain aberrant individuals—there was strict conformity. Only with the consolidation of these communi-ties into a larger society did there emerge that sense of difference within sameness that made partisans, and eventually extreme par-tisans, a possibility. But even with the emergence of parties there was not necessarily extremism. For extremism to exist it was nec-essary that civilization acquire a degree of self-consciousness, as well as a standard of free discourse, which until recently has been the exception rather than the rule.

Among the earliest expressions of something akin to extremism, that is, to a violent rejection of the behavior or the beliefs of the center, are the tragic words of the Book of Job and the warnings of the prophets Isaiah, Ezra, and Ezekiel to the wayward children of Israel. In Greece during the very same period, intense factionalism produced extreme voices among the partisans of kings against tyrants in the seventh century before Christ, and of oligarchs against democrats two hundred years later. In poetry as well, the moroseness of Hesiod and the petulance of Archilochus castigate the center, as do the unimaginable horrors of the tragic poems of Aeschylus and Sophocles. The intention and result of these latter poems was not merely, as Aristotle asserted, to purge the emotions but also, through the momentary and radical rejection of the status quo, to achieve a reinvigorated sense of the center.

And yet the exact nature of the poet's involvement with the center was not always clear. A play like *The Bacchae* of Euripides is revealingly ambiguous. It is the story of the passage of Dionysius from India into Greece. The women of Thebes, driven to bacchic frenzy, take to the countryside to participate in an ecstatic revelry wherein they lose all sense of restraint. The leader of the city, Pentheus, does not recognize the godhead of Dionysus and looks with stern disapproval upon the excesses of the women. His comeuppance arrives in the form of his mother, Agave, one of the leaders of the bacchic frenzy. Goaded on by the god, she eventually slays her own son by decapitating him with her bare hands. But the point of this play is ultimately unclear. Euripides, who is famous for having one of his characters doubt whether the gods even exist, seems himself to be in some doubt as to whether the moral is obedience to the gods or to reason, or whether, at a deeper level, the play is a despairing tirade against the human condition.

The relative restrictions on free expression during much of the Roman Republic and all of the Roman Empire severely limited the amount of extremist behavior that has come down to us in the literature. Such literature as we have is more often than not of a high moral tone, and even poets as racy as Martial and Juvenal are more interested in reproving the sins of their contemporaries than in exhorting them to commit new ones. Truly extreme voices, like that of Tertullian in the middle of the second century, are few and far between. Furthermore, a society as rigorously conformist as Rome was not, in its nature, as prone to radicalism as Greece. This is proved by the fact that the most radical doctrines to preoccupy the Roman mind, such as Cynicism, Stoicism, and Epicureanism, all came from Greece. More quintessentially Roman was the attempt of the elder Cato, also known as Cato the Censor, to stem the tide of foreign cultural invasion by expelling all Greek philosophers from the capital.

In records from the Middle Ages, when religious bonds were far stronger than political or cultural bonds, the forms of extreme behavior that we encounter most often, as well as those most likely to be recorded, are predictably the ones that challenge the centrality of the Church. Often, it is true, there were underlying social and political causes for these convulsions, but almost invariably they took on a religious complexion. In his masterful book *The Pursuit of the Millennium*, Norman Cohen writes of the Brethren of the Free Spirit, one of the most extreme of these groups, that they were characterized by "a quasi-mystical anarchism—an affirmation of freedom so reckless and unqualified that it amounted to a total denial of every kind of restraint and limitation. These people could be regarded as remote precursors of Bakunin and of Nietzsche—or rather of that bohemian intelligentsia which during the last half-century has been living from ideas once expressed by Bakunin and Nietzsche in their wilder moments."[2]

Now in the Middle Ages the overwhelming tendency of society was toward a consensus that preempted individual expression of thought or preference. In religious matters, the Church dictated what one was to think, and there was little possibility or even desire for appeal. What was radical about the members of the Free Spirit was that each man decided for himself, much in the way of modern citizens, the cast and direction of his own conscience. Centered in Paris, the Brethren of the Free Spirit gathered around the learned Amaury of Bene, who died in 1206 or 1207. These so-called Amaurians were essentially pantheists who believed, like so many of the heretics of the Middle Ages, that the end of the world was nigh. As one of their number declared at the Synod of Sens,

"All things are One, because whatever is, is God." Church records go on to claim that the same man "dared to affirm that, in so far as he was, he could neither be consumed by fire nor tormented by torture, for he said that, in so far as he was, he was God."[3]

In time this religious antagonism to the center become more social and political in its expression. Though the Amaurian menace was promptly eradicated by the Church, the seeds of heresy could not be entirely uprooted and came to the fore during the Reformation in the doctrines of the more extreme wing of the Anabaptists. The most radical of all were those who, in 1534, took over the city of Münster in Westphalia and, in the expectation of the imminent annihilation of the world, imposed a kind of communistic theocracy. They were governed by a charismatic young king, Jan Beukelson, whose demeanor and appearance call to mind David Koresh, leader of the ill-fated Branch Davidians. John of Leyden, as he came to be known, even instituted polygamy and acquired more than ten wives. Such was the fervor of the Anabaptists' faith that many of them, rather than flee the besieged city, gladly embraced massacre at the hands of the Episcopal army that eventually restored order.

Such behavior shocked the entire *res publica christiana* for years to come, and the surviving Anabaptists themselves soon adopted a far more conservative stance. But their communistic dream resurfaced a little over a hundred years later during the Civil War in England, in an odd group of fanatics known as the Ranters, because of their habitual use of profanities. According to George Fox, the founder of Quakerism, these uncouth people were marked not only by "reveling, roaring, drinking, whoring" but also by "open full-mouthed swearing ordinarily by the Wounds and Blood of God, and the fearfullest cursing that hath been heard." Like the earlier Amaurian pantheists, their belief in the immanence of God within them assumed some rather odd forms. As one of them declared, "Consider what act soever, yea though it be the act of Swearing, Drunkeness, Adultery and Theft; yet these acts simply, yea nakedly, as acts are nothing distinct from the act of Prayer and Prayses. Why dost thou wonder? why art thou angry? they are all one in themselves; no more holynesse, no more puritie in the one than in the other." Their antinomianism took the nihilistic form of denying the possibility of sin: "As I said before, so I say again, the very title Sin, it is only a name without substance, hath no being in God, nor in the Creature, but only by imagination."[4]

In preindustrial society, however, the kind of society that prevailed throughout the world before 1800, societal divisions had little to do with the activities of the extremists we have discussed. These groups were few and far between, and their influence, except insofar as it expressed a larger malaise, was nonexistent. Rather, such divisions were more apt to be caused by religion and class or by distance and the slowness of transport, which technology was not yet able to bridge. Thus the immemorial difference between Welshman and Englishman and between Breton and Bourguignon remained in full force, alongside that between Protestant and Catholic and between master and man. But it was in the nature of preindustrial society that if it could not resolve these divisions there was also no pressing need for it to do so: the world moved so slowly and remained so localized that there was little interaction, and thus relatively little friction, between the different groups.

In the nineteenth century, by contrast, that part of the world that was beginning to be industrialized suddenly became faster and more efficient. The population began to increase exponentially, and people from every class and nationality were suddenly brought together in the great megalopolises of London, Paris, and New York. Upstart newspapers, whose circulations would have been unimaginable a generation before, provided the first intimation of what the mass media would be like one hundred years later. Suddenly a great many ideas circulated to an ever-growing number of citizens, and like-minded people were able to associate with one another in groups that were distinguished from, and sometimes antagonistic to, the center of society: these came in the form of the more radical German Burschenshaften and other student associations at the beginning of the century, as well as various anarchist and nihilist associations toward the end of the century. Because of massive waves of immigration to the New World, one saw, for the first time on so large a scale, different nationalities living side by side but not yet assimilated into a common culture. For example, in New York

City during much of the nineteenth century, about a third of the population was of German origin and spoke German as its first language, with English a poor second. Nevertheless, even if society could not yet unify the many disparate voices in its midst, still the pull of tradition, the inherent respect that it was accorded, was enough to preserve the stability of the center.

The center as we have defined it first became truly powerful and successfully integrated in the twentieth century, though with sometimes tragic results. It was the work of the earlier part of the century, that is, the latter half of the Industrial Revolution, to bring together and homogenize our culture by way of the mass media and mass transportation. And just as the mass media put the same images and ideas into our heads, so mass production and mass marketing put the same food on our tables and the same furnishings in our homes. Unfortunately, the very technological progress that gave rise to the welfare state and to the increasing homogeneity of the First World also produced the totalitarian regimes that blighted the middle years of the twentieth century. One can plausibly interpret Nazism and Stalinism as the most radically centralized political projects in recorded history, in the sense that they went to the greatest lengths—indeed, to the point of genocide itself—in their desire to eradicate differences within their borders, and sometimes beyond their borders. The case could also be made that the pervasive sense of conformity that characterized America in the fifties was the foremost cultural triumph of the center over the circumference.

But by the end of the industrial age, that is, by about 1970, the First World was beginning to revolt against the tyrannous pull of the center that had characterized the middle years of the century. The whole hippie movement, not only in its radical inception but also in its subsequent embrace by the mainstream, can be seen as a revolt—and a largely successful one—against the pull of the center. In this connection, however, the liberation movements of blacks, women, and homosexuals are ambiguous. On the one hand they demanded for each of these groups the status of sovereign centrality that the white male had always enjoyed. On the other, many of the more radicalized members of those movements sought to separate themselves in almost every way from a white male center that they saw as corrupt and corrupting.

Although the ultimate effect of the sixties and seventies was to leave us a far more integrated culture than we had been, one in which difference is accepted in theory if not always in deed, nevertheless the cultural legacy of those decades was the theoretical, if not actual, endorsement of nonconformity over conformity, and of everything outside the center over everything inside the center. It is this postulated preference for the weaker over the stronger, for the diminutive over the grand, for aberration over sameness, and for the fringe over the center that defines the mentality of the present culture of the First World. And the technology that, in the middle years of the century, brought us more closely together than ever before has been superseded by an infinite proliferation of media that threaten, by atomizing our population into ever smaller groups and subgroups, to fracture beyond recall the centrism of an earlier generation.

This apparent atomization, as well as the now ingrained aversion to the very idea of "the center," has produced, among other things, an increasingly shrill attack upon the center by those who choose to identify themselves with the circumference. It is responsible, perhaps more than any other single factor, for the idea that extremism is rampant in our society and that the center cannot hold. It is the phenomenon that will serve as the focus of the chapters that follow.

3

THE RADICAL RIGHT

As of this moment, the most terrifying threat to the well-being of the center appears to come from the extremists of the right. No group opposes more defiantly, or resents more profoundly, the very centrality of the center. No group in turn inspires in the often divergent factions of the center a stronger sense of common cause. And no group, perhaps, contributes more actively to the sense of malaise that permeates our society at this time, the sense of the world's going crazy. In the vigor of their assault on the center, in the vociferousness of their calling into question everything for which the center seems to stand, the extremists of the right are without parallel in our time. They surface in many different parts of the world, and in each of the lands they have infiltrated, whether Germany, Russia, or the United States, their movements bear distinctive structural and spiritual similarities: a fixation on the past, an antagonism to an increasingly progressive center, an indulgence in conspiracy theories. And yet in each of these lands, as we shall see, the extreme right has acquired attributes uniquely suited to its ever-changing circumstances.

Until very recently most Americans knew little about the activities of the extreme right, aside from a few vague notions about the Ku Klux Klan, John Birchers, and neo-Nazis of various stripes.

Thus, when news of the bombing of the Federal Building in Oklahoma City first got out, many people naturally assumed that Middle Eastern terrorists were responsible. It came as a shock to most Americans to learn not only that the alleged perpetrators were native-born citizens of the United States but also that they prided themselves on precisely the force and fierce integrity of their patriotism.

That was when Americans at large became aware of something called the militia movement, whose more extreme members hated the status quo and were dedicated to overthrowing the federal government, which many referred to as ZOG, the Zionist Occupation Government. For the first time one encountered an entire subculture of hatred, anger, and fear that rejected all that most Americans took for granted and held dear. As the media focused attention, perhaps disproportionate attention, on these tiny splinter groups, it began to seem as though there were dangers all around us, as though, without our realizing it, we had been standing at a precipice all this time. As David H. Bennett has observed in *The Party of Fear*, perhaps the best single book on the extreme right wing in American politics, these groups seem to be "part of an alternative culture. Their books, magazines, newsletters, videos, and Internet links are not seen in academia, not read by the professional or managerial classes, nor part of the life of most Americans outside of the circle of believers."[1]

For anyone examining the extreme right fringe in America, as well as in countries like Germany and Russia, the overwhelming question goes to motivation: what causes a person to engage in acts and to hold opinions of such outrageous extremity? Because we, as a society, are in a general way rationalistic, it seems natural to us that anyone who undertakes so energetic a course of action will have, at least in his own mind, a clear and compelling reason for doing so. And yet, in examining the activities of the extreme right, not to mention other forms of extremism, one is often struck by the divide between the opinions that the extremist offers and the truer motives that underlie his public testimonials. What is important to understand is, first, that the stated aim is seldom the true aim, and, second, that the truer aim is only rarely one motive serving as a pretext for another: more often it is something much vaguer, something as immaterial as a mood, even a whim, which, when joined to a volatile temperament, may beget acts of unspeakable and tragic incivility.

In some cases there is a direct relationship of cause and effect. As Bennett points out, there is a precise correlation between the rise of anti-Semitism in the Midwest and the farm crisis. "As the farm crisis deepened, [Posse Comitatus, a now disbanded neo-Nazi movement] found an audience for its messages. In 1984 and 1985, some desperate farmers, facing loss of their land, turned to violence."[2] Bennett correctly points out that for most of the seventies, farmers had done very well and their land values had increased considerably. Then, seemingly overnight, the boom went bust. As though this wasn't bad enough, many farmers at the suggestion of bankers and government experts, had borrowed heavily to buy new land and equipment. With inflation on the rise and interest rates ever higher, farmers could no longer pay their loans and the banks foreclosed. According to an estimate cited by Bennett, roughly one farmer in three in Iowa lost his home. One disgruntled man declared that "they destroyed everything I ever worked for." When asked who "they" were, he replied, the "Goddam Jews . . . Luciferized bank directors . . . stinking Jewish insurance companies."[3]

Here is a direct correlation between extreme opinions and public calamity, and we need have no doubts as to the sincerity of the farmer in question. In most cases, however, one must learn to live with the very real possibility that, for all the anger and all the vehemence of their declarations, many right-wing extremists quite possibly may not mean a word of what they say. It is important to bear this possibility in mind, because most of the discussions that we hear about the extreme right have assumed a one-to-one correspondence between what the right-wingers said and what they really believed. The result is a discussion that, when not false or misleading, is rather less useful than it might have been.

In fact, the intellectual tenor of right-wing extremism is often more akin to poetry than to clear thought: it is compounded of myth, by which past and present are molded to the wishes of the agitator; metaphor, by which, through leaps of logic, phenomena can be voided of their real significance and made to mean whatever you wish; and finally a sensibility of sorts, a combination of hobbyism and certain aberrational ideas of style. Allied to this is an almost feverish will to believe, the quest for a nourishing, sustaining fiction, if it must be fiction, that will impart meaning, structure, and purpose to one's life. To some extent this need can be found in all humans. But what is exceptional here is the length to which certain extremists will go to establish and sustain the illusion. To preserve the fragile texture of their fiction requires an almost superhuman amount of credulity, arrogant misprision, and poetic fancy in equal measure. This is the point at which mere belief becomes an act of desperate defiance, quite impervious to questioning.

Those on the far right and the religious right, unlike the extreme right (neo-Nazis, militias, the KKK and the like), have many ties to the system and many sympathizers within the system; as such they are essentially practical people who seek to enact legislation, and sometimes they succeed. But the extreme right neither has nor seeks this connection to political reality. Such extremism is more a state of mind than a program that could ever be put into practice. For all its calls to action, the radical right, in its essence, is entirely impractical.

In America today the radical right assumes a variety of forms: the Ku Klux Klan, neo-Nazis, skinheads, and the militia movement. They are notionally separable in the degree and nature of their radicalism—the neo-Nazis and skinheads being farthest to the right, the KKK being slightly less virulent, and the militias being a little closer to the center. But in fact there is considerable interpenetration between their movements, and few of them, despite a habit of drawing up manifestos, have anything like a fixed set of ideas. Thus, although there is nothing inherently fascist about the militia movement, nor anything necessarily religious about neo-Nazism, nor anything intrinsically militaristic about the KKK, their vague sense of common cause, of having the same enemies, results in a considerable overlap in their membership. In this respect, the extreme right, unlike the extreme left, is less intellectual than emotional, as befits a movement rooted in passions, or more often attitudes, rather than in ideas. This is why you find among them none of the *odium theologicum* that often characterizes the antagonism of Trotskyites and Maoists. Surely many of them hate one another, revile one another, break from one another, and occasionally shoot and kill one another: but this is always for personal rather than doctrinal reasons.

What is it about right-wing extremists that makes them right-wing? It is often said that the distinctions between left and right are a fiction, a mere manner of speaking. Perhaps there is some truth to this, but only some. It is true, for example, that both the extreme right and the extreme left hate the federal government. It is true that certain anarchists, like certain militia members, wish to establish communes in order to get big government off their backs. It is also true that America's foremost white separatist of the sixties, George Lincoln Rockwell, was well received when he spoke to the black separatist Nation of Islam. And finally it is true that sometimes the militias co-opt the language of leftism, as when they attribute elements of Nazism to the federal government, which they claim to be combating. Thus, in the publication *Patriot Propaganda*, which is in fact little more than a 'zine produced by Robert Plummer, we find Bill Clinton compared to Adolf Hitler, Gennifer Flowers to Eva Braun, and the Brady Bill to the Decree of 1936. Likewise, when Terry Nichols, a suspect in the Oklahoma City bombing, surrendered to the police, according to Kenneth S. Stern, author of *A Force Upon the Plain*, "he complained that the procedure was reminiscent of 'Nazi Germany.'"[4] Nevertheless, the extreme right, whether in America, Russia, or Germany, tends to favor nationalism over socialism, the individual over the community, and traditional values, as it perceives them, over innovation. More often than not, its members are driven by hatred of nationalities rather than by hatred of classes, and by a preference for their own race over the rest of humanity, which they consider inferior.

The oldest and most famous of the extreme right-wing movements in America is surely the Ku Klux Klan. Indeed, it was the most successful extremist movement in the political history of our country. At its height during the twenties, it boasted over three million members across the United States. Now, however, according to the best estimates, the organization numbers little more than ten thousand. Part of its decline results from the fact that it engages issues that were once seen as problems by the majority of centrist society (like the mass influx of Catholics and Jews, and the emergence of blacks, in what had been a white Protestant country) but that have now been successfully and peaceably resolved by the center. For a variety of reasons, the majority of the population is now neither anti-alien nor anti-black, as a significant number of Americans were in the 1920s. In the aftermath of the abolition of slavery and of the mass immigration of Jews and Catholics, many members of the status quo population grew angry and perplexed. Now this is no longer the case.

Thus the Klan is dated, but it is this very datedness that constitutes its primary appeal to many of its members. There is a triumphant, ornery stubbornness to the Klan and its followers, a defiant assertion that the mere act of belief places them apart from the rest of society; that, in a world in which so much has changed and so little has stayed the same, they alone have not changed, they alone have not been gathered to the center, they alone hate blacks and Jews as much as they ever did. Nevertheless, the Klan's influence is at an all-time low. In part this decline began in the seventies when the several different strains of the movement failed to coalesce. These included the United Klans of America, led by their Imperial Wizard, the Alabama-based Robert Shelton; the Invisible Empire Knights of the Ku Klux Klan, led by Bill Wilkinson; and the Knights of the Ku Klux Klan, led by former neo-Nazi David Duke of Louisiana. These groups were dealt a number of crippling setbacks, such as being forced to pay seven million dollars to the family of a black man murdered by Klansmen, as well as the court-ordered dissolution of the Invisible Empire when some of its members marched against a civil rights group.

Most of those on the extreme right, however, whether militia members, skinheads, or neo-Nazis, often demonstrate a certain disrespect for the KKK, even though, as has been said, there is considerable overlap in the membership of the various rightist movements. The reason for this disrespect is in some measure generational, resembling, in a perverse way, the revolt of the draft-evading Baby Boomers against the traditions of their fathers who fought in World War II and Korea. Indeed, in an even more perverse way, it mirrors the difference between the audience for David Letterman and the audience for Johnny Carson. For many younger racists, the KKK membership seem middle-aged and even square.

It is uniquely the KKK's hatred of blacks that has resonance for the younger generation. In this no one can hold a candle to the KKK. They were hating blacks before anyone else, and, just as anti-Semitism is the province of the neo-Nazis, so hating blacks is the Klan's issue, and it cannot be taken away from them. On the other hand, its once virulent anti-Catholicism has pretty much fallen by the wayside, since that was largely an expression of an older anti-alienism, which means next to nothing to modern extremists.

Perhaps what is most chilling about the KKK is its perverse sense of fun. For it is worth noting that, unlike the extreme left, the extreme right, and especially the KKK, has a hearty sense of humor, even of a distinctly goofy sort. Whereas some rightists wish to be taken very seriously indeed and are persuaded that the fate of the world depends on their actions, the Klansmen, by contrast, often seem to be at play. Their hatred of blacks and Jews is sincere as far as that goes. But this is not an angry hatred, as it is with the neo-Nazis, so much as good sport. The KKK's dopey sense of fun is the more disturbing for being so much at variance with the pernicious malignity of their stated aims: they call their leaders Grand Goblins and King Kleagles, and they meet in groups called Klaverns. Their lecturers are Klokards, their chaplains Kludds, their secretaries Kligrapps. The sacred book of the order is the Kloran, and meetings are called Klonvocations. Furthermore, Klansmen wear silly white sheets and hoods to protect their identities, and this very clandestinity makes them more in the nature of hobbyists, four-square middle-management types who hold down a day job, than hell-bent revolutionaries whose ideology saturates every moment of their waking lives and every pore and molecule of their corporeal being.

For such reasons as these, the next generation does not find in the KKK that manic, Nietzschean edge to which the neo-Nazis and certain militia groups aspire. Thomas Metzger, a leading neo-Nazi and white supremacist, summed up this attitude when he declared, "You don't make change burning the fiery cross out in cow pastures, you make change by invading the hall of the Statehouse and the Congress!"[5]

According to John George and Laird Wilcox, in *American Extremists*, "The neo-Nazi movement in the United States is characterized by two outstanding traits: small size and large capacity to generate media coverage."[6] The authors calculate that there is roughly one neo-Nazi for every half million Americans. Neo-Nazism began in this country almost as soon as the last world war ended, with the founding in 1949 of James Madole's National Renaissance Party. Ten years later, George Lincoln Rockwell, a former navy commander, founded the American Nazi Party, which he led until he was assassinated in 1967 by a disgruntled member of his organization. This organization in turn was followed by the National Socialist Party of America, the creation of Frank Collins. Collins was doing fine until word got out that his real name was Frank Cohn, that he was half-Jewish, and that his father had survived Dachau. Following these revelations he committed suicide.

Today there are a number of such groups, and it is of some interest to pass briefly in review of them. Prominent among them are the so-called Church of Jesus Christ Christian, founded by the Reverend Richard Girnt Butler. This, like many Christian Identity groups, asserts that Christ was not Jewish but Aryan, and that the lost tribes of Israel were Anglo-Saxons and other Aryan peoples. Butler's twenty-acre compound in Idaho—home to some of the most intense right-wing activists—is "patrolled by armed men in blue uniforms modeled on Hitler's SS." In his fiery rhetoric, Butler refers to Jews as "hook-nosed anti-Christs" and the "seed of Satan," the latter epithet pertaining to blacks as well.[7]

Though the link between Nazism and Christianity would have surprised Adolf Hitler, it emerges again in the Restored Church of Jesus Christ in Post Falls, Idaho, founded by Frederick Gilbert, who advocates that *Mein Kampf* be included among the books of the Bible. A similar religiosity inspires Gary "Gerhard" Lauck, who claims to sanctify Adolf Hitler as "the greatest man who ever lived." Faulting Hitler only for being "too humane," he has declared that "we National Socialists declare total war on World Jewry and shall not rest until you have disappeared from the earth."[8]

Thomas Metzger himself, who was once a Grand Dragon of David Duke's Knights of the Ku Klux Klan, is among the most virulent neo-Nazis in America. After being expelled from the John Birch Society ("I learned that you could not criticize Jews"), he founded White Aryan Resistance in order to practice a more energetic form of racism. For some time, this proved to be one of the most effective neo-Nazi groups in the country. Among his many varied activities, Metzger has founded two magazines, one of them called *Blood & Honor*, claiming to be "a celebration of being white." This was followed by *WAR* (White Aryan Resistance). In this latter publication one reads that "almost all abortion doctors are Jews—abortion makes money for Jews. . . . Jews will do anything for money. . . . Jews must be punished for the Holocaust and murder of white babies along with their perverted Lesbian nurses who enjoy their jobs too much."

Metzger's fortunes soon faded, however, through legal action taken when an exceptionally violent group he had helped to found, the Aryan Youth Movement, was convicted in the death of an Ethiopian tourist, Mulugeta Seraw. The victim's estate sued for ten million dollars, and Metzger and his son were named as principals. The jury awarded even more than had been asked for, and this penalty essentially wiped Metzger out financially.

His influence, however, continued through the skinhead movement, in which he and his son John were active members. According to Mark Hamm's book *American Skinheads*, "Were it not for Thomas Metzger the American [skinhead] movement would never have become more than scattered, short-lived groups led by disturbed individuals." Though the movement is still very active, opinions differ as to its importance. According to Bennett it plays only a small part in our culture. Though it comprised some 144 groups in 1991, that figure was down to 87 in 1993, and its hard-core membership is estimated at no more than thirty-five hundred in forty states. A report by the Southern Poverty Law Center, however, quoted by Hamm, asserts that "the emergence of Skinhead Klans represents a unique and frightening phenomenon in the history of white supremacism in America: for the first time, a nationwide movement is being initiated by teenagers who are not confined to any single geographic region."[9]

In the case of the skinheads, at least the extreme examples of that trend, we see for the first time hatred as the overriding point of their association, with little or no pretense to ideology. One has only to consider a representative sampling of their crimes, as provided by Hamm. On 15 September 1987, in the town of Van Nuys, California, several skinheads slit the throat of a Hispanic woman who refused to turn down her cassette recorder, which was playing Latin music. On 1 January 1988, seven skinheads in Dupont Circle in Washington, D.C., attacked a party of homosexuals with bats and knives, fracturing the skull of one of them and chanting, "Die, faggot, die!" Afterward, one of the assailants told the *Washington Post*, "If he'd died, I don't think I would have felt remorse about it." On 15 March of the same year, a pair of skinheads approached a lesbian couple in a bar in Philadelphia and beat them with beer bottles. Less than a week later, in North Carolina, three skinheads abducted an eighteen-year-old black man and killed him by slitting his throat with a knife after torturing him with a boa constrictor. What is evident here, in addition to the slightness or absence of the pretext for violence, is the metaphorical as well as poetical element of the punishment.

One fundamental difference between skinheads and conventional youth culture is that, although mainstream teen culture is almost universally liberal in its pronouncements—advocating things like racial harmony, pot, and sexual laissez-faire—the skinheads are unapologetically odious in the sense of seeking to inspire hate and dissent. "I am a violent person," Hamm quotes one of them as saying. "I love the white race, and if you love something, you're the most vicious person on earth." Less restrained was this statement by another skinhead on the Oprah Winfrey show: "What makes a skinhead? Attitude. White power. 'Cause niggers suck. Niggers and Jews. They're half monkeys. They should all be killed."[10]

And whereas most teenagers try to make themselves attractive, even if that takes such unconventional forms as the grunge look and body piercings, the skinhead, by contrast, seeks to make himself repulsive to the society that—he likes to think—has rejected him. In this he is entirely unlike the typical Nazis, whom he otherwise resembles in certain respects. For Nazism has about it aspects of an aestheticized cult—with its sharp uniforms and spit-polished shoes—in which appearance is all important. It is said that the skinheads' distinctly unappealing name comes from having cut off all their hair in order that it could not be grabbed in a street fight. Perhaps that was the original intention. But now it represents a potent denial of the duty that society imposes on all of us to be as attractive as possible. And as so often in right-wing movements, this particular brand of ugliness, the Doc Martens, dowdy pants, and ungainly T-shirts, is in the nature of a return. It is a return to the blue-collar working-class style of fifties gang members in the heavily industrialized cities of Manchester and Liverpool.

But one must not exaggerate, as some do, the importance of the movement's British origins; it has succeeded in America for very different reasons from those that gave rise to it in England. There it grew out of class struggle: certain unruly members of the working class rose up against what they saw as the hopelessness of their situation, as the impossibility of rising as high as others in society, of freeing themselves from the oppressive class structure into which they were born. In America, by contrast, though there is class struggle of sorts, it does not weigh as heavily on the minds of the young as in England, and it affects them in far different ways. Whatever the employment situation happens to be for young people in America today, at least they do not have the sense, handed down over many centuries, that if they try to get ahead society will punish them for their insolent presumption. Though they might feel, for example, that the American Dream is a hollow hope for them, at least this sentiment will not be aggravated by a rigid class structure. For this reason, Hamm is unpersuasive when he writes that "the Reagan era seemed to have produced conditions conducive to extreme alienation among the white working-class youths in America."[11]

In fact, skinheadism in America, unlike the associated movement in England, has nothing whatever to do with economics. It is far too small a trend to have proceeded from so large a provocation. In part what we are seeing in skinheadism is the perennial rebelliousness of youth, allied to a natural tendency in certain people to hatred, a hatred that our laws sanction and that our culture at times promotes. Surely there have been gangs in our cities for well over a hundred years, and they have largely been the result of economic privations. But skinheadism is a cultural movement that, in its perverse way, emerges out of the same permissiveness in our society, the same liberal openness to all voices, that gave rise to the MTV generation. Most "MTV rebellion" is not really rebellion at all. It is merely a form of picturesque petulance sanctioned by an extremely elastic society that will pat adolescents on the head for wearing torn jeans and swearing and talking back to their elders. The skinheads as well came out of this culture, at least in America, but the results, as we have seen, have been far more explosive.

Compared with these skinheads and with the neo-Nazis, the militias in America seem almost mild, and only a few of them are extremely violent. One major distinction between the militia movement and the neo-Nazis is that the militias are usually inspired less by religious or racial considerations than by anti-liberalism and virulent antagonism to the federal government of the United States. They believe that the United States government is no longer identifiable with that America for whose independence their forefathers (as they deem them) risked their lives two centuries ago. Now, they believe, this very government is plotting to abridge the individual freedoms of all Americans, either because it serves the interests of corrupt corporations and corrupt politicians, or because it has sold out to minorities, feminists, and, most dangerous of all, Zionists.

At their most radical, the militias can be seen as a new packaging for an old product: the rage of the Birchers, the neo-Nazis, and the KKK at an increasingly liberal society that turns its back on the traditions of their forefathers. At the same time, the militias represent something quite new. They represent the radical outgrowth of a peculiar sport that became popular in the eighties: paramilitary exercises and sham battles, amounting to summer camps for grown men, in which they could simulate all the action and adventure of real war as it was portrayed in the Rambo films that obsessed them. As James William Gibson writes in *Warrior Dreams*, "War games took [these] fantasies a step further and allowed men to act out their desires in paramilitary games and theme parks that one would describe as 'better than Disneyland.' Here, away from the ordinary routines of world and family life, men could meet, mingle, and share their warrior dreams." Gibson identifies three main venues for this kind of sport: the National Survival game, a fictionalized combat with groupies throughout the country; the annual Soldier of Fortune convention in Las Vegas; and the firing ranges and combat shooting schools that can be found almost anywhere. "In these special environments," Gibson comments, "the gods of war could be summoned for war games played along the edges of violence."[12]

And yet there came a point at which mere fun and games were linked in certain participants to a deep anger against contemporary society. In order to begin to understand this anger—not the insane anger of the minority of these gamesmen, but the slightly more moderate anger of a far larger percentage of the militias—it is perhaps sufficient to receive a speeding or even a parking ticket in circumstances in which you feel that you were right and that the law officer was taking advantage of you to fill his quota of tickets. As you become aware of the fine you must now pay, the dangers of a repeat offense, and the far greater trouble that will result from noncompliance with the law, all of a sudden the state, which protects and nurtures most of us most of the time, begins to take on the appearance of a malign juggernaut. And the laws that bind our community together, laws that ordinarily seem as self-evident and ineluctable as the laws of nature, suddenly start to seem like the purely arbitrary and possibly sinister inventions of bureaucrats who do not have our best interests at heart. Now for most of us this spasm of antinomianism lasts a quarter hour and is gone. In some few, however, it is in the nature of a festering wound that only grows steadily worse.

Paramilitary movements have been a reality in the United States since the sixties, with the activities of the Minutemen and the California Rangers. Ever since then, survivalist camps for Sunday soldiers have been, for the most part, something of a harmless fad. A few groups, however, have been more virulent than the others, and three have been downright dangerous: the Christian Patriots Defense League; the Covenant, the Sword, and the Arm of the Lord; and the Posse Comitatus. The bearded members of the CSA are a real minority, numbering somewhere between 100 and 150 members.

Much larger was the Posse Comitatus (which has since dissolved), whose name derives from a Latin term in medieval common law meaning "power of the county." Its membership was estimated at between three and five thousand. The name is in keeping with the belief that state and federal laws are worthless and corrupt and that the real unit of power is the county, presided over by a sheriff. This position is maintained through a series of symbolic acts: members do not put license plates on their cars, do not apply for hunting licenses, and resist paying taxes to the state and federal governments. Some have gone so far as to establish a state unto themselves, the "Constitutional Township of Tigerton Dells," on a fourteen-hundred-acre patch of land, presided over by its own judges and equipped with its own "foreign ambassadors." At the entrance are the words FEDERAL AGENTS KEEP OUT. SURVIVORS WILL BE PROSECUTED.[13]

Some have seen this violent distrust of the United States government as a radical extension of the general anti-government sentiment, usually leftist, that emerged in the aftermath of the Vietnam War, Watergate, Iran-Contra, and the ever-escalating national debt. As Bennett writes, "In the post-Vietnam, post-Watergate era, the federal government had become an object of suspicion and contempt for millions of citizens." But if certain elements of the left and right oppose the federal government, they do so in different ways. The conspiracy theories of the left are class-based: politicians represent the interests of the wealthy rather than of the people. By contrast, the far right's hatred of the government is culture-based. Many of its members believe that the federal government is the puppet of various special East Coast interests, usually liberals and minorities, foreign powers, especially Communists, and, of course, the international Zionist conspiracy. At the risk of simplification, the radical left hates Jews because it believes that all Jews are bankers, whereas the radical right hates all bankers because it believes that they are Jews.

In fact, the extreme right's hatred of the federal government recurs not to the sixties but to the fifties; to the Birchers and to

Senator Joseph McCarthy's assertion of treason at the highest levels of government. Nothing fuels the anger of extreme political movements in general, and the extreme right specifically, more than all the recent talk of a New World Order. In part their hatred of big government is linked to the most rabid anti-alienism, the fear of foreign domination of America, as well as to the perennial specter of the international Jewish banking conspiracy. In an interesting symmetry of thought, the far left fears the New World Order because it sees it as the spread of American imperialism, in the guise of the United Nations, throughout the world. For the far right, however, the New World Order is the invasion of the United States by the United Nations, with all its brown and yellow minions in tow.

Furthermore, the New World Order, harkening back to that quintessential East Coast liberal Woodrow Wilson, is the bipartisan love child of the center, indeed, the most exhilarating triumph of the center over the extremes in the history of the world. Its economic arm, comprising GATT and NAFTA, the World Bank and the Trilateral Commission, only strengthens this conviction. What so terrifies right-wing extremists is that, as they correctly surmise, it is the overwhelming tendency of modern times to draw all of us into a common culture. This they see as going hand in hand with the mongrelizing of the races and the effacing of all religious, sexual and cultural differences, or, more precisely, the elimination of that which demarcates white Christian men from the rest of creation. They are, in short, the first to perceive, and the last to accept, that the world is no longer theirs.

As Harold Covington wrote in 1987, in his introduction to *The March Up-Country*, which is something of a breviary for the movement, "Most of what I say here [about the United States] is true for all Zionist Occupational Governments (ZOGs) throughout the Western World. All ZOG's in so called 'democracies' use more or less the same scam—panem et circenses, boob tube mind control, love-thy-nigger brain washing, letting the white peasantry elect a few windbags to a legislative talking shop, etc." On the cover of his book a defiantly athletic Minuteman, proudly bearing a musket, stands over a map of the United States, with the Star of David and the Hammer and Sickle underfoot, as a woman and child cower for protection behind him.

Similarly, we read on the back cover of the novel *Seed of the Woman*, by one Joshua Von Vulcan, published by Four Horsemen Press, "Through the years he [the author] learned the true heritage of Christian Israel, and the manifest destiny of the Aryan Race. . . . Needless to say, he experienced the frustration of knowing the truth and being unable to convey it to his racial kinfolk. Who would listen? Who was courageous enough to defy the Jewish establishment by supporting him? He knew that 'going public' would likely result in his assassination at the hands of the Zionist Occupational Government."

What the militias seek, what they desperately want, is to return to a simpler time when the world was theirs and they were not threatened by the nagging proximity of blacks, Jews, Asians, and women. Their historicism usually is that of the Revolutionary War instead of the 1950s, which is dear to the far right rather than the extreme right. For them the war for independence was a time when freedom-fighting Minutemen protected their family against the forces of imperialism. It is in this spirit that George Bush, popularizer of the New World Order, is mocked as "King George." And it is in this spirit that a flyer published by the Florida State Militia declares, "It is more difficult than ever to convince the American people of the 'peaceful' mission of the federal government toward citizens. The links in the chain grow yearly and now the chain is long enough to wrap every man, woman, and child many times round. As the chains tighten against the strain of the people the promises of rain prove to be nothing more than dust storms. Like a drum, tyranny thunders!"

More explicitly still, the California-based Morongo Militia begins its "Declaration" with these words: "When, in the course of human events, it becomes necessary for the Citizens of this State, to exercise their right to protect and defend their lives, family, property and the right of the State to be free and independent, a decent respect to the opinions of their fellow men requires that they should declare the causes that impel them to exercise their 2nd

Amendment rights, which are guaranteed and protected by the constitution of the United States of America."

A natural question arises: why do these militias appear so
much more prominent now than in the past? There are three events
that have greatly galvanized the movement in recent years. The first
was the incident at Ruby Ridge in which Randy Weaver was
caught in a sting operation trying to sell illegal firearms to a government agent. When Weaver failed to appear in court, the authorities came to arrest him in his cabin atop a remote mountain
in Idaho, where he was holed up with his wife and four children,
as well as his friend and his dog. "I and the children are ready to
stand for the truth and our freedom," his wife wrote to the white
supremacist group Aryan Nation. "We cannot make deals with the
enemy. This is a war against the white sons of Isaac. Yahweh our
Yahshua is our Savior and King."[14] In the ensuing shootout a decorated federal deputy marshal was shot and killed. There followed
an eleven-day siege in which Weaver's wife, son, and dog were also
killed. No one was indicted for these deaths. When Weaver was
brought to trial he was defended by Gerry Spence in what resulted
in an acquittal, though he subsequently served eighteen months on
a lesser charge.

"Are there any damn rights left in this country?"[15] asked one
of his many sympathizers who hastened to the site of the siege.
"All he wanted was to be left alone,"[16] another commented. These
responses reveal one of the recurring themes among militia members: the desire for freedom. Their historicist imaginations are forever returning to the free and unspoiled wilderness of Lewis and
Clark, as yet unclaimed and untamed by the federal government.
In the most charitable construction, one finds among these citizens
a desperate longing to break free from man-made laws—as opposed to what they see as the laws of God—a desire to escape the
corruption of the center, to be disenfranchised from the turmoil of
modernity. For many of them that freedom was symbolized in
Randy Weaver's living atop a mountain in Idaho. And when the
FBI caught up with him, it seemed to prove, as they should never
have doubted, that even here escape was no longer possible, that

the tentacular reach of the government, with all its East Coast technocrats who despise the farmer and the hillbilly, would pursue them, with deadly force if need be, to the very ends of the earth.

But the anger they felt at Ruby Ridge was as nothing compared with their response to the attack on the Branch Davidian compound in April of 1993. David Koresh, the leader of this small religious commune founded in 1936, had originally attracted the attention of federal law enforcement by stockpiling weapons and night sensors, not to mention ammunition and all the chemicals needed for powerful explosives. Things started to run awry when a UPS package destined for his compound fell apart, revealing hundreds of hand grenades. The UPS driver immediately alerted the sheriff, who conveyed the information to the FBI. Though the FBI had intended to raid the premises on 28 February 1993, word got out and the press was there even before the federal agents were on the scene. In the ensuing melee, cultists shot and killed four federal agents as they tried to approach, and in the process Koresh and his father-in-law were wounded.

Now the sympathies of Koresh for the extreme right are unclear. Certainly he could not have been a white supremacist, since he welcomed into his community people of all races. Yet, just like Randy Weaver, he was a biblicist whose literal reading of scripture led him to polygamy. Surely biblicism has considerable appeal in far right circles, yet it was not really this belief that galvanized them to support his cause. Rather it was his obsession with weapons of destruction that made the extreme right see this long-haired messianic figure as one of their own. Furthermore, they identified with his efforts to create his own little state, independent from the rest of the world, and what most appalled them was that his destruction came at the hands—as they believed—of the federal government.

In his book *A Force Upon the Plain*, Kenneth S. Stern likens Waco to Pearl Harbor. And one of those who visited the standoff, Timothy McVeigh, would become the prime suspect in the bombing of the Federal Building in Oklahoma City, which happened, significantly, on the very same day, April 19, that the Waco compound had gone up in flames a year before. As one prominent white supremacist, Eustace Mullins, observed, "The Waco Church Holocaust, in which many worshippers, including innocent children, were burned alive while worshipping in their church [was] an atrocity which surpasses the worst accusations [!] made against the Nazis in Germany."[17]

For many in the militia movement, however, it was the Brady Bill, passed into law in 1993, that constituted the third and final nail in the coffin of the free state. Whereas Waco and Ruby Ridge were more or less symbolic assaults on the freedom of the militias, the Brady Bill was a measure that really hit home. This legislation, which only an extremist would find extreme, imposed a five-day waiting period on anyone seeking to purchase a handgun. This gave the government time to learn if the prospective purchaser was a convicted felon, in which case the sale would be blocked. Though most of us would not find this provision unreasonable, others did not see it that way. As one gun enthusiast declared, "I'm an avid sportsman, and the government wants to do away with my right to play. I've only registered three of my fifteen guns. The government will never get them. They'll have to take them out of my dead hand."[18]

As though the Brady Bill wasn't "extreme" enough, the next year a crime bill was passed banning nineteen kinds of assault weapons and imposing a ten-bullet limit on guns. To many in the gun circuit the implications of this could hardly have been more far-reaching. Wayne LaPierre, head of the National Rifle Association, wrote, "If we lose the right to keep and bear arms, then the right to free speech, free practice of religion, and every other freedom in the Bill of Rights are sure to follow."[19]

To most of us it will not be immediately clear why gun control means so much to the extreme right. After all, its members do not have to defend their lives on a daily basis, and hunting can't be *that* much fun. Why then is it that any abridgment of their right to own firearms is interpreted as being but a step shy of tyranny? That the gun manufacturers should oppose gun controls, of course, makes perfect sense. That common criminals should seek unlimited access to the most deadly ordnance is likewise perfectly sensible, since these implements are essential if they are to ply their trade, such as it is. It is interesting in this connection that criminals seem to take a far more practical view of the gun. Having little or no symbolic resonance for them, it is simply a means to a potentially lucrative end, namely, mugging unarmed citizens and holding up banks and convenience stores.

And yet rightists, and especially extreme rightists, though in a general way law-and-order types, become something less than clear-headed when it comes to guns. As so often with extremists, symbols no longer represent reality—they supplant it. For many men and a few women on the far right, the gun is the reification, the incarnation, of freedom and power. To their historicist minds it recalls Lexington and Concord, the Wild West, and, once again, freedom from the corrupting influence of the big city. The gun harkens back to a simpler frontiersman's existence when the federal government was off our backs, when races were separate and women knew their place. Quite simply, there is something about guns that *feels* so American that even President Clinton, sensing the need early in his administration both to prove his testosterone levels and to quieten the controversy surrounding his evasion of the draft, had himself photographed duck hunting.

Still, the far right sees the gun only as an expensive and thrilling implement. To the extreme right, by contrast, it is something more. It is not so much an ideology (though it is that, too) as it is a lifestyle. In this connection it is worth observing that, whereas the extreme left is motivated largely by ideas—as it sees them—the extreme right is fascinated by accessories, clothing, language, and symbolic acts.

In that case, it may be asked, why don't they join the army? The army can no longer satisfy their interests, not when heads of the Joint Chiefs of Staff are moderate minority members like Colin Powell rather than bloodthirsty killers like George Patton, at least as he is depicted in the movies. Some extremists, it is true, have fought in Vietnam and in the Persian Gulf. Bo Gritz of the Christian Patriots, who is something of a legend in militia circles, was a highly decorated soldier in Vietnam. Timothy McVeigh's movement toward the extreme was hastened only when, in the hopes of be-

coming a career soldier, he applied to become a Green Beret but
was turned down as being psychologically unfit. But most of the
members of the militia are too young to have known conscription
in the Second World War or the Korean War, too young to have
known any other army than a voluntary one made up largely
of minorities. Furthermore, the increasing internationalism of
the United States Army prompted one militiaman to comment,
"Join the army and fight for the UN; join the militia and fight for
America."[20]

As a result the militarists among us, finding little outlet for
their aggressions in the military itself, have resorted to paramilitary
options like the militia movement. At an introductory level there are
the survivalist camps that constitute serious fun for adults. Though
certain observers on the left have tried to see these maneuvers as
sinister and militaristic, in fact they have as much to do with real
aggression as a dude ranch with the Battle of Bull Run. And most
of the men who attend such camps fully appreciate the fact.

Some, however, do not. What they seek is not a temporary
escape but total immersion in a lifestyle. You could not find a better entree into this world than *Soldier of Fortune* magazine, which
can be bought in most of the better-stocked news stores around
the country. The ads tell the whole story. They seem to flatter the
reader by attributing to him a dangerous lifestyle that, in most
cases, has little to do with his sedate, suburban existence. They
implicitly accept the reader as a renegade, a rebel, a mercenary.
There are ads for steroids and bulletproof vests, camouflage pass-
ports and guides on how to "trade in your old identity for a new
start."

There are manuals to show you how to determine if you are
being bugged and how to go about bugging others. For $14.95
you can buy the instructions for a rocket launcher. For the same
price you can have a Hellstorm 2000, which "will allow you to
empty a 30 round magazine in under 3 seconds." Night vision
goggles—"Russia's finest"—are offered at the unbeatable price of
$299. Sniper suits go for $145. You can buy New York Police Department badges and, in a moving testament to multiculturalism,
an SS officer's black visor cap and insignias from the Israeli army.

Books published by companies of which you have never heard bear
titles like *Your Revenge Is in the Mail* (presumably a how-to for
novice letter bombers) and *Screw the Bitch Divorce Tactics for
Men*, whose title is self-explanatory. At the same time, there are
romantic ads with submissive-looking women from Russia,
Guatemala, and Vietnam—"Beautiful. Unspoiled. Romantic"—
who will doubtless provide fewer hassles than liberated American
women.

Just as *Gourmet* magazine assesses wines and patés, *Soldier of
Fortune* rates guns. In a typical article one reads: "We fired more
than 1,000 rounds during our test and evaluation of the Kahr K9
pistol, employing 9mm Parabellum hollowpoint ammunition that
ranged from 115-grain bullets moving at hypervelocities to 147-grain
projectiles plodding downrange at subsonic speeds." Other articles
are devoted to Bosnian mines, nonbounding AP fragmentation
bombs, directed fragmentation bombs, and anti-tank artillery. Despite the magazine's efforts to maintain the appearance of disinterested reportage, Clinton is routinely portrayed as a draft-dodging
Socialist. But the political implications become especially clear in
one assessment of Waco and Ruby Ridge that ends darkly by reminding its readers that there is a duty "to punish—punishment
such as a private citizen could certainly expect—the guilty government parties. Anything less will be a travesty of justice that invites
repetition of these heinous atrocities."[21]

And yet, despite all the posturing and tough-talking militarism, *Soldier of Fortune*, together with the culture that it exemplifies, is really, when all is said and done, in the spirit of play. It
is for hobbyists, after all. Certainly some career criminals and terrorists and hitmen will read the magazine for what we might call
practical reasons. But most who purchase the magazine and the
items advertised—and this includes the militant right wing as
well—simply have a taste for gadgetry of a fairly high-tech order,
a fetishistic fascination that rarely if ever spills over into action. As
one looks at these advertisements for hand cannons, bazookas, and
night scanners, one cannot help recalling the popular expression,
"The difference between the men and the boys is the price of their
toys." This equation with childhood games, cops and robbers,

cowboys and Indians, sounds simplistic, especially relative to anything as odious as the extreme right wing. And yet consider what
one gains by joining in the sport. For most people, life is not a
game; nor is it especially fun. Some—the rich, the famous, the
greatly gifted—seem, at least to those who are none of the above,
to have a life that is far more enjoyable than that of blue-collar
workers. And yet, simply by buying into the gun culture and the
militia movement—a modest investment, after all—one's life immediately becomes dangerous and thrilling.

Now sport, like fiction, entails the suspension of disbelief.
You cannot enjoy a game between the Mets and the Cardinals if
you are forever reminding yourself of what is indeed the case, that
there is no essential difference between the two teams, except that
one wears blue and white uniforms, the other red and white uniforms. What logical reason could there be for our preferring one
over the other? There is none at all. We must suppress this more
adult emotion so that we can curse the umpire and believe the rival
pitcher to be evil incarnate. And so it is, in its perverse way, with
the militias, and so, ultimately, with the KKK, the neo-Nazis, and
the skinheads. What we are seeing is an elaborate blood sport, the
cardinal rule of which is that the participants must never admit to
themselves, and certainly never admit to others, the essentially
ludic nature of the enterprise to which they have consecrated their
lives. Thus Norman Olson, founder of the Michigan Militia,
snapped at one journalist, "Why are you bothering me? Can't you
see I'm trying to stop World War III?"[22] It was in the same spirit
that James Johnson of the Ohio Unorganized Militia said, "When
[the revolution] blows, a lot of us will die, a lot of us will be in-
jured for life, and a lot of us will be in jail. But all of us will be
free again."[23]

Of course this is all arrant nonsense. The revolution hasn't
come and won't be coming any time soon. And though members
of the extreme right have a gift for attracting the attention of reporters eager for a good story, and though they can indeed
threaten, maim, and sometimes murder individuals or groups, their
continued existence is ultimately predicated on the indulgence and
restraint of the federal government, to which they never posed any

kind of threat and which, should it ever feel called upon to do so, could exterminate them without too much trouble.

The extremism of the right, as has been stated, is everywhere different and everywhere the same. Just as the same word, set in a different context, acquires a different meaning, so fascism and Nazism and other causes dear to the extreme right take on very different casts in Germany and Russia because the circumstances into which they are set, and the history to which they respond, are very different. In this respect the far right differs from the far left, which tends to be international and universal in outlook, and thus works to suppress the historicism and specificity of nationalism.

Good people everywhere have been shocked by the resurgence of the far right in Germany. The relative smallness of far right gangs is itself an object of alarm to many who recall that Nazism itself began as small gangs of extremists in the 1920s. Nevertheless, this alarm, though understandable, is probably unwarranted. Whereas German fascism first emerged in circumstances of considerable political and fiscal chaos, now there is order in both realms. And since the vast majority of the population is so determinedly opposed to the extreme right, it is extremely unlikely that they will ever allow a self-proclaimed fascist to gain any kind of power. Nor does the extreme right expect to achieve power in Germany or Russia or anywhere else. The power that the far right exerts in Germany, as in most other countries where it has any force, is of a far subtler and, so to speak, existential kind. Far rightists know that their mere existence is a powerful provocation to the center, and the impossibility of uprooting them, without considerable political cost, is more galling still.

The seemingly miraculous resurgence of fascism in Germany is attributable to one cause, that it never fully died out. It had been suppressed, but never successfully, and the more East Germans hated the Communist regime, the more it became the symbol and instrument of that hatred. As Paul Hockenos explains in his book *Free to Hate*, Erich Honecker, the former premier of the German Democratic Republic, liked to use the following syllogism: because fascism was a reactionary form of monopoly capitalism, and because the GDR was a socialist and thus noncapitalist state, it followed of unalterable necessity that there could be no fascism in East Germany. But when, as early as the seventies, brawling soccer fans broke into a chorus of "Jew Out!" it could no longer be denied that something was afoot. When an official inquiry was made, according to Hockenos, "the earliest top-secret studies of the GDR Skinheads produced results so damning that the state immediately confiscated the documentation and ruled the topic off limits for independent researchers. . . . Nothing less than the state's skilled workers had turned so vehemently on the ideology that claimed to embody their interests above all others."[24] The situation was more trenchantly summed up by the film director Konrad Weiss: "On the surface, [people] lived for forty years as seemingly adjusted, politically indifferent or well-behaved socialist citizens. It is they, I think, who waited patiently for their hour and now pass on the brown baton to their children."[25]

Yet some, like the sociologist Hans-Joachim Maaz, see the socialist state itself as inspiring these developments. For him, there is an essential link between socialist indoctrination and fascism, both of them sternly enjoining discipline and punctuality on children. "One was forced to subordinate oneself to a collective and the collective norms at the expense of individual particularities, possibilities and potentials."[26] Furthermore, though each schoolchild was required to visit a death camp under the communists, Nazism was such anathema that it was hardly ever mentioned in connection with such excursions.

But although it was possible to eradicate most visible traces of the Nazi past, it proved impossible even for the redoubtable Stasi, the East German secret police, to extirpate all memories of that past from the minds of the living. One young man whom Hockenos interviewed confirms this: "My Opa [grandfather] told me that he lived better then than now, earned more for his work. The Nazis built the *Autobahn* and the schools. They took the unemployed off the streets and there wasn't any problem with niggers and foreigners."[27]

As in the United States and most other places, the extreme right in Germany is different from the center right and even the far

right. For these groups are essentially practical, advocating programs that can be realized. Often money and institutional power
are behind them, and they are at least rooted in reality. By contrast, the extreme right in Germany, as in most other places,
emerges from an indwelling temperament, which responds to its
specific circumstances but is really born of something deep within
the individual. The extreme right causes a dismay to centrist German society that is without parallel in other countries. Most Americans, for example, hate neo-Nazis, but they are not ashamed to be
Americans because some Americans are neo-Nazis. In Germany
things are different. For the past half century, the memories and the
guilt of the Second World War have oppressed all Germans. They
understand that whenever they go abroad, even if they were born
thirty years after the end of the war, they will have to answer for
the atrocities of their forebears. There are few parallels to this in
history. It is—to seek only a remote and weak comparison—as
though every white American had to answer to a censorious world
for the institution of slavery.

Thus the extreme right in Germany is a threat to the center
not only in the usual way, by calling its values into question and
by sometimes resorting to violence. Equally important is the fact
that, by its very existence, it reminds Germans of a past they desperately want to forget, while treacherously drawing them into the
vicinity of shared guilt. Neo-Nazism, of course, appears as far
afield as Canada, the United States, and Romania. In this regard it
is a rare, if not unique, example of an internationalist right-wing
extremism. What is different about its manifestations in Germany,
what makes it such a complex phenomenon, is the fact that it is
home-grown, that it does not entail an almost treasonous rejection
of one's own political tradition, as is the case whenever an American or a Briton embraces Nazism.

In Germany, as elsewhere, the extreme right is obsessed with
the past. Marx's famous statement in his *18th Brumaire of Louis
Napoleon*, that the past hangs like a nightmare over the minds of
the living, is far less true today, when we are overwhelmingly oriented toward the future, than it was during the heyday of historicism in the middle years of the last century. But just as the Fascism

of Mussolini and the Nazism of Hitler were the latest and most aggressive mainstream examples of that historicism, so today the extreme right stands implacably opposed to our orientation toward the future, and no one is more opposed than the neo-Nazis. Their embrace of the national past is thus is an echo of an echo. For it embraces not only the recent past, National Socialism, but also the past that that movement had also embraced, the past of Prussian militarism, Frederic the Second and the Neibelungen, stretching all the way back to Arminius. At the same time, unlike other right-wing movements that are avowedly historicist, neo-Nazism embraces a part of history that most Germans would prefer to forget. Most countries take pride in their past. Americans tend to be proud in a general way of the Revolutionary War, just as Russians take pride in Alexander Nevsky and Kutuzov and the French take pride in Henri IV and Napoleon Bonaparte. Only the Germans are denied this satisfaction.

There is this further difference between neo-Nazism in Germany and abroad: Nazism was once a political reality for the German people, as it has never been for the citizens of the United States, Canada, or most other places where it has recently been resurrected. Therefore it can never have in Germany the purely poetic, purely theoretical tone it has everywhere else. Though it was thoroughly discredited in Germany because of its disastrous practical application, it also proved that it could make the trains run on time. Here in America, by contrast, neo-Nazism is akin to Satanism. One does not endorse it in the sincere belief that it has any practical benefits to confer, that it is in possession of some arcane truth that humanity needs to know. Rather it is the palpable evil associated with the movement that appeals to certain members of society who wish, through an act of spiritual violence, to separate themselves from the rest of that society.

Though this is often true among German neo-Nazis as well, the practical reality that Nazism once had complicates their assessment of it. Thus, in a recent poll, many neo-Nazi youths gave their assent to the proposition that "had it not been for the war and the Holocaust, Hitler would have been one of Germany's greatest statesmen."[28] This proviso is important, because it is precisely the reality of the Holocaust—whose existence they deny—that endears Hitler to neo-Nazis outside of Germany and that is seen as the essence of Nazism. In Germany the adherents of Nazism tend to be a little more sobersided, claiming to seek a better standard of living for Germans, as opposed to immigrants, and the restoration of Germany's borders as of 1937, that is, comprising Austria and the Sudetenland, as well as East Prussia and Alsace-Lorraine.

Neo-Nazism in Germany is closely linked to the skinhead movement, and thus is generally younger than neo-Nazism in America and elsewhere. In Germany it feeds into the anxieties of late adolescents, with their restive, wiry strength and deep anxieties about their personal futures. To them, neo-Nazism is the one taboo subject that attests to their rebellious spirit, though it usually lacks the quasi-religious, cultic overtones it has in America. In addition, it calls for summary reordering of the world that the Christian Democratic welfare state of their parents' generation had wrought in West Germany.

In East Germany under Communism, sympathy for neo-Nazism was an indication of resistance to those in power. Without in any way palliating the nature of their views, it must be said of some of them, as can never be said of American neo-Nazis, that there is more moderation in their opinions than one might suspect. What they exhibit is an immoderate, foolish response to a difficult situation, more than one charged with evil. The thrust of neo-Nazism in Germany is really anti-alienism, the fear that one's own job security is being sacrificed to foreign interlopers. In this context, the Jew, when he comes up at all, is a metaphor for the foreigner. As there are relatively few Jews in Germany, anti-Semitism is as nothing compared to the real and disturbing antagonism felt toward Turks, Vietnamese, and Gypsies. The goal, according to one member of the Nationalische Front, is to "make life for foreigners in Germany as uncomfortable as possible."[29]

And yet, "We don't hate foreigners as long as they stay in their own countries," one of them observes. "Vietnamese in Vietnam, Africans in Africa, Germans in Germany. That's only normal."[30] The presence of women among these neo-Nazis, a far rarer occurrence among their American counterparts, is perhaps suggestive of this moderation. One young woman, who fully endorsed the anti-immigrant feelings of the group, nevertheless could say that, although the Nazis had been good for her country, "the extermination of the Jews was inhumane. I couldn't go along with that."[31] Another young man said, "It was bad that Adolf gassed the Jews. That was inhumane. He should have just sent them away. . . . What was good was that Hitler wanted to rule the whole world. If Germany had the power again, everyone would live better."[32] Foolish and misdirected to be sure, but a far cry from Metzger's sole criticism of Nazism, namely, that Hitler had been "too humane." Surely this is not to deny the fact that many of the skinheads and neo-Nazis in Germany are as bad as those in America. Rather it is to suggest that they are different and that they tend to be more practical than mystical, and thus perhaps a shade less odious than their American allies.

The role of the far right in Russia is a little more complicated than in Germany or America precisely because, due to the massive convulsions that Russian society has sustained in this century, and especially in recent years, that all-important sense of a center of society, a center of homing and of balance, is either atrophied or has yet to be born. Political, financial, and spiritual behavior that would be unthinkable in the West, except for small fringes, can often be found close to the heart of Russian society.

Despite this lack of clear centrality, however, most Russians look on the extreme right as clowns or lunatics, rather than as respected statesmen. In Russia, however, the extreme right is a little less violent than in America and far more mystically minded than in Germany. Unlike most American right-wing extremists, who, it is possible, believe not a word of what they say, it seems likely that the Russian extremist is prepared to believe absolutely anything at all. Indeed, the Russians are so prone to conspiracy-mongering that they have even given it a name: conspiratology. The recurring protagonist of these conspiracies is ever and always the Eternal Jew. *The Protocols of the Elders of Zion*, that mother of all paranoid, anti-Semitic screeds, purports to be evidence of a Jewish plot to take over the world. And though it is read as far afield as Canada, Saudi Arabia, and Japan, it owes its existence to the perverse diligence of one Orthodox Christian fanatic, Sergei Nilus, scribbling away in the bowels of the Kremlin.

What is most striking about the present ferment among the Russian far right is that, despite three generations of efficient Soviet suppression, all the old hatreds and superstitions and enthusiasms, whether anti-Semitic, anti-Masonic, or pan-Slavic, should seem to spring back to life at the first opportunity and in almost exactly the form in which they had last been seen at the beginning of the century. But in fact Stalin was neither able, nor did he really try, to extirpate all specters of nationalism in Russia, and his ideal of socialism in one country rejected traditional Marxist internationalism in favor of something quite similar to the old nationalism. As Walter Laqueur says, "Even an extreme Russian nationalist could not have found fault with Soviet communism in 1950 as far as its patriotic fervor was concerned."[33]

Right-wing extremism in Russia is different from its counterpart in Germany because the spirit of the Russian people is fundamentally different from that of the Germans. The Russian, as depicted in the novels of Tolstoy and Gogol, suffers from something of an inferiority complex, which he hardly even tries to conceal. The cultural arrogance often found among the French, Germans, English, and Americans is found only very rarely in Russia, as in that tiny minority who insists that the Slavs, rather than the Teutons, are the real Aryans. Modern Slavophiles, like their nineteenth-century predecessors, tend to be more interested in asserting the decency and purity of Russian culture than in making any great claims for its superiority. Thus the extreme right in Russia tends to be defensive in nature, more concerned with securing its own borders from foreign invasion—of which it has had its fair share—than with conquering the planet. The idea that Russia should take over the world is too foolish even for the most extreme members of the Russian right to contemplate. Instead, the extreme right in Russia is founded on the fear that harm is being done to them, largely by Jews and Freemasons. The parrying of this threat, as their paranoia conceives it, is to the Russian extreme right what global domination is to neo-Nazis in Germany and America.

There is one respect, however, in which the extreme right in Russia resembles its counterparts in Germany and America, and that is its obsession with the past, to which many members desperately want to return. Just as German extremists fondly recall the Third Reich, and just as many American extremists recall the Revolutionary War and the Federalist era, so Russian extremists look for their inspiration to Alexander Nevsky, the proto-fascistic group known as the Black Hundred, and the last of the Romanovs.

Russia is proof that one doesn't need Jews in order for there to be anti-Semitism. The Jews, as of a recent counting, number not more than .69 percent of the Russian population. And this much was acknowledged by Dmitri Vasiliev, one of the leaders of the right-wing group known as Pamyat, who advocated laws that Jews, in view of their relative prominence intellectually and financially, should be allowed only such representation in universities, government, and business as was in proportion to their demographics. Yet the relative scarcity of Jews has not kept certain extremists from attributing to them the most spectacular powers and influence. The Jews, for example, are held responsible for Communism. The fact that few of them ever achieved prominence in the Communist Party is seen merely to confirm the conspiratological suspicion that they were working behind the scenes all along.

At other times, the Jews are accused of being the cause of Nazism, another scourge of the Russian people. Obviously this conviction runs into the inconvenient fact that the Nazis were not famously pro-Zionist. And then there is the by no means negligible fact of the Holocaust. Russian extremists, however, are not deterred by this hurdle. "Who was Eichmann?" Vasiliev asks. "He was a representative of the Jewish people."[34] To the extent that the Holocaust really occurred—some Russians deny that it did—it was staged by the Jews to win sympathy for the Zionist state that did indeed emerge after World War II. Another explanation is that Jewish fascists—that is, Zionists—had arranged for Auschwitz and Dachau as well as the Lvov and Vilnius ghettos in order to "cut off the dry branches of the Jewish people."[35] The not very subtle subtext here is that, since the Jews are so despicable to their own people, why do good Russians have to show them any mercy? It is interesting to note, by the way, that just as certain German neo-Nazis deny that the Holocaust ever happened, so there are Russians who claim to be as skeptical of the pogroms.

There is a crucial difference between the anti-Semitism of the extreme right in Russia and that of the extreme right in America and Germany. The Nazis in the thirties hated Jews for their Jewishness, which was a circumstance of their birth, and from this followed a hatred of the professions they entered and the politics they practiced. Though surely Nazis were willing to attribute conspiratorial and sometimes superhuman powers to Jews, there was an element of realism to their assessment of the Jew. In other words, though it was surely wrong for the Nazis to hate Jews in any circumstances, but specifically for being bankers and liberals, it is true, for what it is worth, that many German Jews in the twenties and thirties were bankers and liberals.

Russian anti-Semitism is very different. It seems as though that country's extremists just lack the basic seriousness of American and German anti-Semitism. In his excellent book *Black Hundred*, Walter Laqueur describes the writings of one anti-Semitic philosopher thus: "The novelty in [Valery] Emylianov's message was that Christianity [to which he was opposed] was a Zionist Sect, that Jesus Christ had been a Freemason and that Prince Vladimir (who had brought Christianity to Russia) was the son of a Jewish Woman and the grandson of a Rabbi."[36] What transpires from this and similar anti-Semitic pronouncements is that, unlike in Nazi Germany, where one simply hated Jews, in Russia that which one hates becomes Jewish because it is hated. "Jew" is the name given to what is hated, and this hatred has little to do with the realities of the Jews in one's midst.

Several cartoons from the popular press, as reproduced in *Black Hundred*, accentuate this point. "Let us smash the reptile—the porno merchant," reads one of them, in which a hook-nosed spider, clearly to be taken as a Jew, menaces a blond Russian woman. In another, two liberal deputies of the assembly, clearly intended to be Jewish and homosexual, can be seen embracing one another. Still another, from 1992, has a repulsive Jewish man, depicted as a rat on its hind legs, leading Yeltsin and Gorbachev in chains. The caption reads, "Shame on the intelligentsia, which has betrayed the Russian people." Now pornography, homosexuality, and the intelligentsia are all despised by the extreme right, so it is natural to associate them with Jews. In a way this recalls the statement of one American white supremacist that "we've let Jews into our country and we've been cursed with abortion, inflation, homosexuality."[37] Though these two positions may appear to be the same, the crucial difference is that in the American one, hatred of the Jew preceded and gave expression to hatred of abortion, etc., whereas in the Russian one the hatred of abortion, etc., took the form of anti-Semitism.

To understand more fully the almost frivolous nature of anti-Semitism in Russia one need only look at the widespread hatred of Masons. This hatred is not uncommon among the far right. Indeed, many militia members in the United States are fond of muttering about the Illuminati, an early form of the Masons, and pointing to the eye above the pyramid on our dollar bill as an example of the secret influence of godless Masons at the highest levels of the federal government. In Germany as well, this antagonism is occasionally seen. But in neither country does that antipathy reach as high a fever pitch as in Russia. Russians even have a word for their paranoia, *zhidomasonstvo*, or Jew-Masonry, since the alliance of Jews and Masons will be clear to anyone who has read (or written!) the Protocols of the Elders of Zion. Wherever it occurs, anti-Masonism is really an expression of entrenched antagonism to liberal and progressive reform, whether that should be, in the past, the emancipation of Jews, serfs, blacks, or women or, more recently, the development of a centrist liberal democratic society. This hatred is a survival from czarist times when the secretiveness and political progressiveness of the Masons made them an object of suspicion and loathing to the authorities. That there neither are now nor ever were many Masons in Russia does not deter those who are bent on attributing to them all manner of malignity.

Of course there are other agents of subversion, usually emanating from the godless, liberalized West. Few are more potent than rock music. "If one takes a rock record intended to be played 33 rpm," Vasiliev believes, "and slows it down to 7 to 14 rpm and

plays it backward, one hears an oath to Satan in English." Another
enemy is yoga, which the same thinker views as "just another strat-
agem to infiltrate surrogates of Western culture."[38]

These ideas would be little more than colorful curiosities were
it not for our fear that they might eventually lead to violent acts.
Despite the outcome of the 1996 Russian presidential elections,
which clearly gave a kind of mandate to the more progressive elements in Russian society, there is a constant and surely excessive
fear that the extremes of one side or another are about to take
over the center. Though the focus of much of this fear falls on
Pamyat, Laqueur is probably right in surmising that "it could well
be that for every member of Pamyat there has been an article in
the Russian and Western press."[39]

This organization, which in 1983 took its name from a novel
by Chivilikhin, was originally cultural rather than political, as be-
fitted the last days of Brezhnev. Back then it was a movement to
preserve various cultural monuments and traditions, as well as to
combat alcoholism, a perennial problem in Russia. It was only
when Vasiliev, who had been a photographer and actor, joined the
movement in 1984 that things started to heat up. Although
Pamyat, strictly speaking, was critical of the Soviets, it had sympathizers within the Communist Party, the KGB, and the army,
since it was seen as an effective bulwark against Western liberals.
This was apparent when one of its most vociferous members,
Valery Emylyanov, founder of the Global Anti-Zionist and Anti-
Masonic Front, killed his wife—hacking her into pieces, placing
these pieces in a bag, and having his assistants burn the bag
(which, by the way, he easily persuaded them to do by telling them
that it contained Zionist literature). When he later claimed that it
was Zionists who had killed his wife, he got off with being committed to a mental institution for a few years before being set free.
"His release," according to Laqueur, "came without the knowledge
of either the Serbsky Clinic or the Ministry of Health."[40]

As is often the case with the extreme right, Pamyat contains
a variety of filiations, most of which are different in name rather
than in substance and are divided more according to the vanity of
their founders than the diversity of their programs. What they all

have in common is, as we have seen, a hatred of Jews and Masons, and this hatred sometimes assumes especially creative forms. One member, for example, Konstantin Smirnov-Ostashvili, founded the Union for National Proportional Representation–Pamyat, the point of which was to make sure that Jews were not promoted. He also advocated that all half-Jews be considered full Jews. Threatening a giant pogrom, he asserted that emigration should stop, lest Jews "escape judgment." When he later came to trial for violently disrupting a meeting of leftist writers, he asked first that he be represented by any German lawyer, then more specifically that he be represented by Kurt Waldheim.

Of a wider importance than Pamyat, though not more compelling intellectually, is Vladimir Volfovitch Zhirinovsky, who garnered fame when he received six million votes in the 1992 presidential election. Like so many others on the Russian extreme right, as well as on the far right in general, from Mussolini to Lyndon LaRouche, Zhirinovsky has displayed considerable elasticity in matters of political doctrine. The right and left have more in common in Russia than they usually admit, and it is not uncommon for someone who has been affiliated with one extreme suddenly to identify himself with the other. Thus Zhirinovsky had been for some time active in liberal circles, even in VAAD, the Central Russian Jewish organization. This is peculiar in light of his subsequent and virulent anti-Semitism. In March of 1990, a virtual unknown, he helped found the Liberal Democratic Party, which claimed to comprise admirers of Andrei Sakharov. Zhirinovsky described this party as liberal centrist, standing, as Laqueur says, "for the rule of law, the rights of man, a multiparty system, deideologization, and a strong presidency."[41]

Five months later, however, in October 1990, gone was all reference to a multiparty system, gone were the human rights, and gone was the emphasis on law and order. Since then Zhirinovsky has revealed himself as a lethal buffoon. As is often the case with those on the extreme right, he does have a strange, perverse sense of humor, which gives rise to a recklessness and mean-spiritedness that are, if anything, still more pernicious for the comical tone in which he expresses them. Thus, sexualizing everything in sight, he famously compared the era of Lenin to a rape, Stalin to homosexuality, Krushchev to masturbation, Brezhnev to group sex, and Gorbachev to impotence.[42] In an interview with a Lithuanian newspaper, he explained his intention, on becoming president, to park nuclear waste on the border with the Baltic countries so that, in Laqueur's paraphrase, "Balts would die of radiation sickness and starvation."[43] He also told a Finnish paper that it was his intention to annex Finland when he came to power.

In the 1996 election, even though Zhirinovsky received about the same number of votes as he had in the previous election, he was pretty much reduced to irrelevance. This was because the press—which had more or less created him in the first place—had directed its attention once again back toward the center. And thus the continuing presence of Zhirinovsky on the world stage proves, if proof were needed, one of the enduring secrets of the emergence and survival of the extreme right: that in any democratic society, even one as strongly centralized as that of the United States of America, you will find a small percentage of the population that is prepared, either through folly or through fear, to subscribe to absolutely anything.

4

THE FAR RIGHT IN AMERICA
AND BEYOND

In one of his election year speeches, Pat Buchanan mentioned within the space of about a hundred words Henry Kissinger and the New World Order.[1] To most of those who inhabit the center, this conjunction of terms would have passed without remark, as Buchanan had intended. Depending upon what they thought of Kissinger and of the New World Order, they might react with pleasure or irritation to the words, but ultimately they would not make much of them. To certain of his listeners, however, this conjunction had another, deeper meaning. It said nothing and yet it spoke volumes. In the same way that flowers are said to contain ultraviolet markings visible only to bees, signaling to them where to alight, so these verbal markers were meant to be invisible to those in the center of society but to signal to certain members of the far right, even the extreme right, that Buchanan understands them.

At a most charitable reading, we might suppose that neither Buchanan nor his listeners consciously grasped what was taking place. They were aware, perhaps, only of a vague and pleasurable sense of connectedness at the remotest levels of instinct and intuition. Still, Buchanan had used code that would be understood pretty immediately by those whose business it was to understand. By mentioning Henry Kissinger—who is seen by many on the far right as the American Jew par excellence—in the same breath with the New World Order, that is, an international conspiracy of sorts that would rob real Americans of their independence, Buchanan was tapping into a deep reservoir of ancient antagonisms: the international Zionist banking conspiracy, the Jew as outsider, the embattled farmer defending his freedom against foreign interlopers. The far right, perhaps even the extreme right, understood very well what Pat Buchanan was doing, and through this almost imperceptible joining of words they felt a connection.

And yet there is a real and categorical difference between Pat Buchanan and the extreme right. In a sense, he is closer to liberal Democrats like Ted Kennedy and former representative Pat Schroeder than to Thomas Metzger and Bo Gritz. He is of the center, of the zone of relevance, whereas the extreme right is categorically removed from that zone. By the same line of reasoning, the extreme right is closer to the extreme left, in methods, rhetoric, sometimes even sympathies, than to anyone inside the center that includes Pat Buchanan. Sometimes, it is true, they will sneak someone into Congress, like the Idaho Republican Helen Chenowith, an apologist for the militia movement; and former neo-Nazi Klansman David Duke managed to win a Republican primary in Louisiana. But such occurrences are exceedingly rare exceptions that prove the rule.

The far right, by contrast, looks to the center and seriously hopes to become the center, by persuading people to outlaw homosexuality, abortion, and pornography and to banish evolution from the classroom. If this could be achieved, then its constituents would be in the center and they would be happy again. This is a practical goal, even if it is highly improbable that it will ever be attained. It is thus fundamentally different from the crazy goals of true extremists, who desire such things as initiating World War III, taking over the federal government, and killing all Jews. The exorbitancy of such a goal, the insane ambitiousness of it all, can be more shrewdly interpreted as what it really is, a way to attract attention to oneself even as one disqualifies oneself from any real possibility of power. The far right, unlike the extreme right, means business.

One of the most consistent features of the far right, as of the extreme right, is the desire to return to what has been and is no more. Indeed, this desire is structurally so pervasive in far right movements in America, Russia, France, Italy, and a good number of other countries around the world, that it can fairly be taken for the linchpin of all the varied and disparate filiations of that much publicized movement to the right that has manifested itself with almost mechanical regularity in recent years. The desire to return to an earlier time is very much in keeping with the spirit of the present age. Today more than ever, humanity as a whole is haunted by the wish to go back in time. Only the love of the future is stronger than this love of the past. The selfsame past which, to invoke once again Marx's mighty phrase, hung "like a nightmare" over the minds of the living has been tamed and turned into an option, a safe haven from an all too clamorous present. Whereas the industrial age indiscriminately destroyed the past, the postindustrial era preserves the past even while rendering its artifacts obsolete. What once was a necessity now survives as an ornament.

For most of the inhabitants of the center, the past has become a recreational zone like the Bahamas in winter or the Alps in summer. Risking nothing from the encounter, we go there to clear our minds of the present so that we can return reinvigorated and ready for more. Popular culture, with its endless reruns and retreads, its ducktails and bell-bottoms and Edwardiana, resurrects the artifacts of the past as so many decorative accessories. Merchant-Ivory and Martha Stewart, with slightly more exacting scholarship, elevate it to a lifestyle. To the far right, however, in America and abroad, the past is a matter of life or death. It is the motherland, the center of one's homing, from which inhabitants of the far right like Buchanan feel as though they have been absurdly exiled and to which they wish desperately to return.

In this emphasis on the past the far right resembles the extreme right, except that the extreme right, as always somewhat lacking in sincerity, merely invokes the past to belabor the present but otherwise uses it, as do the rest of us, for ornamental purposes.

Those on the far right, however, are completely in earnest in their desire to roll back the years. They wish to return to the world of their parents or grandparents, to a world in which the Summer of Love never happened, a world without Watergate or "Sergeant Pepper's Lonely Hearts Club Band." In that world they were the rulers, the lords of the center. When they looked out at that world, they saw everywhere their own reflection.

When they look to the past, they see a realm in which everything is legible, morally as well as politically. Things were not complicated as they have now become. Though the far right surely does not hate women, Jews, or blacks, as the extreme right does, still it fears these people because it correctly grasps that they could not have advanced even as far as they have without the diminution of its own influence. The far right recalls fondly a world in which women retained their virginity until marriage and remained true to their husbands until death; a world where homosexuality durst not speak its name; a world where children respected their elders, learned one standard version of American history, and knew nothing of drugs or pornography.

Now, because of the sixties, as they think, all of that has changed. Worse than that, what has fallen asunder can never be put back together again, though the far right does not yet know this. Furthermore, the very agents of this change, the catalyzing, disruptive, recombinant forces of technology, are the very powers that broadcast this change and make certain that one can neither ignore it nor avoid it. The inevitable result is that the static and noise of modern times can no longer be shut out. These distractions haunt the far right at every step and moment of their waking lives.

If the far right is moved by fear of the present and terror of the future, it is itself, of course, the cause of fear in others. Though the extreme right seems to be an intense and immediate source of fear, in fact the far right is more of a threat to those who do not share its point of view. For, aside from a few terrorist acts, the extreme right is totally impotent. The far right, however, is a different story. Even though they will never win a national election—the far right has never won a majority, by legal means, in the history of Europe, let alone America—still their power comes in the form of an exquisitely honed ability, at least in this country, to exert leverage on more mainstream politicians.

Over the past decade or so, we have witnessed, in most of the major industrialized states of Europe, as in the United States, the resurgence of far right candidates. France has Le Pen's Front National, Italy has Umberto Bossi's Lega Norta and the renovated Fascist Party, Russia has Zhirinovsky, and America has Pat Buchanan. Only England has been conspicuously deficient in this regard. For admirers of symmetry, it will seem strange that, whereas there are no powerful people at all on the far left, let alone the extreme left, a number of national politicians are willing to court the far right, and some essentially belong to it. Though a senator like Edward Kennedy is seen as being left-wing, in fact he is really a centrist, more or less. Jesse Jackson is the closest the United States has come to someone of the farther left entering the mainstream of politics, yet there was no chance of his winning a single primary, as Buchanan did, and his appeal did not extend much beyond black voters. By contrast, you find throughout Congress Republicans who bow to the Christian Coalition, even if, like Bob Dole, they do not really believe in it, and there are other candidates who are true believers. This is in large part because the forces of the far right are much better organized and, perhaps more important, have much more money than those of the far left.

To include the far right in the discussion of extremism that forms the focus of the present book is, it must be admitted, a dubious undertaking, since a point of view endorsed by millions of a country's citizens is not exactly extreme, especially compared to the views of neo-Nazis and militias. Whereas the extreme right revels in and exploits its inassimilable antagonism to the center, the far right aspires at least to the appearance, though often to the practice, of racial integration and decency. Pat Robertson's television programs make a concerted effort to include blacks and Jews in the discussion, and the Christian Coalition bends over backward to support the state of Israel. Though many in the center have reacted, and perhaps overreacted, with visceral rage to the imputations of anti-Semitism in the books of Pat Robertson, the mere fact that he should try to conceal these things, if they are there at all, makes him categorically different from the extreme right.

One other major difference between the extreme right and the far right is that the former completely rejects the center whereas the latter, as we have seen, aspires to become the center, not by coming closer to the center but by getting the center to come closer to it. In order to achieve this goal, those on the far right have demonstrated a certain willingness to negotiate, to make compromises and sustain minor losses, as long as these losses serve their main ambition, the reinstitution of Christian values, or something like them, in America.

Now the regularity with which, throughout the industrialized world, there has been a shift to the right rules out its being merely fortuitous. On a fiscal plain one observes, both in Europe and America, a massive recoil from the world of the later Industrial Revolution, with its swollen welfare system; at the same time, there has been a massive dismantling of the big state that came into being throughout the First World and Soviet Russia in the aftermath of the last world war. The grand strategy of the mainstream, whether center left or center right, is now to save what is salvageable from the welfare state, which has been found to be both inefficient and catastrophically expensive. As a new, overpopulated generation approaches the age of retirement, someone will have to pay for them, and the costs may be crushing. That it is necessary to cut down and cut back is common knowledge, and everyone from Chirac to Jospin, from Major to Blair, and from Clinton to Dole agrees that this is so.

But while economic considerations primarily motivate the center right and center left, the far right is overwhelmingly propelled by cultural and social considerations. Above all, the emergence of the far right can been seen as an answer to that social movement known as the sixties, which, of course, began around 1967 and ended roughly in 1979. Though the eighties are seen as a rejection of the sixties, in fact that decade represents the fullest assimilation of the earlier social movement, so much so that the essence of the sixties now seems entirely ordinary and unremarkable. Even if women and blacks have not yet achieved total parity with white men, few people—not even those on the far right—will express openly the belief that blacks and women deserve inferior status. Nevertheless, the advancement of blacks and women was made at the expense of certain people who felt a lingering resentment. Furthermore, the pervasive liberalizing of society that had taken place from 1960 to 1980 suggested to some that the entire moral fabric of our society was being destroyed.

As a result of similar moral and fiscal considerations there emerged, in the later seventies, what the political analyst Kevin Phillips called the New Right. This movement in effect was the next stage of conservatism in America. The older conservatism, now known as paleoconservatism, had been severely maimed, if not killed, first by the Republican nomination of Dwight Eisenhower rather than Robert Taft in 1952 and then, one generation later, by Watergate, which discredited politics in general but specifically the brand of moderate conservatism that Richard Nixon incarnated. And yet Nixon was essentially a New Deal Republican, who did not seek to roll back the clock or to dismantle—only to change—the welfare state as it was circa 1970. By contrast, the New Right, ten years later, saw the welfare state as a costly relic, a monument to inefficiency and pork. The election of Ronald Reagan in 1980 was the crowning achievement of the New Right.

Four men were especially instrumental in the rise of the New Right: Richard Viguerie, one of the pioneers in direct mail fundraising; Paul Weyrich, creator of the Heritage Foundation with the financial assistance of Joseph Coors; Howard Phillips, founder of Young Americans for Freedom; and Terry Dolan, founder of the National Conservative Political Action Committee. It was in 1974 that, as David Bennett writes, "together, they decided to form a new conservative movement outside the mainstream of the Republican Party."[2] Though they felt better about Reagan than about previous Republican candidates, they did not trust him entirely. Richard Viguerie declared in 1983 that there was "little difference between Reagan's foreign policy and Carter's foreign policy." Paul Weyrich bristled at finding, in the vicinity of Reagan, two relatively moderate Republicans like George Bush and James Baker, which led him to conclude that "Reagan is not the answer; Reagan is not a man of strong character."[3]

What they were looking for, in fact, was precisely the populism—to use their term—that Buchanan would pioneer over a decade later. Like many on the farther right, they saw themselves as being anti-establishment in that they viewed the establishment as liberal and corrupt. Implicit in this belief was a distinction between the establishment and the people, whom the far right now believed to be generally virtuous or, more precisely, conservative in spirit. For Viguerie the establishment constituted a "class of persons with unusual access to the political process gained through economic power or social status or old boy networks."[4] This was the new center from which the far right felt increasingly excluded, and even most mainstream conservatives failed to appreciate fully the degree of alienation that was felt. Here was Buchananism *tout fait*.

The further connection between the New Right and the Christian right, which was to have such a profound impact on the subsequent course of conservatism in the United States, largely resulted from the exertions of these men. As Weyrich asserted, "The alliance between religion and politics didn't just happen. I [had] been dreaming and working on this for years."[5] What evolved from this alliance was the Moral Majority, whose name, it is interesting to point out, was coined by Howard Phillips, a Jew. That Phillips was a Jew underscores the general ecumenism of the Christian right. They are driven more by moral than by doctrinal convictions. Whereas formerly the religious right had been fractured along doctrinal lines, reprising the immemorial antagonisms of Catholic against Protestant, and both against Jews, now, as Jerry Falwell declared, "Evangelicals, fundamentalists, conservative Catholics, and Mormons are all working together." Even some Jews were eventually assimilated into this group. Here the distinction was not between one faith and another but between those who believed in any religion at all and those who believed in nothing.

Though the religious right had prospered through most of the eighties, toward the end of that decade it was rocked by the scandals of Jim Bakker and Jimmy Swaggart, as well as by certain compromising discoveries made about Pat Robertson during his failed presidential campaign in 1988. But the far right, together with the religious right, was to be powerfully revived in the early 1990s, not only in Robertson's reconstituted Christian Coalition, run by Ralph Reed, but as impressively, and most recently, in the presidential bid of Pat Buchanan.

Like so many energetic advocates who are positioned far outside of the mainstream, Buchanan is a dreamer whose thinking has about it whole strata of poetic association, which, given his somewhat drab persona, have most often been ignored. Like the Christian Coalition, this political columnist and television commentator of long standing must be seen in terms of his desire to return to the past. Everything about him underscores this orientation and takes on a new meaning when conceived in such a light. Consider, for example, his pro-life position. On one level, the one of which he is apt to be most conscious, his foremost concern is his desire to protect the unborn, and it is surely possible that he, like many others who have taken up that crusade, feels a genuine dismay at this terminating of human life. It is for this reason that the pro-lifers have made some converts in the center and even among the left.

But it is a larger social vision, a metaphorical fantasy, that drives the enthusiasm of that movement in general and of Pat Buchanan in specific. For them abortion is the incarnation—literally—of sex for other reasons than those of procreation, which is the only reason sanctioned by the Church. The murder, as they see it, of fetuses is a violent and sanguinary confirmation that there exist in this society those who would have such sex in a free and guiltless way. Of course, recreational sex existed in the past, even in the ages to which Buchanan wishes to return. And yet back then the offenders suffered from moral stigma, and those who were innocent of such offenses were filled with a pleasant sense of personal superiority.

A similar spirit of return is the driving force behind Buchanan's isolationism and his rediscovery of the working man. In both respects, Buchanan looks back to an earlier era in our nation's history, rather as certain Romans of the Decadence looked back on the Republic and the austere virtues of Cincinnatus and the elder Cato, that is, to a time before Roman virtue had become tainted by

Persian luxury. Buchanan's foreign policy is thus different from that of Falwell and others on the religious right. As Falwell, a most effective fund-raiser for Israel, once said, "God has raised up America in these last days for the cause of world evangelization and for the protection of his people, the Jews. I don't think America has any other right or reason for existence than these two goals."[6] For Buchanan, however, American support of Israel is costly and dangerous to our armed forces. The fact that the beneficiary of this aid is non-Christian, and more precisely Jewish, does not help, either. Buchanan's isolationism also caused him to oppose American involvement in the Persian Gulf. And yet isolationism's appeal for Buchanan has to do only in part with the practical concern of not becoming entangled in the affairs of other nations. In large measure it is a historicist revival of an earlier stage of Republicanism, that of Senator Taft's isolationism, a point of view that had not been heard from any important Republican since Eisenhower placed internationalism squarely at the center of his party's interests.

It may not be the least appealing thing about Taft Republicans, with their opposition to both the welfare state and internationalism, that they appear to be on the wrong side of history. Taft himself was looking in 1952 for a return to an older stage of the United States such as had existed prior to the Second World War. He did not realize that this was no longer possible, that people could not go back, that the world had become a smaller place and that the United States had become far larger in it. Just as Taft wished a return to the prewar world, so Buchanan wishes a return to Taft returning to the prewar. And like Taft he appears not to realize that it is futile to try to engraft a historicist vision of reality onto reality itself, that the change will be only cosmetic and can never go any deeper.

So, too, with Buchanan's sudden discovery of the working man. Obviously this redirecting of emphasis onto the worker, in itself, is in no way extreme. Indeed, it is not even a conservative issue. And therein lies its appeal. Although we cannot rule out that Buchanan actually feels something for those people who have been laid off in the most recent waves of corporate downsizing, it is at least as likely that he sees this advocacy not only as a way to play against type and to have an issue but also as a return to the idea of the American working man—and the emphasis is on *man*—as he was before and shortly after the Second World War. Buchanan has a vision of a smokestack America of the heartland, a gritty, Steinbeckian world of heavy industry and four-square American values. It is a world a thousand times less sophisticated than our postindustrial age. It is the world of Pat Buchanan's childhood.

In addition to this, his defense of the little man goes against the interests of big business, which have traditionally defined the GOP. Now because the GOP is generally far less conservative than Buchanan, he has as little sympathy for most Republicans as most of them have for him. Thus he feels he owes little to them and their constituency. For him the conflict between big business and the working man is also the conflict between the East and West coasts, with their liberalism, loose morals, and international outlook, and the heartland that is Buchanan's main constituency.

In an age in which most Americans, and certainly most American politicians, bend over backward to give the appearance of tolerance of others' views, Buchanan recurs to an age in which that was not seen as being strictly necessary. It is not so much the outlandishness of any one statement as the cumulative effect of many statements that makes Buchanan appear more than a little racist. But the nature of his racism is somewhat slippery and indeterminate. Discussing immigration, for example, in 1991 he said, "If we had to take a million immigrants in, say, Zulus, next year, or Englishmen, and put them in Virginia, what group would be easier to assimilate?"[7] Now the answer he wanted—and probably the correct answer, at that—would be that Englishmen surely would be more easily assimilated into the land of Washington and Jefferson than would some tribal Africans. But the mere posing of the question, as Mr. Buchanan had to know, was itself incendiary. Second, as he also knew, the use of the funny-sounding name "Zulus" conjures up images of semi-naked savages in war paint and nose rings. In a literal sense, of course, he is speaking only of Zulus rather than of African Americans. But in the mind of the far right, and especially the extreme right, who will recall that Buchanan once referred to Martin Luther King as "a fraud and a demagogue,"[8] the anti-black stereotype will seem to fit, and they will eagerly assent to it. In this respect, Buchanan's use of language is a little like the upscale pornographer's depiction of a young lady and her bird. Those who need to know will understand very well what the bird is supposed to mean.

As for charges of anti-Semitism, one can read his defense of John Demjanjuk as simply an unusually developed respect for the truth as he sees it. This man, who had been living in America for some time, was facing extradition as a Nazi commandant, the so-called Butcher of Treblinka. Whether he was or was not the Nazi in question, he had been, by his own admission, a guard in a concentration camp. And yet not only did Buchanan defend Demjanjuk, but he did so in a particularly noisome way, by comparing Israel's prosecution of the man to France's persecution of Captain Dreyfus. Now this, too, is a fairly complicated equation. Captain Dreyfus, of course, was a Jew falsely accused and entirely innocent, as Demjanjuk, by his own admission, was not. On one level Buchanan seems to be raising his voice against unfair prosecution: what happened to Dreyfus was bad, just as what is happening to Demjanjuk is bad. But more insidiously he appears to be robbing the Jews of the historic fact of their victimization by accusing them of being oppressors themselves. How palliative to the consciences of anti-Semites everywhere that Jews should be no better than they are! This sense is further evidenced in his statement that Congress is "Israeli-occupied territory," which is not so different from the claim, dear to the extreme right, that the federal government is really ZOG, the Zionist Occupation Government. When one combines this statement with his declaring that Hitler, albeit a mass murderer, had "great courage" and was "a soldier's soldier," one can only agree with the famous verdict of William F. Buckley Jr. that "it is impossible to defend Pat Buchanan against the charge [of anti-Semitism]."[9]

In an article in *Time* magazine it is said that "Buchanan's critics have also begun to hear in his speeches code-worded appeals to the armed-militia movement. Much of his agenda—the opposition to immigration, affirmative action, and gun control, the hostility toward international organizations—would be music to their ears in any case. Is Buchanan strumming a few notes just for them?"[10]

The answer, which one can only surmise, is neither simple nor straightforward. Clearly it is not a question of getting their vote. They are too small a constituency to matter, and to the extent that they would have anything to do with the center, there are few other politicians for whom they could vote, because no national politician is more conservative than Pat Buchanan. Since, then, it is unlikely that he is courting the extremist vote, which could only alienate the vast preponderance of more likely voters whom he is wooing, there are only two answers to this question. Either Buchanan is sincerely an extremist, or he and the extreme right emerge from a common intellectual context and use substantially the same language. Probably the latter is true. To oppose the New World Order or to believe that the federal government is overly large is not an extremist position in itself, though it is a right-wing position that surely anyone to the right of Buchanan would believe, though none as energetically as the militias. It is, so to speak, the entry level of the extreme right, and it was perhaps his intention to send a signal, not so much to the militias as to the center, declaring his independence from that dithering acceptance of the centrist liberalism that characterizes the platforms of everyone more liberal than himself.

Pat Buchanan's desire for return, as well as his flirting with the appearance of racism, has many analogues in Europe. Nowhere, however, is the conflict between the old and the new played out with greater risk or for higher stakes than in Russia. As was remarked in the last chapter, the sense of a center is far less developed in post-Soviet Russia than in Europe or the United States. It is easy to see a parallel between Weimar in the twenties and the present state of affairs in Russia. In both cases we find countries reeling from the most catastrophic convulsions in their political and economic spheres. In both cases a great empire has been destroyed, and its citizens are suffering and distraught. Russia now struggles to find its balance, and nothing, it seems likely, will be accomplished without some measure of violence and spiritual upheaval.

Yet there is this difference between Russia and other countries that, in this century, have found themselves in similar circumstances. The usual divisions between its left and right wings have been so distorted as to cease to have any real or useful meaning. The real left exists as various anarchist groups. But the reconstituted Communist Party, despite its attempts at a Laborite platform, appeals primarily to the older generations who fear the rapid rate of change and who wish to secure their pensions. Furthermore, in their antagonism to the unruliness that has supplanted the leaden sameness of Soviet society, and in their desire to return to something like the mood of the country during Stalinism, the new Communists are structurally akin to those in America who, like Buchanan, wish to reinstate the 1950s. At all events, the Communists themselves have made common cause with the far right on a host of issues, and the party's principal appeal is to certain dispossessed former apparatchiks regretting the loss of their dachas and Zil automobiles.

The political life of post-Soviet Russia seems like a circus compared with what we know in the First World. As their culture stumbles toward true representative democracy, the citizens seem to be encountering everything, with varying degrees of adroitness, for the first time. This is one of the reasons that there frequently appears to be such unbridled extremism in their country. In tone, style, and aggressiveness, their centrists conduct themselves the way our extremists behave. As in Weimar, the prevalent fear that everything is out of control only sharpens the desire for what the Russians call *gosudarstvenniki*, a strong centralized state leadership.

Perhaps what has been most galling to the Russian right over the last few years, even more than crime and deep financial uncertainty, has been the sudden loss of their empire. Indeed, the Soviet empire—which was essentially the czarist empire by another name—was the last great empire in the world, after all the others, those of England, France, Austria, Germany, and the Ottomans, had been dissolved. It was the survival of this empire, more than the technology, sports, or culture of the Soviet Union, that gave to its people a sense of greatness that made tolerable the many privations that they had to sustain as members of a socialist society.

Allied to this sorrow at the loss of their empire is the desire among certain far right groups to revive monarchy in Russia. There is nothing necessarily extreme in monarchism nor in the desire to return to that form of government, especially since all but its most lunatic proponents, not only in Russia but in France, Romania, and elsewhere, agree that the monarch must have a largely ceremonial role. Indeed, the restitution of monarchy in Spain was symptomatic of a liberalizing trend, after Franco's many years as dictator. Furthermore, fully a third of the heads of states in Europe at this time are monarchs. Nevertheless, in most circumstances in which people agitate for the restoration of monarchy, in Russia as in France, they are usually sympathetic to the far right, and the secret desire behind their calls for a restored monarchy is the abolition of a few decades, if not a few centuries, of human history.

The new openness that now characterizes the former Soviet Union has given rise to a number of monarchical groups, though they agree on little beyond a desire to restore some sense of empire. Nevertheless, certain Russians who are further to the right than most seek a return to the monarchy as it was before the liberalizing, Westernizing tendencies of Peter the Great early in the eighteenth century. As summed up by Walter Laqueur, they believe that "Russia does not need an ideology but faith, not politics but spiritual values, not democracy but *sobornost*, not a union of republics but Great Power Status." The most extreme monarchists are gathered in the group called Zemschina, whose small numbers believe, like certain Russian extremists discussed in the last chapter, that the church must be bound to the monarchy as of old. As might be expected, they share the anti-Semitism of many on the right.

Most monarchist movements, however, are more moderate. They would reintroduce those titles and ranks that had been introduced into Russia early in the 1700s. Uncomfortable with technology, they favor a return to a peasant-based, preindustrial economy, as well as a strong ruble and an accompanying fiscal policy such as Russia had before 1917. Most of these monarchists differ from the extreme right not only in policy but in tone as well. Their ideas are perhaps foolhardy and quixotic, but they are not vicious or cruel. They wish, for example, to return to the social legislation dating from the most recent czars, as in assistance for young families and twenty-four paid holidays yearly. But because few who wish for a restored monarchy can agree on who should be chosen, "the monarchist idea," Laqueur concludes, "is likely to remain a sectarian dream rather than a realistic alternative."

In America we have nothing comparable to this desire for a return to monarchy. Though there is largely a structural parity between groups on the extreme right from country to country, including the United States, this is one area where we may not follow. But just as we have our militias who oppose a largely civilian society with the lingering appeal of militarism, so the far right in Russia has the Don Cossacks, who despise the chaos and misrule that, especially in their country, seem to be the inevitable corollaries of democracy. And just as the militias look back to the Minutemen of two centuries ago, so the Cossacks can recall their great tradition as freed or escaped serfs who, fiercely loyal and brave, advanced to the Pacific under the Stroganovs in the seventeenth century.

Like our militias, the Cossacks like to march around in traditional uniforms. Infatuated with titles and honors, they are constantly electing their atamans much as our militias elect their sheriffs. And just as our militias try to create their own counties, so the Cossacks wish to have their own state on the Don. Eminently impractical, they call for the return of all lands taken from them and declare null and void all transactions since 1917.

Another unlikely presence on the Russian far right is Alexander Solzhenitsyn, though his affinity for conservatism is somewhat problematic. Nowhere else in the field of contemporary conservatism is there anyone quite like Solzhenitzyn, for the circumstances that produced him and the context that received him are without parallel elsewhere in the world. He was emphatic in his opposition to Marxism-Leninism, which can be seen as a liberal or a conservative opinion, depending upon one's perspective. But he is also anti-militarist, advocating the abolition of the draft and, by implication, of the army, which is the perennial pet of the far right. Furthermore, his tirades against technology and modernity, though suggestive of the Green Party in the West, are largely traditionalist and thus look to the right. In the tradition of the Russian right, Solzhenitsyn is a committed Slavophile who feels that his country has been uniquely appointed for some noble end and that it can never really be understood by outsiders. Thus he sees the West as corrupt, as something that Russians must stay clear of.

Most of all, Solzhenitsyn belongs to the right in the sense that, like all the other conservatives examined in this chapter, he is oriented toward the past. Indeed, he aspires to revive in his own body the massive patriarchal morality of Tolstoy. He resembles this great predecessor not only in his beard—which relatively few Russian men sport these days—but also in the epic sweep that he seeks to impart to his novels (in one of which Tolstoy even appears as a character), as well as in his rejection of what he considers a corrupt Western world and in his desire to return to truer, simpler, and more Russian values. Also like Tolstoy's, his highly personalized heterodoxy conforms neither to the far right nor the far left, though it partakes of both. Ultimately, Solzhenitsyn's politics may be somewhat eccentric, but they are not really extreme. He is no opponent of democracy, let alone a champion of despotism, and, despite his contempt for much that is Western, he is not as virulently anti-foreign as many Russians on the extreme right.

Odd as it might seem for a movement as xenophobic as the Russian far right, one of its main influences is the Nouvelle Droite in France. This is odd because Russia, whose intelligentsia was overwhelmingly Gallicized in the last century, has been entirely free of French influence in the present century. Furthermore, it is a little strange that those on the far right in Russia should be looking to France, since they are the heritors of xenophobic Slavophilia, and France was traditionally the immoral, loose, decadent corrupter of every solid Russian value. Nevertheless, a thinker like Alain de Benoist, one of the leaders of the modern

French far right, is much in demand in Russia, even though his highly developed philosophy is at once intensely personal and very French.

Benoist's philosophy is a vague form of Nietzschean elitism, openly delighting in its Indo-European—some would say Aryan—heritage. He looks with more or less total contempt upon the French Revolution that abolished the ancien régime, as well as on its ideals of Liberty, Equality, and Fraternity. And he is none too impressed with Christianity, either. In this respect he resembles certain strains of American extremism, which also stress a pagan—usually Nordic—background. In *Vu de Droite Social*, he says, "The enemy, as I see it, is not the left or Communism or even socialism, but the egalitarian ideology whose formulations, religious or lay, metaphysical or pseudo-scientific, have never ceased to flourish for two thousand years, and in which the 'ideas of 1789' are nothing but a stage, and in which the current socialism and communism are the inevitable outcome."

From Benoist to Jean-Marie Le Pen, the irrepressible leader of the Front National, is an inevitable but not necessarily an easy step to take. Benoist is situated in the stolidest French tradition of rampant and unrepentant elitism, the direct heir and intellectual emissary of the monarchist party. Le Pen, by contrast, is a vigorous populist. In the battles he has chosen to fight he bears remarkable resemblance to Pat Buchanan. There is this difference: that he is seen as likable though clownish, whereas Buchanan is accorded somewhat more respect and rather less affection. Yet both men emphasize the reform of immigration, which issue is almost invariably allied to a patriotism that fondly recalls an earlier and vanished age; both men claim to be anti-elitist populists—by no means a common thing on the far right; and both stress family values and have trouble keeping away from Nazism, whether in Buchanan's ill-considered defense of Demjanjuk or Le Pen's moronic puns about concentration camps.

The main power of the far right in France is in its ability to shock, an ability that Le Pen has been ready and able to exploit fully. What was so surprising about the 11 percent that his party won in June of 1984 was that it seemed to come relatively soon after the electoral victory of the socialist François Mitterrand. But perhaps this was not so strange after all. Mitterand's victory was a vote against a generation of Gaullism, that is, the party of General de Gaulle. It did not, however, signal a real shift to the left, as evidenced by Mitterand's about-face two years later when he broke off his alliance with the Communists. For 11 percent of the French electorate, Le Pen was an incarnated challenge to a centrist establishment they had grown to mistrust. In the rest of the population, however, he provoked a reaction similar to that of Buchanan, or worse to Oliver North, or worse still to David Duke. His presence on the political stage was a standing reproach to the mainstream. Many centrist Frenchmen felt queasy in his presence, as many centrist Americans feel with Buchanan, as though there were something foul and unclean in their midst. The conservatism that he represented was the name of what they feared and hated, and yet it would not go away.

Like Buchanan, Le Pen is given to saying things which surely do not equal an endorsement of Adolf Hitler—since neither man in his heart really favors Nazism—but which come teasingly close and can be guaranteed to irritate to distraction everyone to the left of them, which is almost everyone. At the same time, such words send signals to those on the right that, if nothing else, these two candidates are not afraid to attack liberal, centrist pieties. For example, one of the most damaging things Le Pen has said—though he said it advisedly—is that "the rise to power of Adolf Hitler and the National Socialist party was characterized by a powerful mass movement, entirely popular and democratic, since it triumphed as a result of regular elections, something which is generally forgotten." Now two things can be said about this statement. In one sense it is false, since the Nazis never garnered more than 37.6 percent of the vote in a legal election and gained control through what was in essence a constitutional coup d'état. And yet they did indeed once get 37.6 percent, which was an impressive tally in a parliamentary system. Naturally Le Pen claims that he has been completely misunderstood—that he was merely making a point, *un peu d'histoire*, as the French say. And yet why bring this up at all? His statement, like Buchanan's comment on Kissinger and the

New World Order, is a way of separating himself from the rest of the more liberal population.

Like Benoist, however, Le Pen's first love may be the French, but his second love is Europeans. When he assumed his seat in the European parliament—which he had won through the parliamentary principle of proportional representation in the European Community—he spoke of "the awakening of the European people . . . translated into massive votes in favor of those who, despite demonization, rise against the dangers of cosmopolitanism and worldwide policies." And yet, though he is stridently anti-immigrant, Le Pen is not a racist in the American traditional sense. Blood means less to him than tradition. Those who come from abroad to settle in France are not the true French, and it is for this reason, rather than for their blood, that Le Pen dislikes them. Though he shares de Gaulle's affection for France as France, he does not have de Gaulle's mystical sense of France's destiny, nor is his vision raised up by that grander humanitarianism that enabled de Gaulle, despite his fierce patriotism, to see beyond his own country and his own people to the rest of the world.

Le Pen has often been associated with earlier nationalist strains in French politics. But there is this difference, that Bonapartism and Poujadism, from the 1850s and 1950s respectively, arose in a context of real French strength and hegemony and tended to emerge from the petite bourgeoisie: Le Pen's constituency, by contrast, emerges out of a depressed middle class, that fears immigrants and takes refuge in its Frenchness. The constituency bears some resemblance to those Americans whose jobs have been downsized or who fear that this might happen, except that such Americans were and continue to be middle-of-the-road and as yet have not turned dramatically to the right.

It should also be said that good people believe in both men. In other words, it would now be difficult to find a pretext for an honorable and benign person to decide to join a Nazi party. But there are parts of both men's platforms, such as their support of working people and their call for traditional values, that find a receptive audience among good people. And one thing that many have remarked on is the degree to which it is impossible to generalize about both men's constituencies. They comprise the young and the aged, workers and professionals, men and women, Catholics and Jews.

Like certain members of the far right in America, Le Pen's adherents are selectively patriotic, denying the Frenchness of whatever displeases them. Just as the militias recur to the Spirit of '76, so many followers of Le Pen wear the red hearts that symbolized the Chouans in the Vendée, who, in 1793, rose up against the armies of the Republic. For them, as for Alain de Benoist, Bastille Day is the *dies ater*, or black day, in their history. There are several reasons for this. One can plausibly see this date as ending the ancien régime and ushering in modern times, not only in France but throughout the Western world. It was this date that essentially marked the death of the aristocracy and the old religion in France. Now many French have feelings mixed about their revolution of 1793—that is, of the Terror—but not of 1789, which is generally thought of as enlightened, as ushering in the democratic reforms that they continue to enjoy. Still, the Front National's assault on the Revolution goes to the heart of French politics.

This also explains why many of its followers have an affection for the well-known Asterix cartoons, which feature heroes from ancient Gaul. This signals, in a good-natured way, a return to the "real" France, as opposed to France of today, a France, they contend, that is hopelessly compromised and corrupted, mongrelized and enfeebled. And much as Buchanan's people look back to the 1930s, when the world—or at least America—seemed safe for Christianity, so they look back to a time, before de Gaulle's destruction of their empire, when France was for the French and not for immigrants, when French literature and art were paramount, people respected the Church, and the welfare state was as yet nonexistent.

And yet, like the far right in America and Russia, in the last analysis the far right in France is really trafficking in symbols. It can never return to the past and at best will retrieve a few superannuated emblems, which cannot satisfy it for very long. What it advocates is cosmetic surgery posing as a coronary bypass. This would be a bad thing if the patient were truly ailing, but the body politic is healthier than it is generally given credit for being, and what ails it does not need, in all probability, such drastic measures as the far right, in America and abroad, has traditionally proposed. What is important to remember about cosmetic surgery, by the way, is that, if it never did much to help the ailing, it never damaged them too much, either. Which is to say that the harm that the far right is likely to do to the center appears, as of this moment, to be rather slight.

5

THE EXTREMISM OF THE LEFT

In the aftermath of Oklahoma City, something happened that was new in the American experience: the extreme right came to be viewed as a clear and present danger to the center. Before this time, from the Haymarket Riots in the 1880s, through the Red Scare in the twenties and the specter of Communist infiltration in the fifties, to the emergence of the Weathermen and the SDS a decade later, it had always been the left that seemed to pose the most terrible threat to the center of society, and it had always seemed to be the right, even the extreme right, that served as the bulwark against such subversion.

Now, however, with the emergence of the militia movement and the apparent reinvigoration of the extreme right, the left has tumbled into such oblivion that you could surely be excused for thinking that there was no left-wing extremism in contemporary America, indeed, that there was scarcely any left-wing activity at all. In fact, left-wing extremism is about as powerful as it ever was—at least in the last two generations. Similarly, despite all the clamor to the contrary, the extreme right is not substantially mightier now than it has been in the past.

Why, then, do we feel so strongly to the contrary? Probably because most of what we know about the subject we glean from the media and because the media's view of the world is dictated in part by what they know will make a good story, in part by a certain lack of perspective on the stories they cover. In the immediate aftermath of the Oklahoma City bombing, for instance, those same militias that had been around for almost two decades, unnoticed and unfeared, suddenly became the subject of intense scrutiny, inspiring hundreds of articles and news programs. This scrutiny, coupled with the initial success of Pat Buchanan's 1996 presidential bid, has filled many people with the sense that we are heading inexorably rightward, just as, during the sixties, the media gave rise to the specter of an imminent takeover by the far left.

Whether in books, newspapers, magazines or television, the media process information, unconsciously or otherwise, in such a way as to satisfy in the center a curiosity largely generated by the press itself. Thus the capture of the man many believe to be the Unabomber immediately provoked a spate of articles and mini-documentaries about radical environmentalist organizations and neo-Luddites even though, in fact, these forces had been in operation for some time already. A more realistic record of the world can be found on the Internet, with its unedited profusion of information and voices. The truth is that there are now in America about as many Stalinists as there were in the sixties, and probably more Maoists, Trotskyites, and anarchists than ever before. But because they have been relegated, with some justice, to the dustbin of history, because they have been branded as old news, you must turn to the Internet to encounter them in all their uncorseted glory.

It has been said of the left that it comprises a thousand different parties and that they all hate each other. The structural difference between the extreme right and the extreme left boils down to this: the extreme right—with a few exceptions like the LaRouchites, who may be crackpots but at least are intellectual crackpots—has its quasi-religious organizations, militias, and gangs, whereas the extreme left has its parties. Another difference is that, whereas the extreme right is oriented toward the past, the extreme left is apt to be inspired by a vision of the future, most often some grand revolutionary plan of Marx or Mao. With sublime condescension, Marxists are forever talking—even today!—of late capitalism, as though, in spite of everything, their communistic vision of the world's future were about to be implemented at long last.

Of course the left as well glances occasionally at the past, albeit more furtively, and for some it is precisely the datedness of their vision, its grotesque stalwartness in an altered world, that constitutes its greatest charm. It is interesting, however, that, in their search for a usable past, few Marxists look back to Marx himself. He is as distant as the Patriarch Abraham and quite as charmless and inscrutable. Above all he is seen as an intellectual who never commanded the masses and who is respected by them more than he is loved. Revolutionary groups have had to look elsewhere for their vision of the past. Some groups recur to the twenties, with its brilliant red banners and its masses marching to the drumbeat of history. This is an especially pleasant point of nostalgia for Trotskyite associations like the Socialist Workers Party, which itself dates from the late twenties, and as such is one of the oldest revolutionary groups in the country.

By contrast, the Communist Party of the United States of America (CPUSA), the grandfather of all contemporary revolutionary movements in America, looks more to Stalin's Russia of the thirties than to Lenin's state a decade earlier. This is because it was Stalin's reforms in 1928 that inaugurated the omnipotent statism that was to fascinate American Communists during the Depression, before the true horror of Stalin's despotism could qualify the fervor of his disciples. It was in the thirties as well that this party reached its highest membership and its greatest prestige. Maoists, by contrast, like anarchists, look to the youth movement and the New Left of the 1960s. For that was a time, once again, when the atrocities of Maoism had not yet become common knowledge and when everyone in the world seemed to own a copy of Mao's little red book.

Collectively these left-wing parties differ from the extremists of the right in the generally secular tenor of their agitation. There is a quasi-religious, almost New Age quality to the extreme right. With all their talk of Thor, the Illuminati, and the Elders of Zion, with all their arcane allusions to Christianity and to the pagan past, they often manifest a distinctly mystical turn. We have seen the almost obsessive awe with which many of them regard the nineteenth day of April, the day of Lexington and Concord, the conflagration at Waco, and the Oklahoma City bombing. Such mystical *Schwärmerei*, however, rarely has any place in the austere rationalism to which the left aspires.

Whereas the extreme right sees itself as being surrounded by a malign confederacy of blacks, Jews, women, secular humanists, and the federal government, those on the far left see themselves in solidarity with "the people" but believe the people to be enslaved to a powerful minority of moneyed interests. And how could the people not want them, since they represent so fully the people's interests? And why, then, does the public persist in not voting for them? Because the power structure has "manufactured consent," to use Noam Chomsky's phrase. And whereas both the extreme right and the extreme left routinely field presidential candidates, they do so for different reasons. When Bo Gritz, the charismatic right-winger, ran for president in 1992, his bid was essentially intended and interpreted as a publicity stunt. When Gus Hall, head of the Communist Party of the United States and a man of remarkably little humor, ran in the very same election, as in every earlier presidential election for the previous thirty years, he seems to have believed that this time around the people would see the light and elect him.

There is still another difference between the extremists of the right and the left. Honesty compels one to admit that the extreme left—when not merely a front for old-fashioned anti-Semitism—genuinely, if misdirectedly, desired the good, as the KKK and the neo-Nazis never did; and that even if the morals of the left frequently fell far short of its stated aims—as in the CPUSA's unprincipled apologetics for the Soviet Union—still most of its members had joined because they sincerely wished good, rather than ill, upon humankind.

Of all the parties of the extreme left, Hall's CPUSA comes closest, in its weird way, to resembling the establishment. Unlike certain long-haired allies on the left, its members are generally indistinguishable from the rest of the middle-class urban population. They tend to be somewhat frumpy and middle-aged, looking more like bureaucrats and homeowners than like firebrands. Gus Hall himself does not wear fatigues, like Fidel, but rather resembles a white-haired midwestern labor boss in a state of permanent middle age. Naturally CPUSA has seen better days. The destruction of the Soviet Union ended, seemingly overnight, the funding, two to three million dollars annually, that the party regularly received and regularly denied receiving from Moscow. Membership is down to a hardcore few, who, it would appear, admire the movement less because they believe in its teachings than because it is so abjectly a lost cause, and because, for some, a certain nobility attaches to lost causes.

In fact, the CPUSA, which had terrified the American right for decades, was always a paper tiger whose foremost utility, a cynic might argue, was to serve as a foil for the far right, one that the far right used brilliantly. Despite typical efforts to inflate membership figures—something every fringe group tries to do—the party, founded by John Reed in 1919, was always marginalized. Even the Depression, the greatest crisis in the history of capitalism, the flashpoint for which Marxists had been waiting for half a century, did nothing to swell the ranks of the CPUSA. Four years into the Depression, the party had no more than fifteen thousand members. The glory days of the party came only at the end of the Depression, when it allied itself with the social programs of FDR and its membership shot up to one hundred thousand. But this increase was short-lived. Most of the members it had gained promptly left when the party, which had formerly vilified Nazism, now asserted its neutrality for the duration of the Hitler-Stalin Pact. What with Krushchev's subsequent disclosure of Stalin's atrocities, among them an anti-Semitism that did not sit well with the many Jewish members of the party, not to mention the Soviet invasion of Hungary in 1956 and of Czechoslovakia twelve years later, the party dwindled to a paltry three thousand members, a condition from which it has not recovered. Consider that there is a tiny organization in Southern California committed to the belief that the earth is flat: at most recent counting, they have five hundred more paying members than the foremost left-wing party in American history.

The first serious challenge to the primacy of the CPUSA came from the New Left in the sixties. To the younger generation that favored a more revolutionary form of Communism, one that possessed the anti-colonial prestige of Mao and the intellectual cachet of Trotsky, the middle-aged conservatism of the CPUSA could no longer be concealed. It was and remains conservative in the strictest sense of the word: despite its constant talk of the future, it has a rigid, backward-looking point of view on most things. With regard to its middle-agedness, the CPUSA bears a passing resemblance to certain groups on the extreme right, especially the KKK, in that both groups are generationally older than the most vociferous right- and left-wing movements of today.

One sees this antiquatedness in Mr. Hall as well. There is something touchingly naive about the way this eighty-five-year-old Minnesotan reacted to the August 1991 coup d'état in the Soviet Union. How, after all, do you explain away the scandalously swift and utter dissolution of that faith to which you have devoted your entire life? Although Hall subsequently denied supporting the plotters in the August coup, there is evidence that at first he did support them. With the same wistful, unshakable nostalgia of French and Russian royalists of the extreme right, Hall cannot accept that his vision has passed away for ever and ever. After claiming in the *Washington Post*, on 2 September of that year, that recruitment in the party was actually increasing, he said in an article in *New York Newsday:* "Headlines like 'Communism Is Dead' are wishful thinking. The setbacks [in Russia] do not signify the end of socialism, either in the Soviet Union or in the world. They do not change the direction of human history that moves society inevitably in a progressive direction." And he went on to explain, with all the logic-defying confidence of a commissar, "The crisis of capitalism is systemic. . . . The crisis of socialism is not systemic."

It should be said that other American Communist groups responded similarly. The *Workers' Vanguard*, an organ of the Sparticist Party, ran an article not long after the dissolution of the Soviet Union about a pro-Soviet demonstration in Moscow. Titled "Mass Protest Against Yeltsin Counterrevolution," it denounced the new Russian president as a traitor and explained that "the Imperialist media and the now anti-Communist Soviet television sought to portray Revolution Day, November 7, as the wake after the 'death of Communism.' . . . The new 'rulers' tried to ban all celebration of the anniversary of the Bolsheviks taking power. The *New York Times* admitted that 'more than ten thousand Communist loyalists' marched, but in fact as many as ninety thousand came out in Moscow in an angry protest against the counterrevolution headed by Yeltsin and Gorbachev."

Nevertheless, the repercussions of the August coup were simply too great not to have a profound and immediate effect on Communism in America. Immediately they plunged the CPUSA into a crisis from which it has yet to recover. At one meeting in Cleveland two hundred members separated from the main body of the party, and fully a third of the party called for a change in its fundamental structure. When dissidents like James Jackson, a critic of Hall, tried to speak out, their microphone was cut off. In the end, the fact that Hall's leadership was ratified by a vote of two to one served only to deepen the divide. As Angela Davis wrote in a letter to one convention: "Like many comrades, I still feel very much connected to the popular progressive struggles of our time. But I do not feel that as a party we have maintained a vital link to those realities."

On this occasion the historian Herbert Aptheker, quoted by Max Elbaum in the *Nation*, asserted quite sensibly that "to speak of a systemic source of the crisis [as Hall had done] . . . is to insist that the nature of the governing parties was the basic source. And what was that nature—it was authoritarian, domineering, brutal, and guilty of colossal crimes—not only suppression but also massive human extermination. . . . It is that authoritarian, anti-democratic and eventually anti-humanistic distortion that must be combated; our party must learn these lessons, must give up denial, must transform its character."

The way Hall dealt with such heretical pronouncements was to purge many of the signatories of the "Initiative to Unite and Renew the Party," among them Angela Davis, for comments about the party's "stagnation in theoretical concepts," "isolation from the progressive developments in our country," and "attempts to stifle debate [that] threaten our party's very existence." Whereas one of the attendees had the wit to tell the *New York Times* that "we don't want to air our dirty Lenin in public," Gus Hall, who had been down this road many times before, knew exactly what to do. He branded his opponents as "traitors to the working class," and the meeting was over.

But there were more problems ahead. Soon afterward, when the more liberally inclined editors of the *People's Weekly World*, the CPUSA paper, arrived at work on 5 December 1991, they found the offices closed and the locks changed. The next week much the same thing happened. Apologizing to their readers for the reduced size of their 14 December issue, they printed a box explaining that it was due to the inability of the staff to gain access to their offices. By the time the issue appeared, however, this had been changed by higher-ups to read that the reduced size was due to "the pressures of convention work."

Other left-wing groups were quick to enter the fray. In the *Bulletin* of the Workers' League, Bill Vann asserted, in an idiom almost as charmingly dated as Elizabethan English, that "every genuine Marxist and class-conscious worker should welcome the shipwreck of this politically criminal organization [the CPUSA], which has long functioned as an instrument of the Kremlin's counterrevolutionary policy. The two warring factions, now at each other's throats over alleged organizational abuse and control of the party's dwindling assets, are equally reactionary petty-bourgeois groups, entirely hostile to the working class."

Of course, all of this happened several years ago. More recently, in a truly moving testament to the irrepressible power of the human spirit to overcome adversity, a fund-raising letter from the CPUSA demonstrated the powers of positive thinking. "We regularly receive letters, phone calls, and visits all over the country from people who say they are fed up with capitalism. They say it just like that. And they add how grateful they are that a Party that works for a different system in our country still exists."

Whereas the CPUSA has looked to Russia for seven decades, other parties, like the Revolutionary Communist Party, have answered to Beijing. In a way this made more sense. Marxism has had two main eras of expansion in the present century, each comprising some twenty-five years. The first was from 1917 to 1946, the second from 1947 to 1971. Though the first was localized in Europe, the second was outside of Europe and went *pari passu* with the dissolution of the colonial empires that Europe had acquired in previous centuries. Traditional Marxism was in no position to deal with this state of affairs. Marx had seen Communism as the inevitable evolutionary outcome of industrialized capitalism, just as he had seen bourgeois capitalism as the inevitable outcome of feudalism. That Communism should emerge directly out of feudalism—which is in fact the only way it ever emerged, except when one industrialized country invaded another—did not make sense to orthodox Marxists. And yet it was a question that Marxism would have to answer if it were to survive. For the real business of radicalism, at least as far as the New Left was concerned, involved the annihilation of colonialism in the aftermath of World War II.

Nor should it be forgotten that for many New Leftists who were rebelling against their own middle- or upper-middle-class background, Moscow looked very much like what they had left behind: middle-aged, potbellied white men who drank gin and tonics and resembled the rebels' fathers. Maoism provided the answer. By embracing a Far Eastern ideology—with all it implied of Orientalism and mystical otherworldliness—the younger generation was mounting an implicit challenge to Western society. Furthermore, because this ideology was peasant-based rather than proletarian, it had the right ecological look that some were then seeking.

Some sense of the ethos of contemporary Maoism can be found in a recent issue of the *Revolutionary Worker*, which is an organ of the Revolutionary Communist Party, U.S.A. (RCP). Published in English and in Spanish—the language of contemporary Maoism—its emblem is a red flag, wind-swept and battle-scarred, tied to a bayonet that recalls the glory days of the Paris Commune. Unlike the CPUSA, the RCP makes a point of embracing minorities. The cover of the 4 February 1996 issue features dreadlocked Mumia Abu-Jamal, the poster boy of the far left, who is on death row for murder. The back page is an appeal to send donations to the Shining Path in Peru. In the same issue appears an inexcusably awful poem on Clinton's State of the Union speech, accompanied by pictures of House Speaker Newt Gingrich and Clinton, wearing snouts and porcine ears. In a retro nod to the sixties, the message here is that the politicians are all "pigs."

The RCP is one of the few remaining parties to survive the crackup of the New Left. It traces its origins to the foundation of the Bay Area Revolutionary Union (BARU) in 1969. Like many of the parties on the left, formed in almost farcical imitation of the parties of the October Revolution, theirs is a tale of constant fissure and regrouping. When one of its members joined the Students for a Democratic Society (SDS) in 1970, the name was changed to the Revolutionary Union. Three years later the organization had some six to eight hundred members in twenty-five cities across the nation.

In the interest of winning over the working class, the party adopted some oddly conservative cultural politics, such as opposition to the Equal Rights Amendment, open hostility to homosexuals (whom the far left traditionally abhors), and resistance to the demands of blacks. One of their organizations, the Committee for Decent Education, opposed busing on the grounds that it created hostility between the races, a position that alienated other leftist groups and lost the party most of its black members. Thereafter the party was pretty much in abeyance, surfacing occasionally to stage stunts like Get the Rich off Our Backs, a counter-Bicentennial march in Philadelphia in 1976.

For most of this time they had been in step with China in much the same way that the CPUSA was in step with Moscow, that is, by piously assenting to everything that the Chinese leadership said or did. The RCP even went so far as to skewer Castro, that sacred cow of the radical left, for his intervention in Angola in 1976, which they saw as being at the behest of the Soviet superpower, an organization they considered no better than the United States. And yet, after Mao's death and the arrest of the Gang of Four, who continued to support him, things began to change and China became slightly more open to the West. Whereas other left-wing organizations endorsed these changes, Bob Avakian, who was and continues to be the leader of the RCP, assailed the Deng government. He inveighed especially against its reintroduction of Western cultural figures like Shakespeare, Beethoven, and Rembrandt, calling the Deng government "a fascist bourgeois dictatorship" and branding Deng himself, in an admirably pungent image, "a puking dog who deserves worse than death."

The party's foreign policy has been equally extreme. According to the historian Harvey Klehr, the RCP "finds all revolutionary governments in the world too moderate. After the victory of the Sandinistas, the RCP attacked them for not instituting socialism and for cooperating with the bourgeoisie. Likewise, it supported Robert Mugabe's guerrillas in Zimbabwe until they agreed to participate in elections; then they attacked Mugabe as a sellout. Bob Avakian even attacked the Soviet Union for fighting World War II on a patriotic, bourgeois, democratic basis."[1]

Such intolerance is as typical of the extreme left as of the extreme right. It is very revealing to find many of the same paranoid attitudes in both camps. Thus rapper Ice T, interviewed in the *Revolutionary Worker*, cites the activist Quincy Jones as saying to him, "If you look at the Persian Gulf, they ended that war in a hundred days. They would not think twice about taking them guns and aiming them on the streets of America. And not one of us can fly a Huey, not one of us can move one of these jets, and those people who can are already indoctrinated and brainwashed with their angle."[2] That Gulf War weaponry is being used against unarmed civilians is one of the recurring alarmist themes on the extreme right as well.

But this is not the only instance of an intolerance among certain far leftists that is similar in degree and in kind to that of the extreme right. Whereas the latter views homosexuals as an abomination against God—or something along those lines—the extreme left satisfies the urge to hate them by accusing them of being the products of capitalist decadence. "The gay men's communities have typically been characterized by the promotion of a very narcissistic and self-indulgent lifestyle," according to one writer in the *SF Weekly*. Once the revolution comes, a "struggle will be waged to eliminate [homosexuality] and reform homosexuals." It is precisely this form of intolerance among Communists that makes certain members of the extreme left, such as anarchists, highly suspicious of the various strains of socialist statism.

Still, although it is generally true that the extreme left cares far more about ideology than does the extreme right, this statement is less true today than it was in the past. There was a time when the fate of the world seemed to stand or fall on the minute doctrinal differences between Bolshevism, Menshevism, and anarcho-syndicalism, a time when the slightest revision in doctrine was seen as heresy, if not apostasy. Now, despite the high-blown labels that radicals sometimes give themselves, it is not Communism or anarchism that they seek so much as any general but energetic form of leftism that serves to oppose the more conservative center of society.

Traditionally Marxists and anarchists appeal to very different sectors of the left: Marxists to the proletariat of industrialized workers, anarchists to those whom Marx somewhat inhumanely dismissed as the *Lumpenproletariat*. Whereas the Marxist traditionally believes that a massive state is the natural and necessary outgrowth of a classless society, the anarchist traditionally wishes to abolish all but the most rudimentary forms of statism. In practice, however, both doctrines are united in their antagonism to the center, and, since neither group has any real power or even the possibility of real power, this antagonism to the center, to established authority, is the true motive behind their agitation.

One can divide classical anarchism into two strains, that of Kropotkin and Sully-Prudhon on the one hand, and of Bakunin and Nychaev on the other. The first, to which Tolstoy belonged, emphasizes humanity's basic decency, which has been corrupted by the state, with its merciless exactions of law and order. The second, which is essentially nihilism, is more concerned with the destruction of established authority than with the construction, along humanistic lines, of a more equitable society. Despite this theoretical division, one is apt to find, especially among more recent anarchists, that the two strains exist side by side.

The essence of anarchism can be found in these words of Tolstoy: "I regard all governments . . . as intricate institutions, sanctified by tradition and custom, for the purpose of committing by force and with impunity the most revolting crimes. And I think that the efforts of those who wish to improve our social life should be directed toward the liberation of themselves from national governments, whose evil and above all whose futility is in our time becoming more and more apparent."[3]

A century later, in a recent issue of the New York–based *Love and Rage, a Revolutionary Anarchist Newspaper*, one writer expressed more or less the same view, "that humans are inherently good, and that it is a fundamental natural law that humans should be free and equal. The existence of authority, whether it takes the form of the state, capitalism, or the family, destroys human nature and perpetuates selfishness and greed: once authority is removed, human goodness will be released and a new society based on goodwill, truth, and mutual aid will replace today's society of corruption, coercion, and avarice."[4]

Perhaps the most prominent anarchist of recent years has been the Unabomber, who, if the evidence is believed, can be identified with Theodore Kaczynski. Close to a million copies of the Unabomber's manifesto were circulated, via the *Washington Post* of 19 September 1995, in accordance with the writer's instructions that he would not murder again if his essay were published. It is questionable how many people actually read its thirty-five thousand densely printed words, or how many who undertook to do so got much farther than the first few paragraphs. Though it would not be accurate to say that they missed out on very much, a reading of the manifesto is not a complete waste of time. In itself it is not especially interesting or remarkable, but because of the circumstances surrounding publication, it makes for fascinating reading. Though roughly the size of other manifestos like Mill's *On Liberty* and Rousseau's *Social Contract*, it is obviously not in their league, either for brilliance of expression or for originality or even cogency of thought. Still, it is a reasonably respectable foray into political science, written in such an even, undemonstrative tone that you need constantly to remind yourself that its author detonated sixteen bombs in eighteen years and that, as a result, three people lost their lives and a dozen others were maimed. Nowhere does the Unabomber sound like the serial murderer he admits to being. In fact, he makes only one allusion, by the way, to his sanguinary path to publication. "To make an impression on society with words is . . . almost impossible for most individuals and small groups. Take us for example. If we had never done anything violent and had submitted the present writings to a publisher, they would probably not have been accepted."

Kaczynski's position regarding the left and liberalism in general is not always clear. "The leftist seeks to satisfy his need for power through identification with a social movement. . . . But no matter how far the movement has gone in attaining its goals the leftist is never satisfied, because his activism is a surrogate activity. That is, the leftist's real motive is not to attain the ostensible goals of leftism; in reality he is motivated by the sense of power he gets from struggling for and then reaching a social goal." Elsewhere he asserts that "leftists tend to hate anything that has an image of being strong, good and successful. They hate America, they hate Western Civilization, they hate white males, they hate rationality." In passages like this he sounds almost cantankerously right-wing.

And yet, if he hates leftists, the Unabomber is scarcely kinder to conservatives. "The conservatives are fools," he writes. "They whine about the decay of traditional values, yet they enthusiastically support technological progress and economic growth. Apparently it never occurs to them that you can't make rapid, drastic changes in the technology and the economy of a society without causing rapid changes in all other aspects of the society as well, and that such rapid changes inevitably break down traditional values."

Perhaps what makes the manifesto so interesting is that, to all appearances, it is written by someone not so very unlike ourselves, someone who takes care to footnote his sources, who tries to make his case as reasonably as possible, who, in tone at least, sounds like a centrist. Unlike that other murderous madman and would-be author Adolf Hitler, there is no foaming at the mouth here. The author does not declaim. He is at pains to be balanced and fair, and he almost gains the sympathies of the center by finding certain things as unreasonable and distasteful as the rest of us do. "Propaganda," he explains at one point, "is used for many good purposes such as discouraging child abuse or race hatred." Elsewhere, inveighing against the growing sense of the pointlessness of life in industrial society, he fears that people "would seek other, dangerous outlets (drugs, crime, 'cults,' hate groups)." In this regard, clearly, he is one of us: he is a citizen of the center.

At other points he even sounds almost likable, presenting us with a Rousseauian view of human nature. Because "the System" (a sixties term he constantly invokes) needs mathematicians and scientists to do research, "heavy pressure is put on children to excel in these fields. It isn't natural for an adolescent human being to spend the bulk of his time sitting at a desk absorbed in study.... Among the American Indians, for example, boys were trained in active outdoor pursuits—just the sort of thing that boys like. But in our society children are pushed into studying technical subjects, which most do grudgingly."

The press has misunderstood the Unabomber. He is instinctively thought of as a leftist because, if he is indeed Mr. Kaczynski, he looks a little like a hippie, and because he was teaching at Berkeley in the late sixties, at the time of the sit-ins. In fact, it is his conservatism that is the most remarkable thing about him. To begin with, he has had almost no exposure to the larger world for almost a quarter century, having spent that time, except for one interval of two years, in a sixteen-foot-long shed in Montana. Though his thinking has not changed substantially since the early 1970s, his real intellectual roots are in the 1950s, in once prominent thinkers like Eric Hoffer, whom he cites, and, far more important, Alfred Adler, whom he does not cite. The influence of this man, the pioneer of such concepts as the inferiority and superiority complexes, is revealed in the Unabomber's constantly recurring to the theme of power and one's efforts to attain it.

It is not for nothing that one of the chapters in the manifesto is titled "The Power Process." For the Unabomber, the desire for power is the drive behind everything we do. The fulfillment of this desire seems to him to be healthy, and it is something that can be found optimally in preindustrial society, where—he imagines—each person was able to produce what he needed and thus to find a kind of fulfillment. Like a moralist of the school of Rousseau, he believes that thwarting this desire leads to decadence. "Thus the aristocrats of the Roman Empire had their literary pretensions; many European aristocrats a few centuries ago invested tremendous time and energy in hunting, though they certainly didn't need the meat; other aristocrats have competed for status through elaborate displays of wealth."

Because, he believes, technology thwarts this power drive, it is directly causative of all the anxieties and all the frustrations of modern times. If his measures are not implemented, he predicts, "human freedom mostly will have vanished, because individuals and small groups will be impotent vis-à-vis large organizations armed with supertechnology and an arsenal of advanced psychological and biological tools for manipulating human beings." What he prefers is something called Wild Nature, that is, the nature that he experienced in the godforsaken wilds of Montana, with no neighbors for miles, no electricity or creature comforts beyond what one could build for oneself, and no food beyond what, through native ingenuity, one could catch or grow.

The Unabomber's thinking consists of a few core convictions, from which he tries unsuccessfully to forge a system. An avid outdoorsman, he opposes technology and especially the industrial society that has caused the massive agglomerations of people into cities. He despises leftists for what he takes to be their falseness and their underhanded will to power. He romanticizes the past and wishes to reinstitute it. Beyond this, there is little texture or even consistency to his thought.

The major intellectual failing of the manifesto—quite aside from its being harebrained to begin with—is that it completely neglects to outline the future of human society if the revolution that it advocates were ever to occur. Would communes develop, or would society consist of a billion monadic nuclear families each governed by a father hunting and foraging for food? Would society not eventually regroup? What steps would be taken to ensure that this did not happen? Such utter lack of attention to the consequences of his revolution is perhaps the surest sign of the Unabomber's madness. One could also point out, of course, that most people, contrary to what the Unabomber believes, are perfectly content to live as they do, or at least would not be happier,

and probably would be considerably less happy, if they were living in the communal or eremitical conditions that the Unabomber
prescribes. One could point out, further, that all of the culture
Kaczynski claims to admire, those writings of Shakespeare and
Thackeray that enlivened his hours in the wilderness, not only
would never be published but would never have come into existence in the first place in his state of nature. But to raise such
points would be, as so often, to answer a fool with his folly.

Given the distinct strain of conservatism in the Unabomber's
manifesto, why, it may be asked, should he be included in a context of left-wing extremism? The reason is that his thinking is in
many respects consonant with the long line of anarchist thought
outlined above. His desire to retreat from civilization and his praise
of the American Indians suggests a Rousseau-ian retreat from civilization as we know it. Like nihilists in the tradition of Bakunin
and Nychayev, he wishes to subvert and destroy the existing power
structure. But like Tolstoy's and Kropotkin's, his politics derive
from the core conviction that man is essentially good—a conviction
that you would never find expressed among right-wing organizations like the Posse Comitatus, despite their advocating a similar
dismantling of the state.

As anarchists go, however, it must be said that the Unabomber
is something of an anomaly. Though he sanctions violence, he is not
really a nihilist, and, indeed, the virtues and civic duties he com-
mends are oddly middle-class. His brand of anarchism advocates
individual cells, monadic nuclear families, rather than communes,
which he considers undesirable and which he associates with the
leftism that he claims to despise. And he implicitly despises other
anarchists because they see politics as an end in itself, whereas he
is essentially apolitical. He is motivated to action more by his desire for a specific result than by any love of the process itself.

Most writers who identify themselves with anarchism are
rather less "action-oriented" and more theoretical, and thus they
are, for lack of a better term, less practical. There is, it must be
said, something dandiacal, something of the poseur in the few remaining downtown anarchists, who seem to believe that, by having
a little bit of taste and some knowledge of poetry and by wearing

picturesquely threadbare clothes, they qualify as the reincarnated Charles Baudelaire. One of the most exuberant of these downtown types is Hakim Bey, who has pioneered the concept of what he has called "temporary autonomous zones," or TAZ. These contexts of temporary freedom, as Bey sees it, are not direct challenges to the state but aspire more humbly to be a "guerrilla operation which liberates an area—of land, of time, of imagination—and then dissolves itself to re-form elsewhere/elsewhen, before the state can crush it." Recalling a party "where for one brief night a republic of gratified desires was attained," he asks, "Shall we not confess that the politics of that night have more reality and force for us than those of, say, the entire U.S. government?"[5]

Sometimes the tone of contemporary anarchism is more strident. In the same issue of *Love and Anger* quoted above, one writer attacks the racism of Farrakhan—something most others on the left would not feel called upon to do—but he does so in a way that ultimately underscores what Richard Hofstedter memorably called "the paranoid style in American politics." The author asserts that "Farrakhan's emphasis on black capitalism, his anti-Semitism, and his attempts to subordinate women within the struggle are all connected. They are each the expression of the way that the ideas of the oppressors are reproduced among the oppressed. And they go a long way toward explaining why Farrakhan, while officially attacked, is in fact not only tolerated but actually subsidized by the white power structure." This sentiment is echoed by another writer who claims that "we can hold no illusions about the US government or the militia movement—it is too dangerous. They both must be destroyed—period point blank! The feds will not destroy right-wing movements, because they are the loyal allies in the war against blacks, queers, wimmin, poor people, and the left."[6]

"They must be destroyed—period point blank!" These are pretty fierce words, and we can only be grateful to their author that he has apparently granted a reprieve to the United States government and to the rest of us. And yet these words are oddly suggestive not only of the nature of contemporary anarchism but of all leftist extremism. For in this frantic call for action, as in so many similar passages in recent anarchist literature, what we are seeing is in fact a retreat from action and from true politics, from the terminally unglamorous, thoroughly unpoetic, and utterly charmless procedures of compromise and negotiation by which alone real social progress is accomplished. If one knows that there is no possibility of success in a course of action, is it not reckless and irresponsible to advocate it anyway, and in the process to allow real gains, less poetical but more material, to slip away into indolent oblivion? The unspoken truth at the heart of all the agitation and all the calls to action on the extreme left—and on the extreme right, for that matter—is the confidence that nothing will ever happen, that no one will ever listen, that everyone will go home and that we shall all carry on as before. The bourgeois will resume his place behind his desk and the worker will resume his station at the factory, and the center will cohere, if anything strengthened by this brush with an impotent enemy so vociferously at odds with itself.

6

THE EXTREMES OF VIRTUE

It has been the ceaseless labor of the past thirty years to expand the center that was once defined by white heterosexual men. During this period blacks, women, and homosexuals, among other groups, have all struggled successfully to gain entry into the center of society. And while this process of assimilation is not yet complete, no reasonable person would dispute that all three groups are closer to equality today than in 1960, and no decent person would deny that the changes that have surely taken place have, on balance, redounded to the profit of humanity as a whole.

Inevitably, however, every liberation movement will beget a fringe that, in the extremity of its measures, resembles its enemies at their worst. When this happens, we are inclined to think that extreme circumstances have begotten extreme behavior. More likely, though, people who are extreme by nature become attracted to a cause because of its opposition to the center rather than its ambition to become the center. And so, the more the group as a whole achieves its long-desired assimilation, the more vociferous the fringe becomes in its opposition. At this point the emerging fringes either clamor for equality without integration or, rejecting the idea of equality altogether, assert their superiority to what they see as a corrupt center.

This desire to oppose rather than to join the center explains some of the weird alliances between the radical fringes of these liberation movements and the most extreme of their perceived oppressors. As the black writer Ishmael Reed asked rhetorically, "Don't you think that the white neo-Nazis and some of these black nationalists ought to get together, to unite so as to save on overhead costs?"[1] His ironic words were almost borne out when the Nation of Islam, at the height of the civil rights movement, provided a forum for George Lincoln Rockwell, the foremost white supremacist of the day, to discuss the founding of separate states for whites and blacks. And one might also point to radical feminist philosophers like Catharine MacKinnon and Andrea Dworkin who, in their opposition to pornography, have made common cause with far right senators like Jesse Helms. Furthermore, in their philosophical rejection of the world of men, they bring themselves into striking proximity to positions usually articulated by the most entrenched male chauvinists. Though such alliances might appear, at first glance, to be unimaginable, the point of extremism is usually opposition to the center rather than to other extremes. The corollary to this condition is that extreme groups are apt to feel more solidarity with one another than with any group in the center.

Yet even when these groups endorse positions dear to the far right, there is a perceived difference. In the popular imagination, whereas right-wingers are associated with the traditions of oppression, leftists are assimilated to the revolution of the oppressed. For this reason alone the far left is freely granted a moral authority that the far right is consistently denied. Thus we, the center, know to reject the anti-pornography of Jesse Helms as boneheaded, philistine conservatism, but we are inclined to look very differently at the essentially similar claims of Catherine MacKinnon. No right-thinking person, likewise, would endorse the separatism advocated by the neo-Nazis, but the separatism of the Nation of Islam, even if a pipe dream, has about it the faintest whiff of moral prestige.

This deference of the center to certain extreme positions on the left results at times in a failure of nerve, a tacit complicity in moral relativism whereby people who are entirely innocent reveal a bizarre willingness to hold themselves accountable for the most outlandish crimes. In time, the morale of the center becomes frayed from this constant challenge to its probity. Some of its members fall to self-loathing before it; others turn that hatred toward minorities.

Most of the center, however, responds with benumbed apathy, combined with the suspicion that the world is going to hell. It was in this way that they greeted the preposterous claims of racial superiority put forward by certain black educators, most famously Leonard Jeffries of the City University of New York. These black supremacists either insist on African culture's superiority to Western culture or, implicitly embracing our culture, assert that what is best about the civilization of the West actually had its origins in Africa or at any rate among blacks. A recent public access program on Time Warner Cable of New York City, titled *The Real Jews Are Black*, tried to prove that Shakespeare was black. The evidence was as follows. The moderator flashed onscreen the well-known portrait of the conspicuously white bard that appears in the first folio edition of his plays. This image, the moderator asserted, was a forgery. As proof of Shakespeare's being black he showed a posthumous bronze bust, though he did not acknowledge or perhaps never even knew that it was posthumous. Now because bronze is a dark material, the Bard was given a swarthy complexion, which was all the proof needed to believe that our greatest poet was a black man. Even Malcolm X was not immune from such folly. As he told Arthur Haley in 1958, trying to convince him that the author of the *Odyssey* might have been black: "Homer and Omar and Moor, you see, are related terms."2

Most blacks and almost all whites would shy away from making any claims about the inherited physical differences between the races. When Jimmy "the Greek" Snyder averred that black swimmers were more buoyant than whites, he was immediately dismissed as a sports commentator at ABC. And yet certain black authors have made assertions that are substantially the same. Ellen Warfield-Coppock, for example, believes that melanin, which causes the darker pigmentation in blacks, possesses extraordinary powers of physical and spiritual strength. "Melanin," she asserts, "can help [blacks] glide in the air like Magic Johnson or hit top speeds like Florence Joyner."3 By the same token, because she believes that the pineal gland calcifies more often among whites than among blacks, she sees this as accounting for a higher rate of sexual perversion among the former.

Of course, such musings are idiotic, and we must hopefully assume that most people, black or otherwise, will recognize this fact. But what is really corrosive about these meditations is that they occur within a context of almost incessant and insidious questioning of science and history. The secret agenda of this interrogation is not to disprove the discourse of the center, though it pretends to do so, but rather to establish the grounds on which all historical and scientific discourses are considered equal to all others, at which point the truth becomes like putty to be formed however one wishes. This agenda was stated almost explicitly by the black social scientist Molefi Asante: "All analysis is culturally centered and flows from ideological assumptions. . . . A total rewrite of the major events and developments in the world is long overdue. Our facts are in our history; use them. Their facts are in their history; they have certainly used theirs. All truth resides in our experiences. Your Afrocentricity . . . is a truth, even though it may not be their truth. With an Afrocentric spirit, all things can be made to happen."[4]

Such pronouncements are of a purely intellectual nature, and insofar as they promote pride in one's heritage, especially when that heritage has been historically disparaged and denied, they are more false than malign. The same cannot be said for some of the more virulent racism associated with black activism. It is the tragedy of certain blacks in America to have learned everything *about* racism, but in the most important sense to have learned nothing *from* racism. What is bad about racism against blacks is not that it is directed against blacks but that it is racism in the first place, that it is an irrational hatred of human beings by human beings. The truth is that many blacks, though surely not all, have understood only that racism against them was bad, though they have no real problem with racism in itself, especially when they are doing the hating. Publicly they profess to fight fire with fire: having been burned by racism, they will use racism themselves. But this specious argument cannot exculpate them from the crime of racism, which comes all too easily to some of their number, a racism they carry out with altogether too much vigor and satisfaction. Perhaps it was only to be expected that a people so discriminated against for so long must beget some members who would retort that hatred upon their former oppressors. Still, one would like to think that they would have learned the deeper human truth of rising above racism, and this, at least among a few of the louder members of the black community, has not happened.

Consider, for example, the anti-Semitism that is expressed by certain blacks—and we cannot repeat too emphatically that we are talking about relatively few blacks who represent only themselves. In *The Secret Relationship Between Blacks and Jews*, a work written and published by the Nation of Islam, slavery is presented as essentially a massive genocidal attack against blacks carried out by Jews. This is the black equivalent of the Protocols of the Elders of Zion. Some of those associated with the writing and dissemination of *The Secret Relationship Between Blacks and Jews* are so far gone in their hatred of Jews as to excuse or pass over in relative silence the white Protestant slaveowners in the South, not to mention the Arabs and, indeed, the black African potentates who sold their people into slavery in the first place.

"The Jews' participation in the slave trade," the document goes on, "particularly their trafficking in non-Jewish slaves, incited the moral indignation of Europe's Gentile population. The Europeans reacted by taxing the Jews and some were expelled from their host country."[5] This claim, of course, is patently false, not least because the Jews were expelled from their various host countries long before the slave trade began. Furthermore, it could be argued that such Jews as were involved in the slave trade—and they were a small minority—engaged in these dealings only after their conversion to Christianity. Though it may come as a surprise to many to learn that, in the antebellum South, certain American Jews owned as much as 2 percent of all slaves, it will come as even more of a surprise that blacks themselves owned 3.5 percent.

It should come as no surprise, however, that, as though in direct support of Ishmael Reed's suggestion about white and black supremacists sharing overhead cost, this implicit exculpation of white Protestants and explicit incrimination of Jews has been seized upon and put to good use by white supremacist groups. The real subtext of *The Secret Relationship* is that, because Jews are supposed to have orchestrated the entire trade in African slaves, it is quite all right for blacks to hate Jews in return. Such an argument, of course, is surely necessary if blacks are to hate Jews at all. The problem with blacks hating Jews—the "problem" being from the perspective of black racists—is that there is little plausible reason for doing so. For them to hate white southerners, in other words, is perhaps a questionable moral equation, but at least there is a plausible link between slavery and the forebears of these white southerners. And yet most contemporary American Jews are descended from ancestors who not only came to this country generations after slavery was abolished but came in a state of destitution precisely to escape persecution themselves. Furthermore, although many ethnic groups have been guilty of anti-black sentiment, and although some Jews have doubtless been guilty of this hatred themselves, nevertheless, Jews as a whole were conspicuous, during the civil rights era, for showing solidarity with blacks in their struggle for equality. Thus it is not clear why it should be Jews who are apt to be singled out for this hatred.

That such reasoning has no bearing on black racists is conveyed in the following distasteful diatribe by Khalid Abdul Muhammad, one of the spokesmen for the Nation of Islam, who pretends to imitate an old Jewish man of presumably Middle European extraction: "Ve, ve, ve suffer like you. Ve, ve, ve, ve marched with Dr. Martin Luther King Jr. Ve, ve, ve were in Selma, Alabama. Ve, ve were in Montgomery, Alabama. Ve, ve were on the front line of the civil rights marches. Ve have always supported you.' But let's take a look at it. The Jews, the so-called Jews, what they have actually done, brothers and sisters, is used us as cannon fodder."[6]

Indeed, it is the very liberalism of Jews that Muhammad attacks. "One people, one planet," he begins, presumably paraphrasing liberal "Jewish" discourse. "Hell, you [the Jews] didn't want to share it with us until it got all out of whack. Until you had messed up the ozone layer. Until you had destroyed much of the rain forest. Until you had tampered with the delicate balance in nature, polluted the very air that even you have to breathe, polluted the very water that even you have to drink."[7] Thus the Jews are responsible for environmental catastrophe as well as for slavery!

It is a mystery why certain blacks hate Jews and why their hateful words find a surprisingly warm reception in many pockets of the black community. Talk of Jewish contamination of the environment and of Jewish involvement in the slave trade is clearly the effect rather than the cause: such talk presupposes a hatred of Jews, rather than causing it. Part of this hatred, surely, has to do with the fact that there have been Jewish slumlords, but this is only a small part. A great deal of the rancor is the product of envy. The Jews have been victimized at least as much as blacks—in itself an intolerable irritant to certain blacks who want the monopoly on victimhood—and yet, in spite of this, through diligence and intelligence they have won their way into the center of society.

But more important than that is the belief—which many Jews share, by the way—that their two ethnicities occupy opposing points of the human spectrum. In this dualism, the Jews are seen as bookish, weak, and pale from not being out in the sun enough. Blacks, by contrast, are viewed as powerful, poorly educated athletes who see school as something sissies go in for. As a result, certain blacks feel, at remote levels of intuition, that the difference between Jews and other whites is that blacks do not have to fear essentially nonviolent Jews the way they certainly have to fear gun-toting white supremacists, who talk violence with such venom that, one feels, even people like Farrakhan respect them. When Khalid Abdul Mohammad imitated the mythic Middle European Jewish liberal, he presented him as weak, suppliant, and frightened—the polar opposite of the brave and athletic young black man who is equally a subject of myth.

Yet it is a myth that characterizes the discourse of black extremists. Notions of fearless physical power and manliness pervade their tough-talking discourse to such a degree that their first recourse is to attribute weakness and effeminacy to those whom they happen to dislike. At one conference Khalid Abdul Mohammad was introduced by the conference's organizer, Mark Shabazz, in the following way: "We want to bring on a man who gives the white man nightmares. We want to bring on a man who makes the Jews pee in their pants at night."[8] Presumably he knew his audience well and knew what they wanted to hear. In a similar vein Alton Maddox, a lawyer for the Nation of Islam, when asked about Farrakhan's famous reference to Jews as "bloodsuckers," commented menacingly, "You'd better be glad that the only thing we are doing is calling you bloodsucker."[9] So, too, Ashra Kwesi, another prominent member of the Nation of Islam, described the top echelons of the Vatican as "a lot of white faggot boys" and referred to the apostles in a painting of the Last Supper as well as "a whole lot of faggot white boys."[10]

Now, because of their genetic makeup, blacks tend on average to be physically bigger than Jews and Asians, whom certain black racists dislike almost as much as they do Jews—and largely for the same reason, that Asians seem to them to be bookish, deferential, hard-working, in other words, unmanly. The "mentality" of the black community, by holding up men like Mike Tyson and O. J. Simpson as models, more than, say, Christopher Darden or Kweisi Mfume, constantly reinforces this theme. And yet any black man who buys into it must address a paradox: despite being encouraged to feel stronger than most of their fellow citizens as individuals, black men corporately feel less "empowered" than almost any other minority. By way of overcompensation, one imagines, Khalid Abdul Muhammad, speaking of South Africa, declared that if the whites "won't get out by sundown, we kill everything white that ain't right. . . . We kill the women, we kill the children, we kill the babies. We kill the blind, we kill the crippled, we kill 'em all. We kill the faggot, we kill the lesbian, we kill 'em all. . . . I said kill the blind, kill the crippled, kill the crazy, goddamit, and when you get through killing 'em all, and when you get through killing 'em all, go to the goddam graveyard and dig up the grave and kill 'em all, go to the goddam graveyard and dig up the grave and kill 'em a-goddam-gain, 'cause they didn't die hard enough. And if you've killed 'em all and you don't have the strength to dig 'em up, then take your gun and shoot in the goddam grave."[11]

What is really going on here? Most white people who subsequently learned about this outburst through the media came away with entirely the wrong idea. Here, they assumed, was the voice of black anger in all its terrible ugliness. Here was something they must guard against at all costs. In fact it was nothing of the sort. Inverting Teddy Roosevelt's injunction to speak softly and carry a big stick, here was a case of speaking loudly and carrying a straw. It resembled the fantastical rantings of children who know that the grown-ups, those really in power, could send them scurrying with a simple flick of the wrist. Nevertheless, it is part of the fantasy life of humans that those who have been trampled upon can derive some emotional sustenance from the kind of talk that Muhammad gave them. To use the word "kill" twenty times in the space of one hundred words was perhaps a quick fix, something to get the adrenaline going. The insistent repetition lulled his listeners into an almost hypnotic trance in which they felt, for a moment, empowered and important. But inevitably reality would set in once again, and those whom these words had exhilarated would come face to face once again with the essential fact of their powerlessness.

As even a brief discussion of black extremists reveals, their mentality is a thing compounded of metaphors and fantasies in equal measure. Not only is slavery seen as a Jewish enterprise, but once we accept this assertion as fact, even though it relates to events hundreds of years old, every black person alive today is given the moral authority to hate every Jew alive. This universalizing of the actions of some very few Jews into the responsibility of all Jews is a metaphorical operation that is in fact nothing less than the extremist's stock in trade. Talk of genocide and of the collective guilt of perceived oppressors haunts the discourse of black extremists at every step. And yet it is not unique to them. Rather it is the stock in trade of extreme feminists as well, not to mention extremists among gay rights activists.

Whereas black extremists essentially hate all whites—or, more precisely, all nonblacks—certain radical feminists are equally virulent in their hatred of all men. For Andrea Dworkin, the diapason of human experience is reduced to male dominance and female submission. As she concludes her book *Intercourse*: "The men as a body politic have power over women and decide how women will suffer: which sadistic acts against the bodies of women will be construed as normal. In the United States, incest is increasingly the sadism of choice. . . . Perhaps incestuous rape is becoming a central paradigm for intercourse in our time. Women are supposed to be small and childlike, in looks, in rights; child prostitution keeps increasing in mass and in legitimacy, the children sexually used by a long chain of men—fathers, uncles, grandfathers, brothers, pimps, pornographers, and the good citizens who are the consumers; and men, who are, after all, just family, are supposed to slice us in the middle, leaving us in parts on the bed."[12] In other words, all men molest children and women!

The source of Dworkin's rage, like that of certain black extremists, resides in metaphor. First of all, the shape of the male and female genitalia, as well as the victorious insertion of the former into the latter, seems to her to emblemize that male aggression against women that, in her vaguely Freudian way, she believes to be at the heart of the patriarchal society. And once this view is accepted, all men, through an even greater metaphorical leap of her imagination, become guilty by association if not by deed in all the aggression ever waged against women by men. In this manner, not coincidentally, all women attain to a global ascendancy over all men.

A similarly metaphorical thrust is exhibited in the diatribes of Catharine MacKinnon. "Imagine," she begins, "that for four hundred years your most formative traumas, your daily suffering and pain, the abuse you live through, the terror you live with, are unspeakable—not the basis of literature. You grow up with your father holding you down and covering your mouth so another man can make a horrible searing pain between your legs. When you are older, your husband ties you to the bed and drips hot wax on your nipples and brings in other men to watch and make you smile through it. Your doctor will not give you drugs he had addicted you to unless you suck his penis."[13]

The artsy second-person narrative is intended both to speak directly to women and to exclude men. Men in this transaction are objectified as menacing implements seen only from the outside. Women, meanwhile, are invited to believe that the experience that is being foisted upon them is really their own. In fact, this is so far from being the case that the experience MacKinnon describes turns out to belong to no one in the world. Her *sotto voce* end note is revealing: "Some of these facts are taken from years of confidential consultations with women who have been used in pornography." That is to say that she has provided a composite of several different cases that are the experience of no one woman. With sedulous care she has stitched together the most extreme circumstances she could imagine and tried to pass them off as the most common in the world.

It is further in keeping with the metaphorical imagination of Catharine MacKinnon—indeed, it is her *idée mère*—to equate pornographic depictions of an act with the act itself. "In terms of what the men are doing sexually," she asserts, "an audience watching a gang rape in a movie is no different from an audience watching a gang rape that is reenacting a gang rape from a movie, or an audience watching any gang rape."[14] Thus the image of a woman being forced to submit to a man, even when the image is the most innocuously comical or blatantly fake, is, in her mind, no different from actual rape.

Her proof of the connection of pornography to sex-related crimes, namely, that certain rapists have admitted to buying pornography, is unimpressive in the extreme. She cites the December 1984 issue of *Penthouse* in which "Asian women are trussed and hung. . . . Not long after this issue of *Penthouse* appeared, a little Asian girl was found strung up and sexually molested in North Carolina, dead. The murderer said he spent much of the day of the murder in an adult bookstore. Suppose he consumed the *Penthouse* and then went and killed the little girl."[15] Now it may be that many rapists purchase pornography: it would seem unlikely that someone capable of so grotesque an act would be too squeamish or principled to purchase nude pictures. But if many rapists purchase pornography, the overwhelming majority of people who purchase pornography do not commit rape. Furthermore, it is elementary human nature that many rapists, if offered the exculpatory escape clause of pornography, will eagerly grab at this straw and piously declare that they were doing fine until they happened to catch a peek at *Hustler*, which spelled their downfall.

It is yet another paradox of MacKinnon's and especially Dworkin's line of thought that, by inculpating all men, they serve to exculpate precisely those who are guilty. In a perverse way, rapists, whose deviancy can be metaphorically described as a private extremism, make common cause—as so often happens—with extreme feminism in their shared antagonism to the center. The newly remorseful rapist can assail society for placing pornography in his hands—an argument with which MacKinnon has armed him—while the feminist can reproach society for having created the rapist in the first place, even though the rapist contravenes everything for which that society stands.

As racists, religious fanatics, and radical nationalists have always known, it is possible to separate humanity however you want. You can divide it up between gay and straight, male and female, white and nonwhite, black and nonblack, Albanian and non-Albanian, Scrabble player and non–Scrabble player. Traditionally liberalism has been seen as the demolisher of the stereotypes that conservatism has erected. In practice, however, one often demonstrates one's liberalism by stereotyping right back at the conservatives. MacKinnon has more than anti-pornography in common with certain voices on the right. For her as for the typical "male chauvinist pig," man is seen as the doer, the active agent, whereas the woman is viewed as passive and receptive. For MacKinnon the act of intercourse, the *intromission*, as she calls it, of the penis into the vagina, is the pattern of all human interaction. History for her is the record of what men have done to women, what women have received at the hands of men.

Though this point of view is ultimately based in Marxism, that is, in viewing history as the dualism between oppressor and oppressed, in certain respects it runs directly counter to Marxism. Instead of class struggle we have gender struggle. "Male dominance is sexual," MacKinnon maintains. "The male sexual role . . . centers on aggressive intrusion on those with less power. Such acts of dominance are experienced as sexually arousing, as sex itself."[16] The problem with the reductivist worldview of MacKinnon and Dworkin is that, even to the extent that it could possibly be true, it can tell us nothing about the aggression between men, nor about issues of homosexuality or race, all of which not only exist outside of their theories but run directly counter to them. Indeed, in their discussion of pornography, there is no mention made of the booming market in gay and lesbian pornography, not to mention images of nude men for the delectation of straight women.

Furthermore, one could be excused for interpreting MacKinnon and Dworkin as seeing sexuality not as a prerogative for women as well as men—which is how sex-positive feminists like Germaine Greer and Susie Bright view it—but rather as something that women give to men or have taken from them by men. At all events, interaction with men is not something that they themselves could possibly find enjoyable according to this line of reasoning. Here we have a perfect example of the ascendancy of theory over reality. As a culture, we can now know, as no one should ever have doubted, that women are as much interested in sex as men are, even if the speed with which they conceive desire and the form that that desire takes are not always the same as in men. To suppose that the woman is merely "thinking of England" is to set feminism back much further than even the most entrenched conservatives would wish.

Thus far, MacKinnon's indefatigable efforts to outlaw pornography have failed. And yet, despite the legal impotence of her reasoning, culturally she is already starting to take effect. "Many more mainstream feminists and intellectuals, like Naomi Wolf and Susan Faludi, among others, pick up threads from her work," writes Katie Roiphe in *The Morning After*. "Many of her early ideas about sexual harassment and pornography are amplified in common feminist positions. It is easy to trace the path from her thoughts to the cocktail-party conversation of an average left-leaning college sophomore."[17]

Consider a much publicized case from a few years back, which centered around one of those Take Back the Night rallies that are now a fixture on college campuses around the United States. The name of the rally expresses the idea that women, who theoretically fear the night in which rapists lurk, can band together and reclaim it from these predators. In general hundreds of women, with some male supporters, march through a campus to various places where open mikes invite each of the women to tell the audience about the sexual harassment, not to mention rape, that she has suffered. Now it is obviously true that many women have been victims of such aggressions, and it is also true that many men may not always be fully sensitive to the effects of their words and actions on women. But it is difficult to escape the impression that, among certain of the participants, the desire not to be "silenced," to invoke the language of these marches, is elided with the desire "not to be silent." What results is that the desire to speak out often precedes having anything to say.

In a Take Back the Night rally held at Princeton in 1991, a senior named Mindy came up to the mike and spoke of a certain young man who had made a pass at her in the dining facility and then forced her back to his room and, "while he shouted the most degrading obscenities imaginable, raped me." She went on to say, "Because I see this person every day, my rape remains a constant daily reality for me. . . . There are some nights when I sleep soundly, and there are even some mornings when I look in the mirror and I like what I see. I may be a victim, but now I am also a survivor."[18]

These words were duly heard and applauded, and Mindy encountered no problems until she took the unusual step of publishing them in the *Daily Princetonian* of 23 April 1991. For certain of the allegations could be easily disproved. She said, for example, that she had reported the rape, but she had not. She purported to transcribe the words of a rape crisis councilor, who, however, denied ever having spoken with her on that score. And she even named the assailant, who threatened take her to court. About two weeks later, just days before her graduation, she issued a formal apology in the same paper in which she had made the allegations. "I have never met this individual or spoken to him. . . . I urge students who are knowledgeable of this situation to cease blaming this person for my attack. . . . I made my statements in the *Daily Princetonian* and at the Take Back the Night March in order to raise awareness for the plight of the campus rape victims. . . . In several personal conversations and especially at the Take Back the Night March, I have been overcome by emotion. As a result, I was not as coherent or accurate in my recounting of events as a situation as delicate as this demands."[19]

Katie Roiphe, who relates this episode in her book, asks the obvious question: "If Mindy's political zeal and emotional intensity blurred the emotional truth of her story, one wonders how many other survivors experience a similar blurring."[20] But what is ultimately interesting here is not that the young woman invented her rape: that has been going on since the beginning of the world and is almost as old as rape itself. It is a tradition stretching from Potiphar's wife to Tawana Brawley, the young black woman who almost precipitated a race war by claiming that she had been raped by white men. What is important about the Princeton episode is the specific reasons for which this woman spoke out. First of all, she had spoken at each previous Take Back the Night rally during her years at Princeton, and she wanted to have something to say on this occasion as well. More important, the immemorial mendacity of Potiphar's wife was resurrected and channeled into a progressive cause. Rather than the older reasons for lying—manipulation or the desire to escape one's personal guilt— now there was the desire to further the cause of the women's movement.

As Roiphe goes on to comment, "Others would claim that the abstract truth in these accusations eclipses the literal falsehood. In a piece about William Kennedy Smith's date rape trial, Catharine MacKinnon . . . wrote that the truth of a given accusation should be weighed in the larger political balance: 'Did this member of a group sexually trained to woman-hating aggression commit this particular act of woman-hating aggression?'"[21] One might say of certain extreme feminists what Bernard Shaw once said ironically of the British, that they will do absolutely anything for the sake of a principle.

Perhaps the supreme fiction of radical feminism is that, in its rejection of liberalism as being complicit in male dominance, it refuses to acknowledge the real gains that the women's movement and social movements in general have made over the past thirty years. Our society has proved to be far more elastic than it is in the interests of many activists to admit. Nothing expresses this malleability of the center better than its shifting views on homosexuals. As recently as fifty years ago, homosexuality in our culture remained, as it had been in most places and at most times, the love that durst not speak its name. It was a thing so hidden from view that many people did not even know of its existence, and some, when informed, literally refused to believe what they heard. The idea that, only a few decades later, pairs of men might hold hands in the street or even marry would have seemed like lunacy. Nor could one have predicted that there would come a time when homosexuals would be readily accepted into the center of society, while those who sought to deny them their constitutional rights, to rebuke or physically harm them, would be seen to stand outside the mainstream.

Though this assimilation of the homosexual to the center has by no means been completed at the present time, it has acquired, like the integration of blacks, a paradigmatic importance. A liberal outlook on homosexuals, as on blacks, is seen by society at large as the litmus test of one's tolerance and humanity. Of course, hatred of homosexuals is far more pervasive and far more tolerated than a similar antagonism to women or blacks. Men who go out of their way to speak well of blacks and women will draw the line at homosexuals. This is because many men feel threatened by homosexuality and because they viscerally consider the activity of homosexuals to be too distasteful even to think about. Still, such admissions are becoming rarer every day.

Recent books like *A Place at the Table* by Bruce Bawer and *Virtually Normal* by Andrew Sullivan differ from most autobiographical books on homosexuality in being written by cultural conservatives, whose foremost desire is to merge invisibly with the rest of the population. What they advocate is not the concealment of homosexuality but the evolution of circumstances in which sexual preference no longer matters at all. Such writers look askance at some of the more boisterous and flamboyant behavior associated with homosexuals. "The only time I ever feel ashamed of being gay," Bawer quotes a friend as saying, "is on Gay Pride Day." Bawer goes on to comment, "I know what he means, though my own emotions on that day are, at worst, closer to dismay than to shame. . . . [I] watch the file [pass], each group behind its identifying banner: the gay senior citizens, the separatist lesbians, the Dykes on Bikes, the People With AIDS coalition . . .

the local chapters of direct-action groups like ACT UP and Queer Nation, the disco-blaring floats advertising various bars and dance clubs, the volunteers from Gay Men's Health Crisis and God's Love We Deliver." After expressing mixed emotions and praising the courage of some of the contingents, he says, "Altogether too much of it is silly, sleazy, and sex-centered, a reflection of the narrow, contorted definition of homosexuality that marks some sectors of the gay subculture."[22]

For writers like Bawer and Sullivan, homosexuality is merely an adjunct to their humanness. It is not their defining characteristic. And yet, for many homosexuals, this is not the case. "Everything I do is gay,"[23] Bawer quotes one man as saying. And for some of the more extreme voices in the gay rights movement, humanity is to be divided unbridgeably between gays and nongays, just as Dworkin divides humanity between women and nonwomen and just as Farrakhan divides humanity between blacks and nonblacks. Within this context, the AIDS epidemic is not merely one more affliction visited upon the homosexual community but the defining issue in radical gayness.

Two main radicalized groups of what might be termed the homosexual left, ACT UP (Aids Coalition to Unleash Power) and Queer Nation, have emerged within the context of this disease. The former group, founded by Larry Kramer in 1987 and famous for the SILENCE = DEATH stickers they have placed all around the country, now has over a hundred organizations from Seattle to Paris. With the stated aim of drawing attention to AIDS and gaining publicity for their cause, members of ACT UP interrupted mass at Saint Patrick's Cathedral in New York, lying down in the aisles and harassing worshippers. On another occasion they caused the New York Stock Exchange to shut down after they raided the trading floor to protest against Burroughs-Wellcome, a pharmaceuticals company, for charging too much for the drug AZT.

In response to ACT UP's apparent moderation in recent years, despite the outbursts of Larry Kramer, Queer Nation was founded in 1990 under the direction of Michelangelo Signorile. Among other forms of protest that proved very newsworthy was their dressing up as priests and nuns in order to interrupt meetings of fundamentalist Christians. They also pioneered, though they have since discontinued, the process of "outing" public figures who are closet homosexuals, especially celebrity actors and singers.

Not the least interesting thing about this group is their reappropriating the traditionally derogatory term "queer." In this regard they parallel the way some blacks have reappropriated the word "nigger." Their reasons for doing so are twofold. On the one hand, by assimilating to themselves, by consuming and internalizing, the terms of the hatred that was traditionally directed against them, they feel as though they have conquered it. More insidiously, however, by labeling themselves "queer" they seem perversely to victimize themselves, or more precisely to cause you, the nongay bystander, to be co-opted into the circle of their victimizers. Now most right-thinking citizens of the center feel nervous around words like "queer," as well as "nigger," especially when these words are employed by their respective minorities. Those in the center tend to cave in before these epithets. Feeling that their liberalism, their tolerance, is being questioned, they are apt to surrender at once all opposition to the arguments of the minority, no matter how ill-considered those arguments happen to be.

Implicit in this self-victimization, it should be said, is a new kind of attack, perhaps without precedent in the earlier history of controversy. As yet the center is not certain how to answer it, and as such it is one of the most brilliant and manipulative ploys extremists have yet devised. The old method of attack tended to be in the nature of simple, straightforward character assassination. One attributed bad things to one's opponent and hoped that those listening would believe what they were being told. But at this late date such a ploy would be seen as too divisive to have an effect. Furthermore, insofar as such attacks are in the nature of direct assertion, they can be directly parried and perhaps refuted. Thus it has proved far more effective for you to attack your opponents by accusing them of attacking you. It is simple and it almost always works, precisely in the way that an enemy's forces are dismayed by new weaponry they have not encountered before. What is so impressively effective about this ploy is that it immediately places your opponent in the position of proving to an audience habitually sym-

pathetic to the perceived underdog that he has no intention whatever of attacking you. The very act of trying to show that one is
well-intentioned almost immediately neutralizes one's ability to fight.

Despite the success of this tactic, the fact that Queer Nation
has become as illiberal and as intolerant as its perceived oppressors
cannot be doubted by anyone who has read such documents as *Ten
Things We Will Not Tolerate*. In fact there are many more than ten
items on that list, and they include "Dykes and Fags who build ca-
reers working for community-based and AIDS organizations—and
think they're doing their part." Another reads "Dykes and Fags
who think we're just like everyone else." What is striking here is
the disqualification of the middle-ground homosexual such as
Bawer and Sullivan describe. Just as the Jewish Defense League sees
the more mainstream Anti-Defamation League of B'nai B'rith as
being complicit in anti-Semitism, just as certain extremists voices in
the Nation of Islam see the NAACP as Uncle Toms, just as the
Revolutionary Workers Party sees the CPUSA as corrupt revan-
chists, so Queer Nation, in tried and true extremist fashion, seeks
to define itself by opposing—indeed, reviling—those who are a single degree closer to the center than they are.

In this regard it is instructive that further points of intolerance include "Red Ribbons. Memorial services . . . The World's
largest Quilt . . . Gay games. Candlelight marches. Rainbow Flags.
Lesbian Chic. Log Cabin Republicans. Compassionate Straights,"
in other words, any form of assimilation to the center. For the red
ribbons, the rainbow flags, the gay games, and the quilt are all
forms of "soft homosexuality," moody gestures that, to the nos-
trils of extremity, smell like scented candles and bad faith. They
are symbols of the degree of the center's compassion for homosexuals. And it is precisely this acceptance—the stated aim of most
gay rights activists—that Queer Nation will not tolerate. This is
made explicit in the final thing that it finds intolerable: "You . . .
and your tolerance!"

Just as the Nation of Islam and certain extreme feminists seem
obsessed with the idea of genocide, so certain extreme voices in the
gay community have exploited the metaphor by seeing AIDS as an
all-out war on homosexuality. The appeal of equating AIDS with

genocide is simply this: that it enables the gay activist to attribute to human agency, rather than to blind biological force, the death of many thousands of people, which in turn permits those with AIDS to politicize this affliction and use it as a point of leverage in the assault upon the center. Furthermore, if AIDS is a man-made affliction, then suddenly there are martyrs everywhere and the field is divided into the oppressors and the oppressed; in other words, it can be realigned along the terms of traditional leftism. For those AIDS activists who buy into this genocide theory, it becomes the equivalent of the far right's international Zionist conspiracy or the Nation of Islam's account of slavery as a massive Jewish plot.

On 14 November 1993, Larry Kramer told the doctors at the AIDS Institute Conference in Albany that "intentional genocide is going on here. It is intentional! It is intentional! It is intentional!" Pointing out that AIDS has been killing people since 1980, he asserted that "nothing has happened. The third asshole president in a row sanctions intentional genocide. You know your government sanctions intentional genocide. . . . But you keep your mouths shut and you do not tell the truth . . . and that makes you murderers of me and of everyone who is sick and dying and dead of this plague. . . . Everything you say and everything you do from the minute you get up in the morning and go into your office until you go to sleep at night implicates you in this perpetuation of the plague." After invoking Hannah Arendt's comment about "desk killer Nazis," he concluded by repeating three times, "Genocide is a crime an entire society commits."

This idea of AIDS as murder at the hands of a genocidal, fascist center was stated most explicitly by Kiki Mason, an activist, shortly before he died. "I am not dying, I am being murdered, just as surely as if my body were being tossed into a gas chamber. . . . Activists now negotiate with drug companies just like the Jewish council in the Warsaw Ghetto . . . negotiated with the Nazis. And where does that leave the rest of us? We're left fighting for ourselves while a group of well-educated affluent white homosexuals sit on community boards and advisory councils while we're left to die in the street." For his part, "I'm going out fighting. This is my message to everyone with AIDS. If you think the end is near take someone with you. Hold the president of a drug company hostage. Splatter your blood across the desk of a politician. . . . Trash an AIDS researcher's home."

But then he says something that is oddly revealing, surely more revealing than he intended. "I truly believe that the current rate of AIDS will not change unless radical steps are taken immediately. If you don't believe me, take a good hard look at the war on cancer." Indeed one should take a look at the war on cancer, or even on the common cold. What one finds is that certain maladies simply resist treatment, even though no one in his right mind would accuse cancer researchers of "killing" their patients because, despite what we can be sure are their very best efforts, they have not succeeded thus far in finding a cure.

One will look long and hard to find anyone who has publicly contested this kind of reasoning, beyond a few members of the far right whom no one listens to in any case. In the presence of the incalculable horror of AIDS, we see the wishes of the dying as sacrosanct and we feel that, no matter what hyperbole they invoke, it is bad form for us to contest their allegations. But the truth about AIDS, what is so intolerable to those who would turn it to political advantage, is that it cannot be pressed into the old categories of victimization, or oppressor and oppressed, or leftism versus conservatism. To do so is to allow metaphor, poetry, to presume upon the status of fact.

All movements have their metaphors, and the more extreme leaders of the gay, feminist, and black rights movements have used theirs more emphatically than any other group. What makes their metaphors different from those of other groups, however, is that they have been granted a whiff of prestige, which, for example, the purveyors of the international Zionist conspiracy have not been granted, even though, ultimately, they are about equal in terms of their intellectual merits. What makes them different, that is to say, is that they enter the mainstream of civil society far more readily than the far right ever will. As a result, discourse is debased, good people respond either with anger or self-loathing, and the greatest achievement of the center over the past generation, its assimilation of women, blacks, and homosexuals, goes unnoticed and unpraised.

7

THE FRINGES OF RELIGION

There is a well-known passage in Boswell's *Life of Johnson* in which the biographer and his subject are discussing the issue of madness. At this point the eminent moralist says, "My poor friend [Christopher Smart, the poet] shewed the disturbance of his mind, by falling upon his knees, and saying his prayers in the street, or in any other unusual place."[1] Dr. Johnson, that lord of common sense, would find few people today who would challenge the correctness of his diagnosis: praying in the street seems to us, as it did to the people of Dr. Johnson's day, to be a pretty clear sign of mental instability.

But then he says something else, something by the way, which establishes immediately and categorically a divide between him and us. "Rationally speaking," he believes, "it is greater madness not to pray at all." Though he goes on to wonder why some of his contemporaries do not pray enough, he is still expressing the opinion of the center of his society, an opinion totally at variance with the opinions of the center today. Up until the early years of the present century, our culture, like most other cultures, was thoroughly saturated with religion. Religion seemed the point of departure as well as the destination of every meditation and every act. Today, of course, at least in our society, all of that has changed. Most of us would be mad by Dr. Johnson's reckoning, and we ourselves might have our suspicions of him.

Though once at the core of the center, religion has been essentially banished from our secular state, reasserting itself only on ceremonial occasions like baptisms, weddings, and funerals. Religion is entirely acceptable to our society—as long as one does not really believe in it. As soon as you start taking the sacraments too seriously, as soon as you believe, as the Church of Rome insists, that the wafer and the wine are the body and blood of the living God, you are suddenly at variance with the center. Surely we have some tolerance for men—and occasionally women—of the cloth. But secretly we have written them off. They are no longer part of our world in the way that, in the novels of Trollope and George Eliot, they were the very pillars of the Victorian center. Though we often profess our admiration for such people, this admiration is really the highest form of condescension.

Given the general malaise that has settled over our society in recent years, as well as a growing uncertainty about the future, it is interesting that our society does not seem to be turning or returning to religion in any significant degree. In part this is because our malaise tends to be more in the nature of brooding melancholy than of energetic despair. Also it may be precisely the cause of our malaise that we are not religious and are not getting more religious. Problems that a more spiritual frame of reference could assimilate without too much difficulty are allowed to fester in minds entirely unaided by the leaven of spirituality.

Religious extremism, or at very least a kind of religious behavior stalwartly at variance with the mainstream, appears either as radical traditionalism or as radical nonconformity. As might be expected, the more established religions—Christianity, Islam, and Judaism—occupy the first category, whereas the second category comprises those who emphatically wish to break free from the center by opposing secularism with spirituality and tradition with individual freedom.

In view of the generally unreligious nature of our centrist society, however, any exuberant embrace of a metaphysical system is, by its very nature, an act of provocation. Perhaps what is most unsettling about religious conversion is its suggestion of a stronger conviction than the social fabric of our society, at present, is able to accommodate easily. Such conviction is seen to be an act of retrogression. Whenever religion ceases to be merely conventional, whenever it partakes too strongly of personal choice, it becomes disruptive to the center, and occasionally it appears downright extreme.

In defining religious extremism, we must acknowledge that one man's religion is another man's fanaticism. To a monotheist, the polytheism of the ancient Greeks or of modern animists seems an obscene fable. To the atheist, by contrast, all religious belief appears equally foolish. Indeed, the idea of virgin birth, if looked at through any other lens than that of faith, may not seem more immediately credible than the fables of antiquity. For our present purposes, religion itself will be defined as any body of beliefs that attempts to answer in an organized way the "ultimate" questions of human life. The emphasis therefore is less on how phenomena are explained than on the ultimate function of a system of beliefs. Certain religions, like Confucianism, are so steeped in ethical rather than metaphysical speculations that there is some controversy as to whether they are to be counted religions at all. Scientology, for example, does not claim to be metaphysical in the least: its adherents would argue that its beliefs—for example, in an afterlife—have a completely scientific foundation, and they could give you an involved defense of this view, which would surely impress anyone who, like most of us, knows little about the laws of physics. Neo-pagans, by contrast, are content to see their invocations of one or another superlunary power as but a metaphor of something within themselves. In neither case is there any summoning of real metaphysical belief. However, as both schools of thought aspire to answer those questions that are traditionally the province of religion, and as they often invoke ritual, it is fair to see them in a religious context.

Christianity is the most powerful religion in the most powerful nations on earth, and it exhibits the widest variety of behavior. There are, especially in the southern United States, nonconformist biblicists like the Branch Davidians, whose adherence to the letter of the Bible includes the practice of polygamy, as well as snake-handling Pentecostals, Jehovah's Witnesses, and an odd little sect known as the Two by Twos. But most of the more radical or energized proponents of Christianity are social traditionalists, who have made remarkable progress in recent years by returning not so much to the letter of the Bible as to a state of mind more prevalent in the country forty or even one hundred and forty years ago.

From a doctrinal point of view they do not differ markedly from most other Christian organizations, aside from a tendency to accept creationism and reject Darwinism, as well as an occasional belief in the laying on of hands and speaking in tongues. What marks off the churches of the Christian right is thus not the depth or degree of their faith so much as the social circumstances in which their faith is displayed, as well as their willingness to conceive faith politically.

Surely the Christian right as now constituted does not represent the first time that politics and religion have been joined in America. Ministers like Rex Humbard and Billy Graham were clearly conservative. But, unlike those evangelists who followed them, their conservatism was only implicit. They at least *appeared* to be nonpartisan, and even if it was primarily conservatives who listened to them, they came to hear the evangelism, not the conservatism. A closer similarity to more recent movements like the Moral Majority can be found in the fifties and sixties among ministers like Billy James Hargis, who at one point declared it his "Christian responsibility to fight godless, atheistic Communism, because I want to save this nation."[2] And yet, even if he served as a model for those who came after him, he did not succeed to nearly the same degree.

Another thing that distinguishes the old old-time religion from the new old-time religion is that, whereas the former merely incarnated the conservatism of its day, the latter represents a concerted effort to return to an earlier form of religion and morality. It seems at once old, in the sense that it promises to reinstate earlier values, and new, in that its ministers are at least a generation younger, having passed through the sixties and come out the other side. Rex Humbard and Norman Vincent Peale were the end of an old tradition. Though the dissolution of their kind of religion was not yet evident in the sixties, by the later seventies it was no longer dying but dead. And it was this death, of course, that was the precondition for its resurrection.

A variety of social factors led to this ultimate resurgence of the religious right. Throughout much of this period, the Republicans Nixon and Ford occupied the White House; in traditional Republican fashion, they were more interested in fiscal conservatism and foreign policy than in attacking moral decay. In response to this failing, the Christian right arose along with, but in opposition to, the presidency of Jimmy Carter, a chief executive whose style and demeanor had been formed and honed during the sixties and early seventies. That the public was now in the mood for religion, that it could see religion as something different from the preachments of Peale and Humbard, was proved by the fact that Carter ran as the most self-consciously Christian president in over a hundred years. And yet his Christianity was different from that of the newly emerging religious right. It was more touchy-feely and New Age. It had little to do with the old-time religion that the religious right wanted and was about to find in Jerry Falwell and others. Unlike the religion of Carter, or for that matter of Graham, this was to be fundamentalist Christianity, which accepted biblical inerrancy and talked of Armageddon.

But most of all it was the Christian right's social program that revealed its conservatism and its desire to go back in time. Its strength, especially at the beginning of the eighties, derived from its sense that, in the sixties and seventies, the world was verging on moral anarchy, that not only had all the old values—respect for parents, abstention from both drugs and sex out of wedlock—ceased to be practiced, but society as a whole was now powerless to advocate these values with any moral authority. Throughout this period, however, many citizens rejected the radicalism of free love and loose morals, though only implicitly. As yet they were an atrophied force, waiting to be reinvigorated. The agent of this reinvigoration turned out to be the Christian right. In part its resurgence represented the mobilization of members of what Nixon had called the Silent Majority. Most of that constituency had come to terms with the sixties, accepting contraceptives, racial integration, and homosexuality. On some of these issues, even the far right had come into the center: these days you find little overt anti-black or anti-Jewish rhetoric among the Christian right. But there were other issues, especially having to do with sexuality, issues like abortion, homosexuality, and premarital sex, in which the far right, the religious right, could never acquiesce.

Of those televangelists who subsequently assumed center stage, it is only fair to distinguish Jerry Falwell and Pat Robertson from Jim Bakker and Jimmy Swaggart. The former two, like true ideologues, appeared to be sincerely interested in promoting their strongly felt social and political agendas, even though this advocacy was in no way incompatible with tremendous skill in soliciting money from their congregations. By 1985 Falwell's Moral Majority was raking in $115 million a year. Nevertheless, it is hard to detect in them the same scandalous cupidity shown by Bakker and Swaggart, who not only enriched themselves personally but directly contravened the morals upon which their ministry was based. What immediately disturbed many observers of this new old-time religion was the unappetizing worldliness it often displayed. "My spiritual gift," Jim Bakker once said, "my specific calling from God, is to be a television talk show host." He admonished his congregations, "If you pray for a camper, be sure to tell God what color."[3]

Surely the last word in hypocrisy was Jimmy Swaggart's calling Jim Bakker "a cancer that needs to be exorcised from the body of Christ," following allegations that Bakker had consorted with prostitutes of both sexes. Yet scarcely had that scandal died down when photographs surfaced showing Swaggart with a prostitute in a sleazy motel in New Orleans. The photographs had been taken at the behest of one Marvin Gorman, whom Swaggart had publicly smeared as a philanderer, because he feared Gorman's competition. Though Swaggart gave a stunning televised performance in which he burst into tears and acknowledged his sin, the council of his church banned him from the airwaves for one year, and when he refused to accept this verdict he was defrocked. He continued to appear on television, but it is estimated that as much as 80 percent of his congregation of 2.2 million viewers quickly disappeared. This was terrible news for the Christian right in general, but it proved disastrous for Pat Robertson, who just then was launching his bid for the Republican nomination for the presidency. He had gotten off to a good start, outpolling Bush and almost beating the favored Dole in the Iowa caucus. But with the fall of Swaggart, and after several mistakes of his own, Robertson's campaign quickly foundered. Even Jerry Falwell broke ranks to endorse Bush, the quintessential liberal Republican.

Yet Falwell, too, would suffer from the Swaggart debacle. In 1989 he formally disbanded the Moral Majority on the grounds that, after ten years, it "had accomplished its goals." More likely his decision had to do with the fact that television ratings for all the televangelists were going down. Combined viewership of this programming had been 7.7 million in 1990, down from 11 million only five years before. As a result, Falwell found it too costly to remain on television and thus canceled his *Old Time Gospel Hour* on most of its two hundred outlets. He also had to auction off some of the grounds of Liberty University, which he had founded.

These scandals were followed by Bush's tepid conservatism and subsequent loss to Clinton, who looked for all the world like a "tax and spend" liberal. As a result, many people abandoned the Christian right, and its days looked numbered. But these observers were wrong. "In fact," writes the historian David Bennett, "learning from the crisis of the late eighties, the movement would reshape itself. It was to become more formidable than even its strongest supporters and most fearful enemies had believed possible."[4]

The main agent in this resurrection was the Christian Coalition, which was created by Pat Robertson shortly after his failed bid for the presidency. Largely delegating authority to Ralph Reed, a pleasant-looking, clean-cut young man, Robertson retreated from the limelight, correctly judging that he would not help his cause if he maintained too high a profile. Instead the Machiavellian Reed proved a brilliant strategist in the political arena. As he told one religiously oriented publication, "What Christians have got to do is to take back this nation one precinct at a time, one neighborhood at a time, and one state at a time." His strategy was simply this: to eschew the charismatic leader, such as Robertson had aspired to be; and to galvanize the nation by going to the grass roots, to conceal the religious allegiances of candidates, to keep the Christian Coalition's name out of the election. As he said in one of his most famous declarations, "I want to be invisible. I do guerrilla warfare. I paint my face and travel by night. You don't know it's over until you are in a body bag. You don't know until election night."[5]

"You should never mention the name Christian Coalition in Republican circles," he wrote in one of his manuals for recruiters, in which he also advised them to stop using the language of Christian redemption. The success of the Christian Coalition can be measured in its growth from about 57,000 members in 1991 to 1.6 million four years later, with a budget of twenty-five million dollars a year. Though tax exempt and supposedly nonpartisan, this organization quickly took over the GOP state committees in Texas, Minnesota, Iowa, and Virginia, and exerted considerable influence on the Republican platform in 1992 and, to a slightly lesser degree, in 1996.

The Christian right as we have described it is not extreme. Though it is far right, it accepts, in its despairing way, the protocols of the democratic process and can manipulate them with some success, as recent elections have revealed. It desires to become the center and imagines somewhat fondly that, if this one bill or that one proviso can be passed into law, it will be that much closer to repealing the twentieth century. In this rejection of modernity, the Christian right resembles certain Islamic groups, except that militant Moslems have proved all too ready to resort to violence, as in Iran, to ensure the victory of their point of view.

Centrist society in the West is not sure what to make of the Moslem. For more than a thousand years he was the enemy incarnate of the society of the center. Unlike the Norseman, he could not be converted; unlike the Jew, he might kill a Christian and directly threaten the survival of the center as it was then known. There were indeed stranger, more alien humans on the planet, Indians, Chinese, and black Africans. But these never impinged on the minds of the center as anything more than distant fables. The Islamite, by contrast, was a bloody-minded foeman just beyond the borders of Europe. The closest parallel in modern times would be that of the Soviets relative to American cold warriors.

Though almost four centuries have passed since the waning of the Islamic threat, Western society still is not quite sure what to make of that religion. To our eyes Islam is a monolith as fixed and immovable as the great Kaaba of Mecca. With the exception, it is thought, of a few enlightened or self-interested monarchs and a few of their rich friends, Moslems are true believers who might willingly walk into a minefield in the hopes of going straight to heaven. What makes Islam so frightening to non-Moslems is the apparent sincerity of its believers. Among them we seem to find little of the hypocrisy that certain born-again Christian ministers have revealed. Though Saddam Hussein and Muammar Qaddafi may cynically invoke religion to sway their populations, who are often very religious, for us the Ayatollah Khomeini, a fanatical believer in his cause, seems far more typical of Moslems in general.

And yet it is probably even harder to generalize about Moslems than about Christians. To the casual inspection of the outside world, the *ummah* of Islam—that is, the transnational community of its believers (resembling the medieval notion of the *res publica christiana*)—is a more or less monolithic structure heeding the words of its religious imams with that totality of submission that is implied in the very word "Islam." In fact, the Moslem world is not united even in its opposition to America and the West; the only point of real commonalty among its disparate peoples and professions is an antagonism to the state of Israel.

Within the context of Islam itself, it would be fair to describe the situation as a war of all against all. There is the immemorial conflict between the Shiites, usually the underclass in any given country, and the Sunni Moslems. There is, first of all, the class conflict of the wealthy against the poor and of the educated against the illiterate, the modernizers against the traditionalists, and the Westernizers against the pan-Arabists. In addition, Islam is more subject to change than is generally appreciated in the West. The revolution in Iran is no longer, under Rafsanjani, as it was under Khomeini, the mullahs having evolved a slightly more propitiatory view of the West. Indeed, even the Islamic victory in Iran in the first place was the result of Khomeini's coup d'état, whereby the clerics gained the ascendancy over Marxists and more moderate politicians like Bani-Sadr and Mehdi Bazargan, all of whom had been, until that moment, part of a coalition united only by opposition to the shah.

In a sense, what is extreme about Islam is not the extremists who adhere to it but rather Islam itself. It alone of major world religions cannot be assimilated easily to the modern age. Or rather, no religion, insofar as it is based on metaphysics or on something other than reason, can be fully assimilated to the modern world; although most of the world's people, whether Christian, Jewish, Buddhist, or Hindu, have resolved this dilemma in favor of modernization, the lands of Islam alone have, through a conscious choice, chosen tradition over progress. And whereas several prominent leaders of the Moslem world, from the shah of Iran to Nasser in Egypt and Bourguiba in Tunisia, have tried to orient their countries toward modernization, this process has been primarily cosmetic, or at most has benefited a small percentage of the ruling elite. For this reason, social revolutions, which in other societies take the form of class antagonism, in Moslem countries often become an antagonism to modernization itself.

It is interesting that modernization is often rejected not because of what it is in itself but because it is associated with the West. If it were possible, practically or conceptually, to purge modernization of this connection, it would be far more congenial to many Moslems. As the philosopher Mawlana Mawdudi avowed, "We aspire for Islamic renaissance on the basis of the Koran . . . but the application of this spirit in the realm of practical life must always vary with the change of conditions and increase of knowledge. . . . On the one hand we have to imbibe exactly the Koranic spirit and identify our outlook with the Islamic tenets, while on the other we have to assess thoroughly the developments in the field of knowledge and changes in conditions of life that have been brought during the last eight hundred years."[6]

In this quest he was fundamentally wrong. To achieve modernization without Westernization would be to square the proverbial circle. It would seem impossible at this late stage of history, that is, the postindustrial phase, to achieve modernity without also allowing for an open and liberal society, with all that implies of dissent and civil liberty. A century and a half of modernization has confirmed that, although it can exist in a context of religion, it cannot thrive in circumstances where traditionalism is absolute. Modernization is not one of a number of competing traditions: it is opposed to the very idea of tradition. And since modernization comes from the West and has been brought thus far to its highest perfection in the West, probably it is impossible to remove it conceptually from the West. All Islam can do is to co-opt some of the utensils of modernity, but not the mentality that engendered those innovations. In other words, it can have premodern people operating modern machines, but their society as a whole must forever remain in a state of stunted development.

The general failure of this experiment in the lands of Islam has caused them to appear fundamentally backward, the atavistic remnants of an early stage of civilization, eternally opposed to the center of society as conceived by the First World. In part, this is because Islam, to the extent that it has become modernized at all, recalls the Roman Empire around the time of the Germanic invasions. Then, "civilization" existed only in the scattered cities of the empire and had not spread to the hinterland where most of the population lived. So, in the case of Islam, the fruits of modernization have benefited relatively few people, who found it in their interest to modernize industry but not the mentality of the population as a whole. Where Moslems have profited from modernity, rather than merely serving it, as in Turkey, they are less apt to look to radical Islam.

Because Islam was always strong among this disaffected underclass, religion, rather than Marxism, proved to be their ideology of first recourse. Whereas the far right in the United States seeks to resurrect a religion in which most of the citizens no longer believe and which, in a real sense, is socially dead, the aim of the more religious Moslems is to preserve and protect from decay a religion that is generally in force and has not yet died out.

Yet religion is not sufficient to explain the behavior of many Moslems. They resent imperialism for the usual reason, that they have been vanquished by a superior power that has profited from their misery. Their hatred of Israel stems not from an inherent hatred of Jews—historically Moslems were more tolerant of Jews and of other religions than Christians tended to be—but from the fact that, for them, Israel represents an inassimilable presence of Western Imperialism, not overseas but in the very heart of their hegemony. Israel confirms what the more thoughtful among them secretly fear to be inevitable, that the Western world, which exemplifies modernity itself, is their manifest destiny.

Despite what is often reported, Islamic radicalism is frequently rooted in secular causes. It is not so much the fakirs or the dervishes who are driven to extremism but the urban masses energized by the eloquence of some cleric. In addition to their hatred of modernization and Westernization, what motivates fanatics has a great deal to do with the perceived suppression of some Moslems by others. In both Iran and Lebanon, where the Shiite population is very large, it invariably represents the poorest sector of the social and economic hierarchy. The Shiites did not rebel against the shah because of his famous taste for pagan processions but rather because of their misery, which shrewd Islamic fundamentalists were able to exploit to their own advantage.

It stands to reason, then, that this sense of social inequity most often inspires extremism in those who are exposed to the inequity long enough to become disillusioned by it. And this is why, very often, the most radical and active Islamic fundamentalists are the products of their societies' unsuccessful attempts at modernization. The majority of violent Islamic factions tend to be not its semi-literate peasants but disaffected members of the urban population, whose origins, it is true, are often in the countryside. In the words of the writer Sa'ad Eddin Ibrahim, "The typical social profile of members of militant Islamic groups could be summarized as being young (early twenties), of rural or small-town background, from the middle and lower middle class, with high achievement motivation, upwardly mobile, with science or engineering education, and from a normally cohesive family. It is sometimes assumed in social science that recruits of 'radical movements' must be somehow alienated, marginal, anomic, or otherwise abnormal.

Most of those we investigated would be considered model young [Egyptians]."[7]

These young Moslem extremists are merely the latest avatar of the archetype of the Moslems as murderous outsider, that is, the disrupter of the center. To label him an archetype, however, is not to mitigate the threat that he represents. It is merely to acknowledge that he is the latest example of a type that dominated Western thought through the middle years of the seventeenth century, became a standing jest for the next three hundred years, and returned in full force only in recent years, through the threat of terrorism.

For many years, the Jew as well was seen as an outsider and a threat to the center. In Europe in earlier ages, the Jew was the incarnated fringe. He was perhaps the strangest thing a Christian would ever lay eyes on, since he was the only non-Christian in sight. Moslems might be encountered in battle, but one did not live among them, as one did among Jews. Furthermore, the Jew's refusal to convert to Christianity stressed his inassimilable difference from the rest of society. In the past two hundred years, of course, Jews have succeeded in occupying the center of Western society in a way that makes them the envy not only of other minorities but also of those whose places they have taken in the center. Furthermore, there are now many other groups in our society—Asians, blacks, and Moslems of a more traditional cast—whose very appearance is far more at variance with the perceived center than that of Jews.

And yet there are some Jews who actively resist this assimilation, most conspicuously the Hasidim. Like many other religious conservatives, the Hasidim express their rejection of the center by wearing a style of clothing that harkens back to an earlier age. And though they participate in mainstream society to a far higher degree than, say, the Amish, especially in the sale of diamonds and electronics, they seem to exist in this larger world but not to belong to it. At day's end they retreat into their closely knit communities, where they encounter only others like themselves.

But the Hasidim are merely a fringe; a group like the Jewish Defense League (JDL), founded by Meir Kahane, is a radicalized extremist organization. Though the relationship between politics

and religion in this group is not as close as among Islamic fundamentalists, religion is consistently invoked to make a political
point. In 1984, for example, Meir Kahane called for an "end to the
Arab jackals who do not serve in national service or remotely pay
the required share of taxes and who go into the Jewish night with
money in their pockets seeking Jewish women. They defile the seed
of the Holy People, they strike at the God of Israel through the
daughters of His people." This xenophobia goes beyond Arabs to
embrace all non-Jews. "Cleanse the land of Israel of the foreign
pollution of gentilized culture. The foreigners vomit their sickness
onto us and we swallow it eagerly. We are to blame; we are the
desecrators. Let us vomit them out and purge the Holy Land of all
vestige of impurity."[8]

Since their stated reason for being is a fierce devotion to Judaism, it must come as a surprise that they hate many, perhaps
most, Jews as much as they do non-Jews and even Arabs. In this
they recall the intense factionalization found among fanatical Muslims. They have three times staged takeovers and sit-ins that damaged the property of the Park Avenue Synagogue in New York.
They have attacked the Washington bureau of B'nai B'rith, and at
the Israeli consulate in New York one man accosted Colette Avital,
Israel's consul general at the United Nations, in a synagogue and
shouted, "Bitch, we will kill you!" In the time-honored tradition of
the extreme right and left, they imagine that their more centrist
coreligionists are complicit in what they see as the subjugation and
victimizing of Jews. And, as so often among extremists, their pro-
fessed love for their one group is really an excuse for hating all
who are excluded from that group. In the process, they tend to attract those who are very good at hating.

Yigal Amir, the assassin of Israeli prime minister Itzak Rabin,
is not known to have been a member of the Kahane group but
rather was associated with something called Eyal, a Hebrew
acronym meaning "Jewish Fighting Organization." Still there was
surely sympathy between the two groups. As one commentator,
Rabbi Benjamin Hecht, explained, paraphrasing the JDL's position,
"[They believed] it was permissible according to halakha (Jewish

religious law) to kill Prime Minister Rabin because of the alleged danger to other Jews caused by his government's peace policies."[9]

The movement that Kahane started in 1968 contains several splinter groups: the Jewish Defense League and the Jewish Defense Organization in the United States and the Kach and Kahane Chai parties in Israel. Like many racist extremists ranging from Farrakhan to George Lincoln Rockwell, Kahane was a separatist who wanted to keep Jews apart from other Americans in the United States and from Arabs in Israel.

It is interesting that these extremely politicized Jews look nothing like the Jewish stereotypes circulated by the extreme right or the Nation of Islam, nor like the image that many Jews have traditionally had of themselves. For neo-Nazis and members of the Nation of Islam, the dangerous Jew is the wealthy banker or the bespectacled middle-class intellectual. He is seen to be physically and morally weak but to have acquired through illicit means an ascendancy over more robust and honorable men than himself. Yet the members of the Jewish Defense League are determinedly working class in their dress and speech and in their willingness to push back if anyone pushes them. They recall, in this regard, street fighters from the tougher neighborhoods of Brooklyn, from which many of them come. As a result, to many Jews they seem, despite their proud claims to being one thousand percent Jewish, oddly un-Jewish.

But then, the JDL is concerned with nothing so much as the destruction of stereotypes. The first stereotype that the JDL wanted to explode was the image of the Jew as weak and bookish. To this end, Kahane established an eight-week boot camp in which Jewish teenagers learned to fire weapons and engage in hand-to-hand combat. As he wrote in a chapter titled "Violence" in his *History of the Jewish Defense League*: "Vandals attack a synagogue? Let that synagogue attack the vandals. Should a gang bloody a Jew, let a Jewish group go looking for that gang."[10] It was in this spirit that, in 1970, Abraham and Nancy Hershkovitz, responding to the Palestine Liberation Organization's hijacking of El Al flights, attempted to hijack an Arab airplane but were stopped before they could board the plane. Other stunts involved the attempted abduction of a Soviet diplomat and the interruption of the Bolshoi Ballet with a smoke bomb.

Perhaps the closest historical parallel to this militancy of the Jewish Defense League can be found in some of the sects of ancient Judea, like the Zealots and the Sicarii (whose name essentially means "assassins") who both rose up against the dominion of Rome. This connection with the past was made explicit by Kahane, who wrote that, where violence was the only means possible, "the JDL was prepared to lay aside the Jewish book and raise the ancient Jewish fist."[11] Though contemporary Judaism, like most religions, has a deep and abiding sense of the past, this reference to the ancient image of the Zealots and the symbolism of the raised fist is, if the term will be allowed, morphologically akin to the neo-Nazi references to Arminius or to Hezbollah's references to the sword of Mohammed. Like many far right movements of a historicist slant, the Jewish Defense League opportunistically supposes that earlier circumstances continue in force, that nothing has changed since the last century, that Jews everywhere in the world are still menaced by pogroms and by the imminent recurrence of the Holocaust. As is written in a report published by the Anti-Defamation League of B'nai B'rith, "Kahane and his followers have constantly compared the current situation of Jews in the United States to that of the Jewish community in Nazi Germany prior to World War II. With the view that every anti-Semitic incident that occurs in the United States is merely a foreshadowing of the next Holocaust, Kahane claimed to be sounding a wake-up call to all Jews in America that they must fight back before history inevitably repeats itself."[12]

Indeed, Kahane wrote in his book *Time to Go Home*, "There is a dark cloud on the horizon of the American Jewish future. It signals a storm such as we have never seen. It warns of the beginning of the end for the American Jewish community. The time to leave is now, before it's too late. It is time to go home, to return to the land of Israel."[13] In another book, *Never Again!*, he went even further: "It is imperative that the Jew mount a massive and total war on these groups and their existence."[14]

What Kahane's writings fail to take into account, of course, is that the world is no longer as it was in the 1930s, with its prolonged economic depression, its entrenched rear guard, a host of atavistic conflicts that had not yet been resolved. And while some Americans are anti-Semitic, their number is surely smaller than it was one or two generations ago, and, at all events, the mass of Americans were never anti-Semitic to begin with, in the way that, one could argue, the Germans were. In other words, in order for such an attack to be mounted against Jews in the first place, it would be necessary for everything to be radically different from what it is now. Through a neat symmetry, the far right of Judaism exaggerates the power of the neo-Nazis precisely as the neo-Nazis exaggerate the power of the Jews. In this sense each is essential to the other's survival.

Though Kahane was born in America and saw himself as an American, he soon came to feel that the future of Judaism lay in Israel. As soon as he moved to that country, his target became the Arabs and Israeli moderates. According to one Anti-Defamation League report, "Replaying the events of World War II in a Middle Eastern setting, Kahane cast the Arabs as Nazis, the Israeli government as quislings, and the rest of the world as indifferent."[15] Soon he was calling for the expulsion of all Arabs from Israel. "I want to remove the Arabs of Israel because I do not want to kill them every week as they grow and riot."[16]

And yet, for all the vociferations of Kahane and his associates, the influence of the JDL is almost nonexistent. Though the Jewish Defense League in America is tiny compared to the Nation of Islam, the former having about a thousand members, the latter about twenty thousand, its influence is reduced even further by the fact that it enjoys almost no sympathy among the mainstream of American Jews; by contrast, Farrakhan's influence extends much further into the African American community than its twenty thousand members would suggest. Even if the Million Man March bore an inflated name, at least it drew a crowd of several hundred thousand. Were the Jewish Defense League to attempt anything of the sort, at best it would draw only its most diehard members, and even that is not certain.

One characteristic shared by the JDL and the more conservative elements of Islam and Christianity is that their members are almost always born into the faith. And yet there is a considerable variety of religions that no one inherits as a birthright but that one adopts only later in life, through an act of conscious rejection of the religions of the center.

An alternative to the unbelief of the center and to the dogmas of the far right is a kind of recreational religion. More often than not, such stirrings of spirituality take the form of quick fixes like the Psychic Hotline or the daily horoscope, which are the spiritual equivalent of snacks, if not junk food. But some people, dissatisfied by this temporary salve of superstition, are looking for more substantial creeds. At the same time, they no longer find what they need in the religions into which they were born, that handful of religious options sanctioned by the center. In order for their religion truly to be *theirs*, they feel, they must acquire it for themselves.

Herein lies one of the defining differences between our society and that of the past. Time out of mind you were stuck with the religion you were born into. Only with the Reformation in the sixteenth century did choice enter into the picture, and even then it was apt to be a matter of life or death, and the choice was limited to a fairly circumscribed number of denominations and an occasional heresy. Now, however, precisely because of the general abeyance of religion in contemporary life, one is offered a religious menu—if the sacrilege will be permitted—with almost as many options as ethnic cuisine presents. Obviously this analogy between food and religion is somewhat facetious, but it is not entirely so. The very same social and technological forces that, in the last generation, have greatly increased culinary variety—a rapidly accelerated world, constant cultural cross-fertilization, and endless innovation—have not only precipitated the collapse of much traditional religion but have also given rise to a great variety of religious options. Today one can choose between the ornate ceremony of the Roman mass or the comparative austerity of the Lutheran. If Christianity is not to your taste, there is Judaism or Islam or, ranging farther afield, Buddhism, Hinduism, or Baha'i.

Now all religions derive their strength from the twofold process of inclusion and exclusion. There is one kind of pleasure in a sense of community, a sense of being among one's fellows, and there is an entirely different pleasure in separating oneself from the mass of humanity, in gaining entry into a select group. Cults with massive followings like the Church of Scientology and the Unification Church, also known as the Moonies, appeal to their members by providing a sense of community and fraternity to those who are apt to feel alienated and alone in contemporary society. Satanism and witchcraft, by contrast, are more self-consciously elitist. They appeal to a far smaller community, which takes satisfaction partially in being among a few like-minded souls but more in standing at variance with the rest of society.

But whereas the Church of Satan appeals predominantly to men whose quest for self-actualization suggests vaguely right-wing, yuppie leanings, witchcraft is closely associated with feminism and tends to look leftward. Formerly the religion of disaffected old women from the countryside, Wicca, as this faith is sometimes called by its adherents, has more recently become urbanized, at least in the sense that its practitioners tend to be college educated and to have spent time in big cities. This movement, though ancient, looks back to the sixties, with its soulful young men in da Vinciesque beards and its moon-eyed young women with high cheekbones and flowing black hair and outlandish jewelry. Some hold secret midnight covens in the nude; others, like the New Reformed Druids of North America, put on their robes, take up their eremitical staffs, and march into the sun-bleached California wilderness.

By claiming to return to a pre-Christian past, Wicca implicitly—and sometimes explicitly—criticizes orthodox religions like Christianity, which it sees as essentially phallocratic, hypocritical, and ultimately inhibiting to healthier, more natural instincts. In place of God the Father they have reestablished an ancient female deity whom they call, portentously, the Goddess. But, as with many modern, left-leaning religions, adherents of Wicca tread delicately over questions of metaphysics. In this regard, they resemble progressive Christians and Jews, who generally try to fudge these issues, not for fear of being wrong but for fear that, if they are right, then everyone else must be wrong. If there can only be one God, then all those who assert the existence of many gods must be wrong. It is far better to see both the traditional deities and the powers attributed to them as a kind of metaphor of internal experience, which permits one, in practice, to believe more or less anything one wants.

According to Isaac Bonewits, one of the principal theoreticians of Wicca, the main difference between science and magic is that the latter is an art and a craft, which "has not yet been fully investigated or confirmed by the other arts and sciences." He elaborates by resorting to a kind of New Age semi-science that is the stock in trade of this and all related movements. "The physical Universe (assuming it's there) is a huge Web of interlocking energy, in which every atom and every energy wave is connected with every other one."[17] Most of his coreligionists are likewise content to accept that some as yet inscrutable and undiscovered link between their science and magic will one day give legitimacy to their beliefs, and for the time being they are content to leave it at that.

Cults, by contrast, tend to be far more doctrinaire than Wicca, and their requirements of rigor and obedience in part explain the censure the have received in the press. But this antagonism is further fueled by the fact that, in flagrant defiance of our secularized world, cultists have chosen to believe in something spiritual in the first place. Implicitly they seem to threaten our way of life by their radical rejection of it. They are like nuns and monks, whom we also regard with considerable suspicion. The only way we can account for this rejection at the hands of our sons and daughters, our brothers and sisters, is to suppose that they have been seduced into their respective allegiances against their will, or through so insidious a process of manipulation that free will was no longer in force.

But what the present generation of secularists refuses to understand is that coercion is not always the case, that the decision to join a cult often represents a kind of meeting of minds. Surely the leaders of a cult are consumed by the ambition to further their cause, and more often than not their goals entail some sort of psychological conditioning, not to say coercion. But it is important to remember, though difficult to understand, that many people who join cults are not only susceptible to such influence but go to encounter it in a state of full and eager preparedness. Most of us who inhabit the center would not feel this yearning, but others do.

If, for example, you inquire into the background of some of the members of Sun Myung Moon's Unification Church, you find not only that they were susceptible to influence by the cult but that, for some time prior to their joining, they were looking for precisely what the Unification Church had to offer them. As the sociologist Marc Galanter says of one Moonie, "Jerry effectively joined before he even realized the group's identity, but throughout the conversion process had been fully mentally competent and able to query his hosts at will." He became a member when, during one of the weekends sponsored by the Unification Church, he found himself "increasingly attracted to the group's ideals of universal brotherhood and its commitment to [the Divine Principle.]"[18] Like most of the other guests, however, he saw no connection between the present meeting and the Unification Church. He admitted to Galanter—while he was still a member of the cult—that if he had seen it at that time, he would not have participated any further.

Toward the end of the meeting, he and the other guests were asked if they would like to spend the rest of the week in a retreat. Five declined, but Jerry and two others accepted and were driven to the retreat. Only in the van did he hear someone mention the word "Moonie" for the first time. He asked why no one had brought it up before. He was told that "people criticize Reverend Moon unfairly; they would turn you away from joining the workshop, and you would lose the chance to hear his words. We just want you to have the chance to find out what he has to say."[19]

What is most interesting about this episode is the five applicants who went away in peace. In this way the church succeeded in separating those who were willing from those who were not. Those who chose to leave felt no coercion to remain. Perhaps their departure proved that they were ultimately unsuitable anyway. The point of the process, in other words, was not to hold guests against their will but to find which of them would be willing to stay of their own accord.

In his doctoral dissertation on the Unification Church, Roger A. Dean records something similar. "[The Moonies] have come to realize that ritual involvement with a cult (often under questionable pretenses) promises no guarantee that a potential recruit may not be [entirely] disruptive in future interactions. Therefore, the dinner meeting provides a comfortable, low-key atmosphere in which members can observe and evaluate the likelihood that a particular recruit will comply with more regimental church indoctrination techniques."[20] In other words, there are certain people who are predisposed to join the church, and it is the church's function to understand who they are.

The Unification Church, a Korean-based Christian organization that established itself in this country in 1972, is peculiar, though not unique, among alternative religions in that, even though outside of mainstream conservatism, it is politically to the right. As a result, the political right in America is not sure what to make of this strange bedfellow. Moon is the owner of the *Washington Times*, essentially an organ of the Republican Party and points right, and, as far back as the days of Watergate, Moon and one thousand of his followers met in front of the White House to show support for Nixon. But, although the Unification Church stresses traditional values, it has torn families apart in a way that has seemed to many, including those on the right, to represent a fundamental challenge to centrist society.

What strikes outsiders about the movement, what seems to them so strange about it, is the rigorous conformity that characterizes all its proceedings and that we experience as un-American. Americanism can be defined, in the popular mythology, as the ascendancy of the individual over the group. And while we are surely suspicious of radical nonconformity, we prefer that to its opposite. Now something about Asian culture strikes us as profoundly conformist. For one thing, as the saying goes, Asians all tend to look the same to Western eyes. For this reason it was a catastrophic miscalculation for the Unification Church to rent out Madison Square Garden, that most American of public spaces, to stage one of its mass weddings, in which cult members of opposite sexes, having met only minutes before, were to be joined for life. The idea that so big a step could be undertaken so lightly by the participants, and that they could do so at the apparent command of an authoritarian figure, was deeply unsettling to many, if not most, Americans. When one added to this that Moon and many in his inner circle were literally as well as figuratively aliens, and that the language they spoke and the country they came from were almost entirely unknown to most of our citizens, suddenly the traditional American fear of foreign invasion and secret subversion came roaring back to life.

People were further frightened by what seems to be the strange, treacly pleasantness of the sect. Here was not fire and brimstone, such as certain religious fanatics have promoted in the past. Rather it was all smiles and amenities, allied incongruously to a sense of robotic efficiency just beneath the surface, but infinitely inscrutable. In this respect, the Moonies occupy the popular American imagination rather as the Jesuits did that of the English of the seventeenth century: they appear infinitely clever, scheming, and manipulative in the furtherance of their cause. Nor did it help appearances that Reverend Moon himself seemed to be living high on the hog. He had bought a five-acre house on the Hudson for half a million dollars and the New Yorker Hotel, largely to house his followers, for over $5.5 million. It was in this spirit that, in 1981, a Senate subcommittee found "evidence that Reverend Moon's international organization had systematically violated the United States tax, immigration, banking, currency and foreign-agent registration laws, as well as state and local laws on charity fraud."[21]

Such legislative measures as these confirmed and escalated the antagonism to cults that characterizes mainstream America. In the starkest way possible, they drew the line of demarcation between the center and the circumference. They also brought forcefully into the open the manner in which society, feeling its values to be fundamentally at risk, will take action against any fringe organization whose success has raised it to a level at which it begins to threaten the fundamental well-being of the center.

8

THE AGE OF DOUBT

It will not be obvious to everyone why O. J. Simpson's name should appear at the head of a chapter that touches upon Darwinism, the Holocaust, and French poststructuralist philosophy. And yet, for those who care about the truth, the fact that, to all appearances, O. J. Simpson murdered two human beings in cold blood and then persuaded twelve sentient adults to acquit him not only challenges all our standards of evidence but may fairly be said to precipitate a crisis in our notions about truth itself.

What appears to have happened in the O. J. Simpson case is this: the standard of reasonable doubt was replaced, while most of us were looking away, by the standard of conceivable doubt. The question was not whether it was at all likely that Simpson did not commit the crime but whether it was possible or even conceivable that he did not. Since most things are possible, and since well-nigh everything is, in the strictest sense of the term, conceivable, Simpson went free.

This conceivable doubt extended beyond the particulars to the whole case: it was conceivable that the blood found on the crime scene was not his (though the chance, as even his attorneys implicitly agreed, was only one in seven billion); it was likewise conceivable that somebody had planted at his home a blood-soaked glove perfectly matching one found at the crime scene; and it was conceivable that Simpson's many evasions and inconsistencies, though they certainly looked suspicious, were merely fortuitous. And though none of the doubts that the defense raised could be taken seriously in itself, all of them together succeeded in generating in the immethodical minds of the twelve jurors a fog through which O. J. Simpson could literally get away with murder.

The Simpson trial has been taken to be emblematic of many things: the corruption of the Los Angeles Police Department; racial division between blacks and whites; the abuse of women at the hands of men; the entrenched violence of American society. Though the trial may have involved all of these things, it touched upon something more fundamental still: the philosophical impossibility of attaining absolute a posteriori certainty, of proving beyond doubt, beyond contingency, that what seems to be known for certain really can be known at all. It is this minute deposit of doubt at the core of the center's most deeply held convictions, this fly in the ointment of the center's moral or intellectual certainties, that holders of radical and extreme opinions have exploited throughout the recorded history of thought. Though Simpson surely looked guilty a hundred times over, who could say for certain that he was? Who finally dared aspire to the omniscience of God? An earlier age might have sustained this possibility of doubt with greater equanimity than we could muster today. For though skepticism has haunted philosophy from its very inception, subject to periodic revival and abeyance, there has never been an age in which it was so deeply entrenched in our thinking as at this time. Indeed, in a perverse way, this doubt has become the dogma of the day.

According to Allan Bloom, "There is one thing a professor can be absolutely certain of: almost every student entering the university believes, or says he believes, that truth is relative."[1] In the past such skepticism was limited to elite circles, far removed from that *sensus communis* that is usually content to accept the world as given. Today, however, it saturates every level of society, from the tenured academic who presumes to deconstruct reality, to the man in the street who "knows" that all politicians lie, who routinely disbelieves everything the police say, and who has gotten wind of just enough radical philosophy—even third or fourth hand—to insist that, because you mustn't believe everything you read or hear, you must believe nothing that you read or hear. As a result, the foundations of centrist belief have become radically destabilized, a fact in no small measure constitutive of the spiritual malaise that, as stated in this book's introduction, qualifies so severely the happiness of our society.

In practice, however, the real problem and radical corollary of such pandemic doubt is a willingness to believe anything at all—as long as it is at variance with received opinion or with unadorned common sense. The jury in the O. J. Simpson case attests to this. For the same twelve men and women who did not find the blood evidence quite conclusive enough, even though it established the probability of Simpson's guilt by a factor of seven billion to one, could yet surrender their credulity to the proposition that he had been framed, though they were presented with not a shred of evidence to support this claim.

This doubt erodes not only the old certainties but, more insidiously still, even that expectation of certainty that our forefathers took for granted. It is a doubt so automatic, so reflexive, that there is hardly a province of human knowledge whose traditions have not been called violently into question, precisely because they are traditions. And yet nothing has been called more emphatically into question than the twin disciplines of history and science. This fact is paradoxical, since they seem more fully in possession of the truth than any other discipline, having gone furthest in purging themselves of bias and subjectivity. In our century, the triumphant application of the scientific method, which has produced so many medical breakthroughs and so many important discoveries about the natural world, is matched among many professional historians by the sedulous weeding out of bias, as well as by the evolution of standards of evidence far more exacting than those of previous centuries.

Yet we are seeing now in both disciplines a revolt against those hundred years of certainty, from about 1850 to 1950, when history and science had been brought to a greater standard of veracity, and had achieved more impressive results, than would have been imaginable in earlier times. For historians, this was the age in which it seemed possible once and for all to record the past, in Ranke's famous words, "*wie es eigentlich gewesen ist,*" as it really was. For scientists, it was the age of positivism and the belief that science could solve all of mankind's problems by purging it of its ancestral doubts and superstitions.

And yet, as T. S. Eliot remarked, "humankind cannot bear very much reality." In retrospect the burden of attention that such veracity required, the toll it took upon the collective spirit of our culture, was simply too great. We have released our grip, and often, in rejecting the arrogance of the last century, certain members of the academic community have made acceptable again the dubious doctrines that the scientists of a hundred years ago presumed to extinguish forever. This assault on science takes two forms. In place of the older superstitions of the uneducated masses, we have a reconstituted pseudo-science of crystals and pyramids. And among academics, Nietzsche, Kuhn, and Feyerabend are invoked to subvert the very intellectual underpinnings of science. Indeed, science itself, in the form of technology's present obsession with virtual reality, presumes to deal a crippling blow to our very sense of what is real. If we are to believe some of the more enthusiastic advocates of the cybernetic revolution, reality has become a kind of putty to be molded to our whims.

We have all heard of the so-called Culture Wars, that ongoing and unresolved contest between the cultural elite and the common man, between those who favor multiculturalism and those who uphold the standard curriculum, between those who admire transgressive art and literature in the name of nonconformity and those who condemn it in the name of old-time religion. This conflict has been in the news so much of late that surely there are very few people who are unaware that it is being waged. And yet as great a conflict is under way in universities around the country, between the laboratories where traditional science is being produced, with ever more fruitful results, and the philosophy departments where the foundations of science are being called radically into question. It is a conflict that goes, quietly, by the name of Science Wars.

What is it about Western science that certain academics so despise? Whatever cultural or political claims can be made about the

West, after all, it seems, at least to the man in the street, as though our supremacy in science and technology is incontestably secure. In the present century it has been technology, more than anything else, that has accounted for the West's cultural prestige. For many philosophers of science, however—who, by the way, tend not to be scientists themselves—science seems more arrogantly and provocatively to assert its self-evident truth than any other discipline; to act as though truth were possible and, with enough industry, easily attained; to presume, contrary to the most cherished dogma of our time, that the truth is *not* relative. Furthermore, the fact of Western science's ever-increasing dominion in the Third World is seen as proof not of its self-evident correctness or superiority but of its imperialism in overwhelming all "competing paradigms." All of this taken together makes it quite obvious to some academics that science must be taken down a few notches.

In a recent issue of the journal *Social Texts* devoted to assailing the arrogance of Western science, Stanley Aronowitz vehemently and sarcastically inveighed against its practitioners, not on epistemological grounds but on the basis of what can only be called his sense of justice. Asserting that science constitutes a "regime of truth," he declared that it "is no more, but certainly no less than any other discourse. It is one story among many stories that have given the world considerable benefits including pleasure, but also considerable pain." After quoting with approval one writer's comment that science is "politics through other means," he adds that "the question is whether science can evade what every other discourse must face: its dependence on, as well as struggle for autonomy from, culture. Feminists, ecologists, AIDS activists, and those who, from a scientific standpoint, have examined the use of imputed racialized genetics to explain differences in school performance are acutely aware that much of established science remains in a state of deep denial [regarding these issues]."[2]

As for scientists themselves, researchers, doctors, and physicists, those who humbly work in the laboratories and do the research, he offers this condescending assessment: "The vituperation that accompanies the dogmatists' defense, not only of science but of empiricism and positivism, is rather quaint. . . . They are not usually sufficiently philosophically sophisticated to grasp, let alone refute, their opponents' claims." Faced with the cool reception that his arguments have received in the scientific community, he argues that "members of the faith are circling the wagons against what they perceive to be a serious threat to the church of reason."[3]

One of the more radical examples of anti-science is offered by one of Aronowitz's cocontributors to this issue of *Social Text*, Ruth Hubbard, a professor of biology at Harvard University. Her article, "Gender and Genitals: Constructs of Sex and Gender," examines what she considers the purely artificial construct by which the world is divided into only two genders, male and female. "Built-in biases," she writes, ". . . are especially prevalent, but also especially well concealed, when it comes to understandings of sex and gender, since in Western societies sex and sex differences are linchpins of the way we conceptualize ourselves and our culture. . . . When it comes to sex, the Western assumption that there are only two sexes probably derives from our culture's close coupling between sex and procreation. Yet this binary concept does not reflect biological reality. Biologist Anne Fausto-Sterling estimates that approximately 1 or 2 percent of children are born with mixed or ambiguous sex characteristics. . . . Lately, however, a more radical change has occurred. Some transgender theorists and activists have begun to insist that the binary model is hopelessly flawed and needs to be abandoned. They argue not only for an increased fluidity but want to have gender unhooked from genitals and speak of a 'rainbow' of gender."[4]

More radical still, however, and destined to cause far greater consternation, was "Transgressing the Boundaries: Toward a Transformative Hermeneutics of Quantum Gravity" by Alan Sokal of MIT. In this article he asserted that "in quantum gravity, . . . the space-time manifold ceases to exist as an objective physical reality; geometry becomes rational and contextual; and the foundational, conceptual categories of prior science—among them, existence itself—become problematized and relativized. This conceptual revolution . . . has profound implications for the content of a future postmodern and liberatory science." What Professor Sokal had just declared was that existence itself was a relative and highly dubious concept.[5]

What drew attention to this article, however, was not its outlandishly dogmatic relativism, which was qualified only by its impenetrable prose. Rather it was the author's proud admission, in a subsequent issue of *Lingua Franca*, that the whole article was a hoax, a flawless parody of the philosophical school known as deconstruction. Not least remarkable was just how well Sokal had gotten down the tone of the articles he parodied, the articles published in the very same journal. It is a tone marked by the superb confidence that everyone whom you are addressing, everyone whose opinion matters, speaks your language and already agrees with you. Sokal pretends to challenge those scientists who, by maintaining a traditional faith in science, "cling to the *dogma imposed* [my italics] by the long post-Enlightenment hegemony of the Western intellectual outlook, which can be summarized briefly as follows: that there exists an external world, whose properties are independent of any individual human being and indeed of humanity as a whole; that these properties are encoded in 'eternal' physical laws; and that human beings can obtain reliable, albeit imperfect and tentative, knowledge of these laws by hewing to the 'objective' procedures and epistemological strictures prescribed by the (so-called) scientific method."[6]

Though Sokal's hoax received front-page attention in the *New York Times*, one has to see the publication in the flesh, so to speak, in order fully to appreciate the author's success. There is nothing at all about the publication that would suggest to anyone that there is anything in the least special about Sokal's argument. His article is placed inconspicuously at the end, perhaps as the crown to the issue, since it was almost alone in being written by a working scientist—the other contributors were philosophers of science. It is only when you see the article in this context, when you consider that it was accepted by the editors, and doubtless by most of their readers, according to precisely the same criteria of evidence and argument as the fourteen other articles in the same issue, that all the other articles suddenly seem to take infection from the fraud. And yet the infection does not stop there but expands beyond the issue itself to the works that the other contributors have published else-where, and beyond that to deconstruction itself. For Sokal's argument implicitly accuses deconstruction of a fundamental failing: either it is made up of fakes, or it lacks the intellectual resources to distinguish between fakes and the real thing. It is difficult to say which, in the long run, is intellectually more catastrophic.

It is not the least interesting thing about such academic opposition to science, which it would be fair to characterize as generally leftist, that there is a precisely parallel movement mounted by opponents of science who might be described as "low-brow" conservatives. And just as certain right-wing racists have adopted the language of civil rights, for example, the NAAWP (National Association for the Advancement of White People), so do many of these anti-science conservatives invoke the modish doubt of elite postmodern opinion to gussy up an essentially premodern point of view.

One had thought that the evolutionary doctrine pioneered by Darwin, though subject to modification and refinement, had been proved essentially beyond doubt. Even at the time of the Scopes case back in 1926, the last time the opposition to evolution was brought to prominence, it was a backward, outlandishly conservative opinion. That this conviction should recur now, so many years later, shocks most of us. It should not. Here, as in so many other cases involving the far right, it is precisely the oldness of the doctrine, precisely the fact of its seeming dead beyond recall, that endears it to its more recent proponents. That is to say that there are few people today who innocently accept the words of Genesis, innocently in the sense that it would not occur to them to think otherwise. For most of them, merely to maintain such an opinion in the first place is an act of intentional defiance, an image-conscious decision that has about it, because it is so calculated, more than an element of bad faith. Though many people who hold this opinion sincerely believe in it, one often finds among their ranks those whose main ambition is to disrupt the accepted discourse of the center, to get back at it for having so thoroughly vanquished their cherished traditions.

The number of creationists in the world is larger than one might think. In the late 1970s, according to *The Creationist Move-*

ment in Modern America by Raymond A. Eve and Francis B. Harrold, 42 percent of those in a Gallup poll agreed that the word of scripture was literally true. Another poll in the *New York Times* reported in August of 1982 that over 44 percent of those polled assented to the idea that "God created man pretty much in his present form within the last ten thousand years."[7]

Nor is the creationist movement to be found in America only, though surely it is more vigorous here than anywhere else. England, for example, can claim several hundred thousand creationists, and the movement is even bigger in some of its former colonies, like Canada, South Africa, and New Zealand, not to mention India, Korea, and Nigeria. It seems especially energetic in Australia, where the separation of church and state is not upheld as in America, and where it is frequently taught in state schools. An organization established in Brisbane in 1980 and calling itself the Creation Science Foundation has a full-time staff that puts out a newspaper, *Creation Science Prayer News*, and a glossy magazine, *Creation ex Nihilo*, which is sent all over the world.

Creationism, however, is not a monolith. Those who hold to the biblical account of creation can be divided between old-earth creationists and young-earth creationists. The old-earthers believe that the world may indeed have been created billions of years ago but that man came about through a separate and divine dispensation. The young-earthers insist that the world was created in six days some six thousand years ago. Then there are the so-called scientific creationists, who do not reject science out of hand but try to assert that, in fact, it confirms their point of view, which is based in the Bible.

An interesting parallel can be found between the emergence of creationism and of the KKK, both in the twenties and more recently. Without our suggesting any necessary connection between the two, it should be said that both movements were and remain a backlash against the overwhelming thrust of centrist society. In other words, it would be imprecise to classify them as merely the atrophied survivors of an earlier time. Rather they represent the strenuous rejection of contemporary circumstances of which they are intensely aware. According to Eve and Harrold, the emergence of the creationist movement in the twenties can be attributed largely to the exponential rise in the number of high school graduates in America. By 1900 most biology textbooks wholeheartedly endorsed Darwinism. A generation later, almost 50 percent of the nation's youth were graduating from high school, a figure almost ten times that of half a century before. These students were no longer the sons and daughters of the elite alone but increasingly of the middle and working classes. At the same time, there was considerable unrest among traditionalist Protestants at the arrival of Catholics and Jews. This influx of strangers, combined with incidents like the Red Scare, created among the traditionalists a sense that everything was coming apart and that radical steps had to be taken.

But in time, as the Red Scare abated and as immigrants were increasingly assimilated to the center of society, the tide of creationism also abated. In the forties and fifties the fruits of science—electricity, television, and telephones—reached for the first time to every corner of the population. Everything from Tupperware to cars was designed in a sleek futuristic way that indicated, if nothing else, an almost religious faith in, and enthusiasm for, science. But then the faith in science began to subside. There is a peculiar parallelism, in this regard, between the back-to-nature movement in the sixties and the revival of creationism, which began around the same time but got fully under way only in the eighties. This time, as well, its reemergence was a response to a fundamental shift in the nation's makeup. The nation was being invaded, it seemed, by Moslems and Koreans, who were even more divergent from the mainstream than Jews had been in the 1920s. And this fact, combined with the ongoing liberalization of society as a whole, caused traditionalists to feel as strongly as ever that their worldview was in peril of extinction.

This connection is made clear in a statement made in 1981 by Braswell Deen, chief justice of the Georgia Circuit Court of Appeals: "This monkey mythology of Darwin is the cause of the permissiveness, promiscuity, pills, prophylactics, perversions, pregnancies, abortions, pornotherapy, pollution, poisoning, and proliferation of crimes of all types."[8] And in a way Judge Deen was right, except that he inverted cause and effect. For Darwin in the last century was not the cause but the symptom of the dissolution of an older world. And yet creationists seemed to think that, if it were somehow possible to repeal Darwin, then the world they had lost would suddenly be reborn. This hope, even more than the creationists' visceral rejection of the obscenity of man's descent from chimps, was and remains the real power behind their movement.

One of the headquarters of academic creationism is the Center for Creation Studies at Liberty University, established by Jerry Falwell in Lynchberg, Virginia. All students at Liberty are required to take a semester-long course in creationism, and the university lays claim to having the largest "creationist" museum in the world. An even larger center is the Institute for Creation Research in Santee, California. Founded in 1970, it has a full-time staff of eight, including a Harvard Ph.D. in ecology. Its stated aim is not only to do research into creationism but also to encourage its dissemination. Though some of its money goes to funding archeological exhibitions, one of which went to Armenia in search of Noah's ark, most of it is spent on research that aspires to identify errors in the thinking of more mainstream scientists.

At the heart of this intellectual project is what might be called a kind of hyperscience, which, as was outlined in the chapter "Center and Circumference," finds many parallels in other fringe movements. On the one hand, academic creationists require of traditional science a degree of proof to which even the best empiricism is rarely equal. In this they resemble the Simpson jurors for whom the one-in-seven-billion chance that the blood was not Simpson's was sufficiently reasonable doubt. On the other hand, as with the Simpson jurors, when the proof they demand is not forthcoming, they are willing to surrender their understanding abjectly to an article of faith. Thus, having heard somewhere that science has to do with empirical observation, they assert that, since no one was present to witness the creation of the world or the birth of man, science has no greater claim to authenticity than the book of Genesis. Thus, through a shrewdness that doubtless satisfies them quite well, they level the very same charge against traditional science that traditional science levels against them: that they are merely purveyors of fables.

Elsewhere they invoke a kind of ersatz science, as when they dismiss carbon-14 dating on the grounds that the half-life of the carbon-14 isotope might have been shorter in the past than today. Another one of their arguments, paraphrased by Eve and Harrold in *The Creationist Movement in Modern America*, asserts that "evolution is precluded by the second law of thermodynamics, under which the universe's constantly increasing entropy (disorganization and loss of energy available for work) makes the evolutionary growth of systems of increasingly complex organization impossible."[9]

In addition to such purely academic attacks, creationists have proved quite litigious, although their court cases have not always been successful. In 1973 they succeeded in getting the Tennessee legislature to mandate that textbooks present evolution as theory rather than fact and to provide equal time for creationism. More interesting still was the passage, in 1981, of an Arkansas law advocating a two-model curriculum that would teach both evolution and "creation-science," defined as "the scientific evidences for creation and inferences from those scientific evidences."[10] In doing so, creationists adopted the language of the left, or at least of the center, both to further their cause and, we may suppose, to confuse their opponents. Their stated aim was "to protect academic freedom by providing student choice; to ensure freedom of religious exercise, to guarantee freedom of belief and speech; to prevent establishment of religion; . . . to bar discrimination on the basis of creationist or evolutionist belief."[11]

The law was immediately attacked by the American Civil Liberties Union, not to mention a number of religious groups. It is worth noting that the creationists' case ran aground in the ensuing legal confrontation when one of their expert witnesses, Norman Geisler of Dallas Theological Seminary, asserted that UFOs were engines of Satan. Another witness said that one would have to be "crazy" to think that the earth was only a few thousand years old. Nevertheless, through something perversely called an "anti-dogmatism policy," textbook writers were henceforth required to fudge matters when it came to creation. What had been written, "As reptiles evolved from fishlike ancestors, they developed a thicker scaly surface," was made to read, "If reptiles evolved from fishlike ancestors, as proposed in the theory of evolution, they must have developed a thick scaly surface."[12]

One cannot forbear from offering the personal opinion that religious conservatives have no more right or reason to expect scientists to offer equal time to creationism than religious liberals would have to insist that at every pulpit the books of Darwin be made to stand beside the books of Moses, that priests and pastors be required to present the views of science as well as of revelation. In fact, science and religion inhabit two entirely different realms, each being sovereign within that realm. Science claims to offer up the self-consistent claims that are the product of observation and experimentation. Religion presumes to uphold the revealed word of God. They exist on two disparate plains and need never meet.

Thus far, we have divided the anti-science fringe between generally leftist academics and far right religious traditionalists. In fact, there is a third group, which cannot always be placed on the right-left spectrum: a conspiracy-minded fringe that delights in a radical mixture of skepticism and credulity. One of the typical prepossessions of this fringe is the conviction that man never landed on the moon. "NASA couldn't make it to the moon," Bill Kaysing contends in his book *We Never Went to the Moon*, "and they knew it." The author, who worked in the Rocketdyne research department between 1956 and 1963, goes on to say, "In the late 50's, when I was at Rocketdyne, they did a feasibility study on astronauts landing on the moon. They found that the chance of success was something like .0017 percent. In other words, it was hopeless. . . . They, both NASA and Rocketdyne, wanted the money to keep pouring in. I've worked in aerospace long enough to know that's their goal."[13]

His proof for this extraordinary claim is that, in photographs supposedly taken on the moon, no stars are visible around the lunar module, nor is there any crater underneath the craft, and there is light all around the astronauts—or "astro-nots," as some of his followers call them. "It all points to an unprecedented swindle," he concludes.[14] His arguments are all easily rebutted by NASA. There are no stars for the same reasons that you see none when you are gazing up from under a street lamp. There is no crater under the lunar module because the vehicle emitted most of its propulsion force miles above the moon and then floated to the surface. And what does Kaysing make of the fact that thousands of people at the launch site saw the massive Saturn V rocket take off? It did indeed take off, he contends, but it jettisoned its inhabitants over Antarctica, where they were picked up by air force planes, only to be dropped into the sea two weeks later at the appropriate time.

It would be easy to dismiss Kaysing as a crank were it not for a poll of 1,721 people taken a year after the first moonwalk in 1969. It found that 30 percent were suspicious of its ever having occurred. Even one of NASA's spokesmen, James Obey, a "NASA agent" according to Kaysing, agrees that as many as ten to twenty-five million people, or about 4 to 10 percent, of the population doubt the moon landing. It is of some interest, by the way, that the official position of the Hare Krishna movement, as well, is that the moon landing never took place.

Another group that doubts the moon landing is the Flat Earth Society, which comprises about thirty-five hundred men and women and is based in Lincoln, California. The reasons for its denial of the moon landing, however, are somewhat different from those of other critics of NASA. As its name implies, this group believes that the world is flat; further, it holds that the sun and moon are thirty-two miles above the earth and revolve around it, as do the planets, which are very tiny. Yet there is nothing traditionalist about this conviction. Like the creationists, flat-earthers advocate their own kind of hyperscience, except that they do so in the name not of religion but of reason—as they conceive it. In one of their flyers, the head of the society, Charles K. Johnson, asserts that we should "replace the science religion . . . with Sanity." His position is not so much proved as stated categorically. "One thing we know for sure about this world . . . the known inhabited world is Flat, Level, a Plain World. We maintain that what is called 'science' today and 'scientists' consist of the same old gang of witch doctors, sorcerers, tellers of tales, the Priest-Entertainers for the common people. 'Science' consists of a weird way-out occult concoction of gibberish theory-theology."

Flat-earthers, who sometimes call themselves Zetetics, from the Greek for "seeker," describe themselves, according to one brochure, as "the Few, the Elite, the Elect, who use Logic, Reason, are Rational." Their stated mission is to "rediscover forgotten facts." And yet, for all their combativeness, there would seem to be an essential insecurity at the heart of their militancy. The same brochure that offers membership for only ten dollars concludes with this oddly moving, almost pathetic plea: "We do not want members . . . whose only aim is to scoff or in some way 'harm' our work." To this end prospective members are asked to sign a form declaring that "I hereby affirm that my aim in joining is not to harm, degrade, damage, or [defame] the society."

What links the flat-earthers and the moon-landing deniers to the otherwise far more malign deniers of the Holocaust—in other words, to those who would pervert history rather than science to their own ends—is that, in both cases, the very fact of belief, which in most circumstances is merely a passive state of mind, takes on the characteristics of an activity. It defines who you are and how you comport yourself, and it distinguishes you from those who subscribe to that body of beliefs that defines the center. Although in all cases the stated aim of these deniers of centrist belief is the desire to change men's minds, to force them, at long last, to see what is held to be the self-evident truth, in fact the real aim is to stand apart from the mainstream of public opinion and to delight in that pleasantly unbrigeable gap that eternally separates those who hold such opinions from the rest of the human race.

There is, however, this difference between those who choose to attack centrist notions of science and those who inveigh against centrist notions of history: whereas the former tend to be apolitical cranks or to be vaguely leftist in their assault on the perceived centers of power, the latter usually have some fairly obvious political agenda. As Orwell put it, he who controls the past controls the future. In a well-intentioned article on the op-ed page of the *New York Times*, the historian Arthur Schlesinger Jr. summed up the present state of historical inquiry in the following way: "Militant monoculturalists of the right want history to instill and to extol patriotism, religion, Ozzie and Harriet, Harry and Louise, and in general, the superior virtues of unregulated capitalism. Militant multiculturalists of the left want history to dump the big names of the past, those deplorable dead white males, and build the self-esteem of minorities by telling them how wonderful and creative their ancestors were."[15]

Just as certain creationists pretend to a higher standard of evidence than science can satisfy, rejecting Darwinism on the grounds that no one was there to witness the creation, so do those who attack mainstream history batten upon the doubt that is inseparable from the historical act. As Schlesinger says, "History is, in an ultimate sense, impossible. The past is past—and beyond discovery. Objectivity is an illusion. These doubts are perennial. Now they surface once more, this time decked out with postmodernist jargon of deconstruction, discourse analysis, textuality and narratology. All history in is seen in this light as ideology by other means, as the projection and manipulation of power relationships."[16]

The real point behind the exertions of historical revisionists is not so much to persuade others of the correctness of their opinions as to create a climate or context of doubt, in which it is possible for them, if not to prove their case, at very least to establish the grounds whereby all historical narratives become equally sensible or foolish, equally believable or incredible. Once this doubt has been established, any discourse is as good as any other. The burden of proof shifts a few degrees, and suddenly it is incumbent upon us to prove that the ancient Egyptians were not black and did not fly around in primitive airplanes. Now those of us in the center can prove this fairly easily and in good faith to our own satisfaction. But the very fact that it is we who are proving it means that, because we are seen to have as much of an agenda as our opponents, it is no more incumbent upon them to believe us than it is likely that we shall ever believe them. That is where the conversation usually ends, with each side abandoning the other in despair.

The case of the Holocaust deniers is in some ways unique, having much to do with the unique role of the Jews in Western culture. Most historical revisionists, like the authors of *The Portland Research Project*, a black revisionist manual, serve their own self-aggrandizing ends, in pursuit of which it may be necessary to attack the interests of other groups, though only as a consequence.

Thus the point of black revisionists is primary to assert the grandeur of the black achievement, which entails only secondarily a depreciation of whites' achievement. In Holocaust denial, however, there is no question of personal aggrandizement. True, certain black groups, like the Nation of Islam, may question its veracity because it challenges their claim to absolute precedence in the annals of victimology, and because they find it intolerable that anyone, especially a people as ostensibly affluent as the Jews, should have been more victimized than they.

In most cases, however, Holocaust deniers have nothing like these aims in mind. They claim to have a disinterested attachment to the historical record, although that claim as well is obviously untrue. Yet there is little practical gain in denying the Holocaust. No money stands to be gained, no territory to be redeemed. Why, then, do some people persist in denying what is probably the best-documented crime in human history, a crime whose surviving witnesses number in the hundreds of thousands, while the implements of attempted annihilation lie all about?

The real motive of the Holocaust deniers is not to prove that the Holocaust did not take place. Indeed, it is not to prove anything at all. Nor is it, as Deborah Lipstadt speculates in her admirably thorough book *Denying the Holocaust*, to rehabilitate fascism, which is unlikely to happen in any case. Despite what many Jewish groups fear, it is not the possibility of persuading the center that is the point of the deniers' activity but the apparent impossibility of our persuading them. This refusal to acquiesce in the opinions of the center is the one and only locus of their victory. Many people are antagonized by the Holocaust denier because they assume that his argument has at least this much good faith, that he really believes or wants to believe what he asserts. In fact all he wants, and all he can ever really hope to attain, is the status of being an ineradicable source of provocation to the center.

Nor is it sufficient to say that the Holocaust denier hates Jews, though there is surely a large element of that as well. More than anything else he is sincere in his passionate refusal to conform to the norms of centrist society and in his desire, for whatever psychological reasons, to stand at variance with the center. And in achieving this goal, nothing attracts the attention of the extremist as much as the Holocaust, the greatest historical outrage of the century, an outrage as great as any in human history. It is the point of greatest departure from the conventions of centrist society, the festering wound at the heart of contemporary history. That is why the Holocaust comes up again and again in extremist discourse, on the left and the right, among Queer Nation, as we have seen, as well as in the Nation of Islam.

Furthermore, Holocaust denial is seen by those who practice it as continuing the Holocaust by other means. In a perverse way, they deny the Holocaust precisely because they believe it, because they realize that their intractable denial of it is the only defense they have against the total and overpowering reality of the historical record. In the postwar world, and to an extent today as well, the Jew has been seen as the victim par excellence. Because support for the victim is one of the most cherished principles of centrist society, their denial becomes a Parthian shot at an opponent against whom they are otherwise powerless.

Certain people began to deny the Holocaust almost as soon as its atrocities were fully revealed at the end of the Second World War. One proponent of this view, Paul Rassinier, was a camp survivor who subsequently developed various delusions about the Jews, among them one that doubted the existence of the gas chambers and claimed that the Jews themselves were responsible for their own deaths. This line of thought was developed in the sixties by a college professor from Pennsylvania, Austin App, who asserted that the Holocaust had been orchestrated by the Jews themselves to further the cause of Zionism. But these claims were summarily rejected by almost everyone due to the generally uncouth and harebrained manner in which they were presented.

It was only with the arrival of Arthur Butz's *The Hoax of the Twentieth Century* that this line of thought acquired what appeared to be a dispassionate, footnoted authenticity. The fact that those notes were largely spurious would have gone unnoticed by most of his readers, who in general were not especially interested in the finer points, anyway. Things really went into high gear, however, with the involvement of Willis Carto. It was he who founded both the Liberty Lobby, a far right group, and the Institute for Historical Review. Behind this august and fair-sounding name, Holocaust deniers would erect their most ambitious and well-funded organization. And yet, as so often among fringe groups, animosity arose between Carto and those followers who, being uniquely interested in denying the Holocaust, refused to go along with his larger white supremacist agenda. In time-honored anti-Semitic fashion, he retaliated by attributing this conflict to the behind-the-scenes infiltration of the Jew. The Institute for Historic Review, he proclaimed to universal astonishment, was being secretly run by the Anti-Defamation League of B'nai B'rith.

Whether or not this institute had any success, its members could take heart in the famous Roper poll showing that as much as 30 percent of the American people doubted that six million Jews had died in the Holocaust. Likewise they could take comfort in the words of other dissenters like the French writer, Robert Faurisson, who referred to the Holocaust as a "falsification of history,"[17] or Pat Buchanan, who, having questioned whether the gas chambers in Treblinka could have worked, labeled the Holocaust Survival Syndrome "group fantasies of martyrdom and heroics."[18]

One of the most effective Holocaust deniers is David Irving. This scholar of the Second World War, who refers to himself as a "moderate fascist" and denies being a denier, asserted that Auschwitz, where two to three million people died, was "built by the Poles after the war as a tourist attraction."[19] He was also quoted by the British columnist Bernard Levin as saying that someone should "put an end to the blood lie of the Holocaust which has been told against [Germany] for fifty years."[20] Furthermore, he endears himself to the far right by claiming that the diary of Anne Frank was a forgery. However, he admitted under cross-examination during the trial of Ernst Zundel, a prominent publisher of denial literature, that he had not read all of the transcript of Eichmann's trial, in which the latter admitted that he had acted on the idea of the Final Solution.

Historical denial, of course, goes beyond the question of the Holocaust. In Paris, recently, I was astonished to meet several educated and entirely Westernized Lebanese women who asserted with total confidence that the Gulf War had never taken place. It had been orchestrated by the United States, they said, with the connivance of Saddam Hussein. But why would Hussein, who had proved especially intractable in his dealings with the United States, suddenly wish to acquiesce in his own humiliation? This question the three women were unable to answer, but, as they did not have much respect for Hussein to begin with, they could easily persuade themselves that the real goal of the war was the humiliation of Arabs, despite all the Arab states leagued against Saddam.

The point they were making was that it was absolutely out of the question to have defeated an Arab army so easily; therefore, denial was the only solution. As with deniers of the Holocaust, of the rotundity of the earth, and of O. J. Simpson's guilt, all of reality was made to curl around this one core conviction; reality became what it took to maintain the conviction undisturbed. All questions could be answered because all premises would be called into doubt, as necessary, in order for that initial conviction to remain intact.

Interestingly enough, a very similar attack against the reality of the Gulf War, although in an entirely different context and with an entirely different agenda, was mounted by the French intellectual Jean Baudrillard in three separate articles written for *Libération*. The first, "La Guerre du Golf n'aura pas lieu" ("The Gulf War Will Not Take Place") asserted, as its title implies, that the war would not take place for a variety of conventional reasons, which, since indeed the conflict had not begun, could not yet be rejected out of hand. Furthermore, similar arguments had a fair number of proponents in the mainstream press. In other words, Baudrillard was involved, at this point, in nothing more mysterious than simple prognostication.

In the years prior to writing this article, Baudrillard had risen to prominence in France and in America for his contribution to the intellectual movement known as poststructuralism. It is so called because it is the main tendency in French, and therefore in American, philosophy after the demise of structuralism some fifteen years ago. But where structuralism had aspired, at least early on, to a brittle, impassive methodology that resembled mathematics in its rigorous examination of how meaning was generated in a given text or discourse, poststructuralism has emphatically reintroduced the subject, the author, the voice into the study of discourse. As a result, Foucault, Derrida, Lyotard, and Baudrillard tend to be far more literary than Lévi-Strauss or the early Roland Barthes. And yet there is surely a similarity of mood and motive in their respective schools of thought. Both assail, though from different angles of assault, that subject-object relationship of traditional philosophy, for reasons which, if nothing else, are pleasant to those whose leftism has made them antagonistic to the center of society. Poststructuralism, like structuralism, attacks received ideas about reality and truth, but it favors a jauntier and more spontaneous style rather than the earlier school's grim little system.

Thus one must not expect, for one will not find, anything approaching systematic thought in the writings of Jean Baudrillard. Rather he has three or four intuitions about contemporary society, which can occasionally enhance our understanding of life at the end of the twentieth century. To acknowledge this benefit, however, would be far too modest and indefinite an appraisal for Baudrillard. It is his intellectual vanity to suppose that, at this late date, all of reality has become a sham, a virtual projection of the real thing, a global Disney World. For him, human beings are caught in a war of signs from which they can no longer escape back to any tangible sense of the real. Everything has already been seen a hundred times before, and the mind, saturated with symbols and imitations, is no longer capable of direct and immediate response.

Now war in general, and the Gulf War in specific, would seem to contradict such a contention in the most immediate way possible: there is no faking one's response to the death and destruction that war entails. Something in warfare, with all its bloody immediacy, cannot be trivialized or palliated by metaphors and figures of thought. As such, it threatens directly to contradict one of the core convictions of Baudrillard's philosophy, that everything in our postmodern age is somehow a pallid reflection of what had gone before, in earlier history.

For this reason, it was of pressing interest to him, before the Gulf War began, to deny even the possibility of the war. Much was at stake. In the same way that, if Columbus was right about the earth's being spherical, then one must be able to reach the East by sailing west, so, if Baudrillard was right in his diagnosis of contemporary civilization—indeed, right about reality itself—then it must follow that postmodernity could never produce a real war. It could produce a cold war; it could produce a series of *promenades militaires* like those in the Falklands, Haiti, or Panama; surely Third World countries could slaughter one another; but—and this was crucial—the postmodern nation par excellence, the United States of America, simply would not be able to wage a blood-and-guts war as it had in the past.

The Gulf War now seems an accomplished fact, but it was hardly that in the days immediately before the air strikes began on 15 January 1991. When Baudrillard wrote the first of the three articles on 4 January 1991, it was not obvious that the war would take place. A month had passed since the United Nations resolution demanding Saddam's unconditional removal of his troops from Kuwait. There was even money that sanctions would be imposed, that Saddam would yield, and that the war would not come to pass. Thus Baudrillard's article was not so implausible. "From the beginning," he wrote, "we knew that this war would never happen. After the hot war (the violence of conflict), after the cold war (the balance of terror), here comes the dead war—the unfrozen war—which leaves us to grapple with the corpse of war and the necessity of dealing with this decomposing corpse which nobody from the Gulf has managed to revive. America, Saddam Hussein, and the Gulf Powers are fighting over the corpse of war."[21]

One must retain a certain admiration for anyone with the courage or the recklessness to predict so emphatically that the Gulf War would not take place. Clearly he was laying his life's work on the line. For, although Baudrillard would become more theoretical, or perhaps evasive, in subsequent articles, what he meant when he said, *before the fact*, that the war would not happen was not theoretical at all. When one recalls that hostages had been taken and were being used as weapons in what remained a war of diplomacy, it did not seem so far-fetched to assert, as he had, that "nonwar is characterized by that degenerate form of war which includes hostage manipulation and negotiation. Hostages and blackmail are the purest products of deterrence. The hostage has taken the place of the warrior. . . . The warriors bury themselves in the desert, leaving only hostages to occupy the stage, including all of us as information hostages to occupy the world stage. . . . This impossibility of proceeding to the act, this absence of strategy, implies the triumph of blackmail as strategy."[22]

He goes on to say that "the most widespread belief is in a logical progression from virtual to actual, according to which no available weapon will not one day be used and such a concentration of force cannot but lead to conflict. However, this is an Aristotelian logic which is no longer our own."[23] In other words, the entire epistemology of Jean Baudrillard was riding on the nonexistence, in the most literal meaning of that term, of the war in the Persian Gulf.

Of course, scarcely was the ink dry on his article in *Libération* when the fighting started in earnest. Whole legions of the Iraqi vanguard were wiped out, many parts of Baghdad were reduced to rubble, and its citizens began suffering terrible privations. The war, in short, had begun. But just when it seemed certain that Baudrillard would be forced to retreat from his position, metaphor came to his aid, as it has always come to the aid of purveyors of extreme positions. In his next article, "The Gulf War: Is It Really Taking Place?," Baudrillard more or less allowed that it was taking place, but he would not say so explicitly. It cannot be a real war, he asserted—through a circular argument that troubled him not at all—because, however much it looks like war, it no longer has the wholesale carnage and the indiscriminate bombing that he chooses to define as war.

It is truly unfortunate that this arch-postmodernist was so concerned to make a grandiose, if foolhardy, case for the impossibility of war, and so concerned to defend this conviction in the teeth of insurmountable evidence to the contrary, that he completely failed to appreciate that, in fact, the Gulf War was the first postmodern war, both in the weaponry that the victors brought to bear on the losers and in the spirit with which the war was prosecuted. But that would be a humbler argument than he was interested to make, an admission that the Gulf War was a war like any other, using different means to the same end.

In the third and final essay, Baudrillard took still another tack. "Since this war was won in advance, we will never know what it would have been like had it existed. We will never know what an Iraqi taking part with a chance of fighting would have been like. We will never know what an American taking part with a chance of being beaten would have been like." Though admitting that some blood was spilled, Baudrillard still could not admit that a war had taken place, because he had already committed himself from the beginning to the prediction that it simply would not take place. So he adopted the semantic tack that what occurred did occur but was not really war. "This is not war, any more than ten thousand tons of bombs per day is sufficient to make a war. Any more than the direct transmission by CNN of real-time information is sufficient to authenticate a war." At this point, interestingly enough, he invoked with approval the denial of extraterrestrial travel. "One is reminded of *Capricorn One* in which the flight of a manned rocket to Mars, which only took place in a desert studio, was relayed live to all the television stations in the world."[24] Thus he implicitly leagued himself, somewhat improbably, with flat-earthers and deniers of the moon landing.

Most people, of course, will never read or even hear of Baudrillard's book about the Gulf War. As such, its influence is nonexistent. And yet it is not without importance, even if it is more important as a symbol than anything else. As is so often the case with philosophy, the deconstruction exemplified in Baudrillard's book presumes to challenge the orthodoxies of the present age, to point up its follies and falsehoods, and in so doing to undermine the opinions of the center. That, at any rate, is what the practitioners of deconstruction tell themselves and tell the world at large.

But things are a little more complicated than that. Without their knowing it, these thinkers are themselves obedient to the directives of the center, which not only tolerates but even encourages and ultimately subsidizes the skepticism of which Baudrillard, O. J. Simpson, flat-earthers, and Holocaust deniers are so many varied manifestations. Ever since Hegel wound up his convoluted metaphysics with the conclusion that the Prussian state of 1820 was the highest pinnacle of human evolution, it should have been pretty clear to any sensible reader that even the most radical thinkers, in the end, rarely think thoughts that the center, for all its feigned amazement, has not sanctioned well in advance.

Thus we can predict that, if and when the center rediscovers its older confidence in its own beliefs, suddenly a more pragmatic, perhaps more dogmatic system of thought will come back into fashion. All that will be left then will be those fringes who stubbornly resist the center, like the flat-earthers and the Holocaust deniers. Fortunately for them, they need never worry about tenure or the mainstream publishing and merchandising of books, all of which are in the gift of the center alone.

9

THE REMAINS
OF THE COUNTERCULTURE

The countercultural movement of the sixties and early seventies was the most massive and perhaps most successful spiritual assault ever mounted by the circumference against the center. One has only to consider what the center had been and what it became during that period to appreciate the degree of the movement's success. For in that period the world—or at least the Western world—underwent a change in its appearance and its character as great as anything sustained in the transition from the ancien régime to the Industrial Revolution or from the nineteenth century to the Roaring Twenties. By the end of the sixties, it seemed that there was scarcely a human artifact that had not undergone serious modification. It felt as though the gray shadows of the postwar world, with all its privations and all its conformity, had been dispelled at last.

Of course, the world was changing anyway, and one can make the case that the counterculture was no counterculture at all but really the vanguard of a larger change that society was undergoing during that period. In this sense the members of the counterculture, with their loud music and their long hair, were the overly zealous allies of the very society they imagined they were opposing. Such a view is supported by the ease with which, in the seventies, the center succeeded in assimilating their assault by taking from it everything that was of use to the center, like sexual permissiveness and rock music, while discarding everything that was not, like the drug culture. In effect, the counterculture became engulfed by the center. In the process, the counterculture was endowed with such prestige that, to this day, rebellion against the center, rather than an earlier conformity to the center, is the model for a certain kind of social behavior, not to mention being what it takes to sell music and films to the culture at large.

But in another sense the counterculture aspired, and it continues to aspire, to overturn all accepted values while radically rejecting or vehemently assailing the center. To understand the oddity of the counterculture as it emerged in the sixties, consider that there is, or until recently there was, one dominant culture in any given society, to which all of the members of that society subscribed. Of course, any society is apt to have its immigrant populations and its eccentrics who do not acknowledge or who strenuously resist the pull of the center. But that is different from the counterculture of the sixties, which almost mechanically opposed the views of the majority. This was a new occurrence in human events.

Before that time, social fashions and ideas were dominated by a single trend to which almost everyone paid obeisance. The Beats were one of the first movements not merely to differ from the establishment but to conceive it as an establishment at all, to see it as an oppressive monolith to be opposed. Another way of conceiving of the Beats would be to say that they were at the forefront of the center's postwar efforts to rejuvenate itself. They were the first to take an interest in the East as opposed to the West, the first to oppose the organization man, the first to reassert those elements of individualism that had been slowly eaten away during the transition from an agrarian to an industrial society.

But it was their successors, the hippies and related strains in the later sixties, who created something that looked strikingly different from the culture of the mainstream. Their numbers appeared to be more impressive than, in fact, they were. Though the counterculture could fill the Mall in Washington and the covers of the glossies, most Americans between the ages of eighteen and twenty-five voted for Nixon in 1972 over George McGovern. The way the center dealt with the counterculture was, through a natural process, to meet it halfway, to take from it its more visible and obvious ornaments, from tie-dyes to long hair to words like "groovy," and in the process to give itself a makeover.

Much has changed since then. In the sixties, the counterculture emerged in response to some real problems that beset American and Western society. Its rebellion was fueled by the twofold desire to oppose the war in Vietnam and to expand the freedom available to the individual in postwar America. Today, however, the counterculture, to the extent that it survives at all, has no pressing and immediate function to perform. If anything, society as a whole is immoderately resistant to restrictions on behavior, opposition to which was one of the main selling points of the earlier counterculture. And, following the very success of the sixties, nonconformity has become so much the fashion in music, clothing, and comportment that it could almost be called the conformity of choice for a large portion of the population. Perhaps more important, there is no sanguinary conflict weighing upon the conscience of the republic, and the liberation of women, blacks, and homosexuals has been largely achieved. It should also be said that the very idea of the counterculture—represented in the popular imagination by the aging, pot-smoking, tree-hugging hippie— has become so dated at this point as to be something of a standing jest on sitcoms and op-ed pages. In the last analysis, the main function of the counterculture today is to serve as a nurturing ground for rock groups and designers, whom the center more or less conscripts to provide it with its music and its style.

But what has happened to that part of the counterculture that survives, the real counterculture? Revisiting it one generation later, you find that much has changed and much has stayed the same. One main difference is this: as we have seen, the present counterculture makes no plausible or pressing claim to moral authority. There is no war in Vietnam to oppose. Thus it survives as a lifestyle and little more, one that society at large, which felt genuinely challenged by the counterculture of the sixties, can scoff at with impunity. This is precisely because the turmoil of the sixties, by challenging the often false values of the postwar generation and by changing many of those values, left society in possession of values that it confidently believes to be the right ones.

It was the argument of Theodore Roszak, who coined the term "counterculture," that the youth movement was reacting against the increasing industrialization of society and with it the emergence of the corporation man. Now, however, precisely through the success of the rebellion of the sixties, the technocracy—which was really an effect of the late Industrial Revolution—is not nearly as powerful as it once was. The technology that matters is no longer that of machinery, which businessmen created, but of computers, which were largely the brainchild of hippies and hobbyists. The result is that the nonconformity that had once been channeled into the counterculture has been integrated into corporate America.

In considering the present state of the counterculture, one must not seek, because one can never find, much that is entirely new. Rather what one finds is that the same tendencies in fashion, as in art, are almost universally present but are allowed greater or lesser prominence in a given cultural context at one time than at another. Thus, although sadomasochism, pedophilia, and other such things can be easily found among the counterculture of the sixties, they were private preoccupations, which went almost unnoticed by most who would have identified themselves with that movement. Now, however, those same tendencies that had been latent have been elevated to glaring prominence.

Today's counterculture, like the original one, can be found at many points across the country. But, like the original counterculture, it is primarily a bicoastal phenomenon, being most vigorous in places like San Francisco and Seattle and that part of Lower Manhattan known as the East Village. Despite a brush with celebrity in the early eighties, the East Village, stretching from about Third Avenue and Fourteenth Street down to Houston and over to the East River, has largely resisted gentrification, unlike SoHo and Chelsea. No one is on the make in the East Village. The artistic movement known as the East Village Scene, which was this area's one moment in the sun a few years back, quickly fizzled out, returning the place to those eccentrics, minorities, and working-class families who had inhabited the area long before the graffiti artists ever showed up.

It is here that you will find the largest quantity of occult bookstores, herbal shops, leather and S&M paraphernalia, and body-piercing establishments. Here anarchist newspapers are not only published but even read. Tompkins Square Park, the famous haunt of the homeless before their recent eviction, has been taken over again by several kinds of unquiet youths—Goths, Punks, S&M types—though they must leave the area by midnight. What you will not find are yuppies or "bridge and tunnel" types, as suburbanites are sarcastically labeled in these parts. And you can find here almost every conceivable form of extreme behavior (aside from that of the extreme right) mentioned in the present book.

Even casual exposure to today's counterculture reveals that the most striking change it has undergone since the 1960s has been in its tone. There is much less peace and much more anger among its members in their opposition to the center. Now that the center has accepted the dictum to make love and not war, the best way to oppose the center, it has been found, has been to resuscitate a violence that the center has rejected.

The archetypal hero of this new counterculture is the madman. The madman is seen as the anarchist and artist par excellence, someone to be embraced and imitated. Most obviously, this imitation of madness can be found in the multiform verbal and artistic expressions of the counterculture, with its riotous performances, incoherent poetry, and grunge attire. But there is another sense in which adherents to the counterculture imitate madness: in the anger they often express against society itself, in their stubborn embrace of what society cannot or will not assimilate. Though most members of the counterculture are obviously not mad themselves, there are few elements of madness that have not, on one occasion or another, figured in their outlook on life, from a fixation on abasement and abjection—to use their term of choice—to an indulgence in voguish conspiracy mongering, and with it the belief that one is persecuted from all directions.

An example of this latter tendency is something called Doom, the Society for Secular Armageddonism, defined as "an organization founded upon a fundamental belief: the earth is on the brink of a monumental catastrophe of apocalyptic proportions, a catastrophe that promises to wreak havoc upon the entire planet. In short, the end of the world is at hand. This conviction is based not on religious prophecy but on observance of a multitude of critical world threats, including nuclear proliferation, chemical/biological weap-ons, terrorism, ozone depletion, global warming, deforestation, acid rain, massive species loss, ocean and air pollution, exploding population, global complacency, and many more."[1]

Such points of view surely do not find their way into the mainstream media, but they flourish and proliferate on the Internet. This new medium, together with public access television and 'zines (small-circulation desktop publications), is the great equalizer, whereby the largest corporations and the smallest cranks and charlatans can, at least for the time being, compete on terms of apparent equality. This information superhighway is the *via regia*, the royal road, of the counterculture.

Another constantly recurring theme is hatred of the corporate world and of the Middle American "normalcy" with which it is associated. We find this in "The Cereal Box Conspiracy Against the Developing Mind," a garden-variety jeremiad by Michelle Handelman and Monte Carazza about the way cereal boxes "indoctrinate" children. "The biggest conspiracy of all," the authors assert, ". . . is that we are victims of our birth. Thanks to the often accidental result of a conjoining of simpletons . . . we are doomed to fit into someone else's plan until we become cunning enough to find a way out. By the time we figure out where we stand, it's too late to leave, and even suicide becomes a felony. The second biggest conspiracy comes into play soon after birth—the weaning and shaping of new lives into the Consumerist Reality, which is what the behavioral science of marketing children's cereals is all about. . . . It's not just the mood-elevating refined sugar product they are selling. (You could make a good case for food manufacturers' collusion with the AMA, ADA, and FDA, supplying a ready quantity of sugar-addicted children with juvenile diabetes and dental carries [caries?])." In fact cereal is "only a Trojan Horse into the hearts and minds of the little Nickies and Debbies. Food manufactures are training children to gorge themselves on style, on pop culture. . . . Children are to have a TV show, a top movie, a record album, a video game, and a toy doll to accompany their eating experience."[2]

The contrarianism implicit in this declaration, the manifest antagonism to the customs of the center, was put more succinctly still by Anton LaVey, founder of the Church of Satan and a fixture in countercultural circles. "I've always gravitated to the *opposite*—whatever that opposite may be! Almost as though it were the natural direction for me to go, shunning the average or the usual or the predictable, very much like I would shun a poison. Because I know that no matter what *it* is that is immediately grasped upon as the *norm* . . . it's immediately going to be the *wrong* thing for me."[3]

The Church of Satan has become something of an anarchist institution, if the paradox will be permitted, a pillar of contrarianism. Like Wicca, the goddess-based religion related to witchcraft, the Church of Satan underscores the counterculture's perennial interest in the occult and the search for religious fulfillment outside of the orthodoxy of more mainstream religions. But if Wicca seems benign, the Church of Satan is militant in its opposition to established order, in standing *counter* to the culture of the mainstream. A brief flyer asserts that the organization was founded in 1966, "thus opening the floodgates to a revolution designed to smash the hypocrisy and unreason which have reigned for the past two thousand years. . . . Those who proudly carry our cards identifying themselves as members have the strength and dedication to implement the tools of Satan, the imagination to confound and confuse, the wisdom to recognize the Unseen in our society, and the passions of a classical Romantic soul. . . . We are a group of dynamic individuals who stand forth as the ultimate Underground alternative, the Alien Elite."

The central text of the Church of Satan is LaVey's *Satanic Bible*. The personality that emerges from this book, and that to some extent informs the whole movement, is not, on the face of it, very evil. As the author says plausibly enough, "Satan represents indulgence instead of abstinence! Satan represents vital existence instead of spiritual pipe dreams. Satan represents undefiled wisdom instead of hypocritical self-deceit! Satan has been the best friend the church has ever had, keeping it in business all these years!"[4]

What sort of person would join such an association? And, since it is mystical without really being metaphysical, and pessimistic rather than optimistic, what reasons might one have for doing so? One member of the Church of Satan for a year and a half, whom we shall call Andrew, does not look exactly as one might expect a Satanist to look. And yet he does not defy the stereotype, either. As befits the self-actualization that defines the movement, he seems to work out quite a bit in the gym, has close-cropped blond hair, and dresses all in black. He is quite frank about why he does so. "I don't *have* to dress in black. I just like the way it looks. It goes well with my hair and skin tone."

As for the metaphysics of his religion, he seems disinclined to think of Satan, that figure known to millions from Goethe's *Faust,* horror films, and old operas, is an actual living being. Rather he sees Satan as a projection of one's own impulses. Nevertheless, he does believe in ESP and in his own psychic powers, but even these he can rationalize by saying that eventually scientists will discover a physical basis for the occult. He feels that, through the focusing of his spiritual energies that Satanism encourages, he has seen a marked turnaround and improvement in his life. Because he dropped out of high school and only belatedly, in his mid-thirties, has gotten his college diploma, he believes that he is only now hitting his stride. "Satan has been good to me," he says, with a knowing sidelong glance, referring to a few business ventures that have proved profitable. Furthermore, he has made good friends and his life has become more interesting. "Praise Satan!" he says.

"There is this difference between witches and Christians and myself," he concludes, "that when a witch is not in her coven, she is no longer a witch. When a Christian is not in church, he isn't interested in religion. But I am a Satanist at every moment of the day and night. I have an altar in my apartment which I pray to every night." This statement is revealing. Herein consists not only the charm of Satanism to those who embrace it but the appeal of many other fringe groups: they offer their followers the possibility of a secondary life, a kind of virtual life that coexists with the actual one but is infinitely more thrilling, colorful, and alive. Such movements permit a person, by sheer force of imagination, to think himself out of his drab circumstances, to live life as part of a pageant, an unending command performance for that all-important audience of oneself.

This theatrical sense of life is fundamental to the counterculture, in which the twin impulses of self-exhibition and activism are combined. It is suggestive that Anton La Vey had his all-important Satanic epiphany at the circus, where he used to play the organ and the calliope: "On Saturday night I would see men lusting after half-naked girls dancing at the carnival, and on Sunday morning when I was playing the organ for tent-show evangelists at the other end of the carnival lot, I would see these same men sitting in the pews with their wives and children, asking God to forgive them and purge them of carnal desires. And the next Saturday night they'd be back at the carnival or some other place of indulgence. I knew then that the Christian church thrives on hypocrisy, and that man's carnal nature will out."[5]

The theatrical, circus side of the counterculture also expresses itself in the taste for tattoos and body piercings, which had their place in the culture of carnivals and big tops. Most of us see the body as something rented rather than owned: we inhabit it, and it changes and decays during our inhabitation, but we are not inclined to change it beyond a few minor corrections of cosmetic surgery and a change of decor, that is, wardrobe. But some people would disagree with this assessment.

To some extent, tattoos and piercings have moved in the last decade from the circumference to the center. They are, thus, only the latest example of a style migrating from the counterculture into the center, as long hair and tie-dyes had done a generation before. What had once been the exclusive adornment of sailors, bikers, and Maoris can now be found on Roseanne, Julia Roberts, and Christy Turlington, not to mention an entire generation of nice girls from suburbia. Furthermore, men who are not pirates or homosexuals can now pierce their ears, as well as much else. In each case, the presumptive point of the piercing or the tattoo is to stage an act of defiance, a protest, against the mores of the center, which are vaguely imagined to be stilted and ossified. In fact, this exercise manifests nothing more than the elasticity of the center and the ever-changing nature of conformity.

Precisely because of the center's partial co-opting of tattoos and piercings, there has emerged, as there always will, a vanguard that remains profoundly dissatisfied by these compromised bodily modifications. A fascinating book, *Modern Primitives*, examines the present interest in tattoos, piercings, and scarification. Though the book's title invokes the term body artists often apply to themselves, it is somewhat inapt since it conjures up people living off the land or in mud huts, whereas most of the practitioners of this odd subcult are very urbanized and dress in entirely Western, if somewhat funky, clothing.

Though most people have never heard of Fakir Musafar, there are certain circles in the East Village and in San Francisco where he is almost universally known. The authors of *Modern Primitives*, Andrea Juno and V. Vale, describe thus their first encounter with the man, in an Italian restaurant in 1982: "Dressed in an expensive business suit and tie, Fakir looked the part of a fifty-two-year old Silicon Valley advertising executive. But during the course of dinner he proceeded to remove his tie, insert a large bone through his nose and work two ⅜″ steel circlets into each earlobe, remarking, 'There—I feel *much* more comfortable.' Then he unbuttoned his white broadcloth shirt and inserted twin pearl-handled daggers into two holes in his chest, forming an open *V* pattern." One can interpret this transformation, before their very eyes, as an incarnated illustration of the precise boundaries between center and circumference.

Fakir Musafar is not merely chameleonic: he is virtually amphibious, able to inhabit the circumference and the center almost interchangeably, but never at the same time. The book reproduces a photograph of him in his office: on the phone, presumably closing some big deal, he seems the very image of the corporation man, pleasant looking, with regular features. Another image shows him hanging from a tree by two meat hooks attached to his nipples. In still another he has two eight-ounce weights and twelve four-ounce weights of lead sewn into his very chest. Among other forms of pain, he has laid himself on a bed of nails and a bed of blades and has hung from fleshhooks attached to about thirty hooks sewn into his body. He has "elongated [his] scrotum by slowly adding a series of metal rings," which is supposed to enhance one's sexual experience. As he confides in words reminiscent of those of Anton La Vay, "At a very early age I was aware that I was an alien; I didn't belong where I was. Whatever was natural, rational, and sensible to me was unnatural and repulsive to other people. From the very beginning I just didn't seem to fit."[6] This could almost serve as a credo for the counterculture.

What piercings are for Fakir Musafar, tattoos are for the late Michael Wilson, another fixture of the current counterculture, who goes by the name of Tattoo Mike in the Dick Ziggun Freak Show at Coney Island. Tattoos, for him, "signify a possible way of going through the looking glass for me to achieve a whole other frame of reference and to elicit experiences beyond the normal."[7] His reasons for getting tattooed all over his body differed, however, from those of earlier tattooed men in the circus and in freak shows. Whereas they emerged from working-class environments, there was something intellectualized, "collegiate," in Wilson's cosmetic alterations.

In this he is akin to many other recent recipients of tattoos, who have infused the art with a whole register of irony and New Ageism that had never been there in the past. For example, one tattoo artist who goes by the name of Manwoman claims to have had a dream that counseled him to rehabilitate the swastika from the evil esteem in which it is now almost universally held. Accordingly, he has covered his body all over with swastikas of every conceivable size and shape until they do indeed look fairly benign. "The symbol of the swastika," he explains, "has done nothing in itself— it's innocent. It's intrinsically just lines on paper, a graphic design that's found in all cultures all over the planet for thousands of years. So it's a question of educating the public about its tremendously complex, multicultural past."[8]

Allied to this almost narcissistic fascination with one's own body, as well as to the politicizing of the body in feminist and gay theory, is an attitude toward sex that is quite different from what it used to be. "Make love, not war" summed up the counterculture's attitude toward sex three decades ago. Love and war were seen as antithetical, and sex, which was more or less the same thing as love, was understood to be a pretty straightforward affair. What was rebellious in the counterculture's emphasis on sexual liberation was the fact that they were indulging in sex at all, in the face of a society that was still entrenched in the real or imaginary mores of an earlier generation that advocated extramarital chastity and abstinence.

But today, when the views of sex held by the counterculture of the sixties have been largely embraced by the center, the new counterculture has had to go farther afield in its desire to oppose that center. A far more strenuous form of rebellion had to be found, and was found, in such "alternative" forms of sexuality as coprophilia, pedophilia, and especially sadomasochism. The taste for S&M underscores how, through an alliance of Freudianism and Marxism—each individually antagonistic to the society of the center—sexuality has come to seem the expression of power relations, rather than of the touchy-feely togetherness of the sixties. Thus, instead of the Beatles, "I Wanna Hold Your Hand," which was radical enough back in 1964, we now have a hit single from Nine Inch Nails whose chorus goes: "Bow down before the one you serve."

And in place of sexual liberation we now have sexual exploration, the goal of which is to depart as far as possible from the presumed morals of the center. In the next chapter, on extremist tendencies in high culture, we will point to the sexual deviance, not to mention murderous sadism, of such novels as Bret Easton Ellis's *American Psycho* and A. M. Homes's *The End of Alice*. Though these are, of course, works of fiction, a similarly dark sentiment is conveyed in such midtown Manhattan S&M clubs as the Vault, Den of Iniquity, and Mistress Elizabeth's Dungeon, where many people come to witness and occasionally to participate in sadomasochistic demonstrations. Similarly, in one of the more talked-about social events to take place in the East Village this past year, the annual Black and Blue Ball, each person came dressed according to his or her S&M persona.

This same taste for violence and sex can be found as well in what has been called the Cinema of Transgression. This form of filmmaking warrants discussion in the context of the counterculture rather than of artistic expression not only because its artistic ambitions are almost nonexistent but because it surrenders all artifice to the aim of making what it sees as its point, which is to have fun and also to shock, in the most outlandish way possible, the mores of the center.

These highly amateurish films, which even revel in their rough-cut appearance, are usually comedies, though not always intentionally so. The sound quality is bad, the prints grainy, the acting graceless, and the plot simple. Drawing much of their inspiration from B films and low-brow culture of the fifties and sixties, their goal seems to be to assail the sensibilities of the center with the most gruesomely outlandish forms of sexual and criminal excess. Such titles as *Submit to Me Now* and *You Killed Me First* give a good idea of what these films are about. The latter film is an outlandish remake of film noir suspense, all blood and guts, rape and pillage. *Fingered*, by contrast, is little more than a single scene in which the well-known underground actress Lydia Lunch is being masturbated by a man. In the coyly titled *Sewing Circle*, another underground starlet, Kembra Pfahler, is having her labia sewn together—the procedure is not simulated but is actually taking place—by two other young women.

These four films are the works of Richard Kern, who is something of an underground institution in that he is known to almost everyone in the so-called counterculture and to almost no one outside of it. Nevertheless, even he has had a brief flirtation with the mainstream: the well-known art publisher Taschen brought out a series of his photographs, and a number of prominent rock groups, including the Breeders, had him make their videos. Thus are the most radical tastes subtly injected into the cultural mainstream. And yet Kern himself is dismayed by this process. "I was into [bondage] in my twenties . . . and now it's become so mainstream, bondage and fetish gear and all that stuff. . . . And it's become really boring, to me anyway. . . . I was totally into anarchy . . . the whole concept of anarchy and creating chaos to fuck everything up and make everything change faster. And what it's changed into is MTV, what it's changed into is the New World Order."[9]

Ultimately, however, he need not have worried that his vision of the world, like that of previous countercultures, would be stolen from him through assimilation to the center. The counterculture as it exists today is a truer counterculture than the first, because it holds almost no potential within itself to be assimilated into the mainstream. Aside from a few eccentric tastes and a whiff of attitude, it offers little that society really needs along the lines of the sexual liberation that the counterculture of the sixties was able to offer to the center. For the foreseeable future, then, the counterculture is likely to remain entirely marginalized, and one suspects that its devotees in the East Village wouldn't have it any other way.

10

EXTREMIST CULTURE

This is the age in which a conceptual artist cut a cow down the middle, shoved it into a vat of formaldehyde, and called it art. It is the age in which a highly fashionable and successful film depicted the torture and immolation of one man by another man dousing him with gasoline. It is also the age in which one well-regarded novelist depicted an obese middle-aged man sodomizing the corpse of a thirteen-year-old boy, and in which another acclaimed novelist depicted a sleek young man introducing a rat into the vagina of the woman he had just murdered. In every province of the arts, with the possible exceptions of poetry and dance, we see the same thing: an assault upon the morals of the center such as no other culture has ever leveled at itself with the same vigor and persistence.

Given the subjects that this book has treated thus far—racism, terrorism, and the threatened overthrow of governments—it may seem that anything as immaterial as film, literature, or painting would pale into insignificance. But insofar as such films and novels shape as well as reflect the perceptions of their audience, it would be hard to exaggerate their importance in creating that sense of malaise and lingering sadness that characterizes the present cultural moment. Through the daily accretion of image upon harrowed image and word upon profane word, through the endless repetition of the despairing laments of the suicidal Kurt Cobain in car radios and elevators and on MTV, through the sadomasochistic images of Joel-Peter Witkin insinuating themselves into rock videos, films, and advertising, we have allowed—indeed, invited—these apostles of despair to saturate our sense of reality.

Of course, it is possible to exaggerate culture's power to shape reality: happy people can hum the songs of Kurt Cobain because they like the melody, or they can watch the more sadomasochistic portions of *Reservoir Dogs* because, despite being good citizens, they enjoy being revolted on occasion. And yet these cultural artifacts, if they did nothing else, would be a graphic representation of how the present age chooses to see itself. The same blue sky shone and the same dark clouds lowered upon Caravaggio's Rome as upon Tiepolo's Venice. But the Baroque age to which Caravaggio belonged chose to see itself in a much more dramatic and tortured light than did the age of Tiepolo, the Enlightenment, in which serene order was supposed to reign. And our age is culturally closer in sensibility to the anguished, tenebristic Baroque than to the much maligned Enlightenment, except that our culture has gone further in the way of self-flagellation than any other culture before us.

The arts, by their very nature, have always tended toward extremity. Often in literature, painting, and cinema the unspeakable is spoken and the unimaginable is bodied forth. The arts challenge the center, exposing it to that which is outside the pale of polite society. For some reason it is part of the spiritual makeup of humankind that we do not mind being exposed to depictions of acts we would never either commit or endorse if we knew them to be true. Scanning the annals of art and literature, we find many cultures and ages that favored promiscuity and violence, just as many others favored chastity and complaisance. All cultural contexts can be interpreted, if we choose, as tending more toward one than the other. We discover a preference for the former in the tragedies of Aeschylus and Marlowe, in an anonymous Hellenistic depiction of the flaying of Marsyas and in Ribeira's horrific Baroque rendering of the same subject. Regarding sexual license, there are passages in the epigrams of the first-century poet Martial, as well as in the Renaissance satires of Aretino and the Restoration poems of the Earl of Rochester, beside which the most pornographic enormities of *Screw* magazine seem tame. Sometimes these impulses toward violence and sexuality even coincide with piety, as in the numerous homoerotic depictions of Saint Sebastian that preoccupied the artists of the mannerist age.

But over and above these native tendencies to extremity, modern culture, which we can date, if we choose, from Hugo's *Hernani* in 1830, from Berlioz's *Damnation of Faust* in 1846, or from Courbet's creation of Le Salon des Refusés in 1855, is a rebellious culture par excellence, whose strength and authority are seen to derive from the degree of its newness rather than of its conformity to preordained canons of taste. We expect and seem to want our artists to be rebellious, and it is very difficult today, perhaps impossible, to find a single important artist, director, or novelist who has achieved success by touting his obedience to the center. Ours is the age in which the misdirected dictum of Herbert Read is finally made flesh: "Art . . . is eternally disturbing, permanently revolutionary."[1] In the visual arts especially, from impressionism through symbolism, dada, the Bauhaus, surrealism, abstract expressionism, and conceptualism, we have witnessed one act of rebellion after another. Each of these movements has seemed to accept that the manifest destiny of art was to see how far one could go, how much one could get away with.

Throughout the march of modernism, from about 1875 to 1975, this rebelliousness appeared as an attempt to go ever further in formalism, starting with the dematerialization of the visual world in impressionism and ending in conceptualism with the dematerialization of the very art object itself. Today, increasingly, the imperative obedience to formal progress, as it was understood, no longer exists, but the rebelliousness remains. As though through a necessary reapportioning of energy, artists have transferred that same rebelliousness to a social program rather than to a merely formal one. And, since it is in the nature of the arts to accept no compromise, to take everything to its logical conclusion, what had previously been the purity of form has become, almost by default, a purity of rebellion. In fact, the conflict between center and circumference is so central to our art that you find it being played out in a thousand different shapes and forms in contemporary society. The conflict between center and circumference, usually in the interests of the latter, is now the constant underpinning of most of our "high" culture.

Though one sees this conflict played out in films as well as in the visual arts, it is nowhere more explicit than in recent literature. Three novels, *Try* by Dennis Cooper, *The End of Alice* by A. M. Homes, and Bret Easton Ellis's *American Psycho*, all of which were put out by mainstream publishers, epitomize this penchant for morbidity and violence, this relentless questioning of morality. The violence revealed in these works, however, is not the sort that we would have expected only a few years ago from what, for lack of a better term, we can call "quality literature." Generally speaking, there has been a dichotomy in our culture between pop-culture fiction and movies, which are violent and action-packed, and high-brow culture, which is "boring," that is, nothing much seems to happen in them.

This dichotomy, however, no longer holds true. Instead two very different forms of violence have emerged, a middle-brow violence and a high-brow violence. The first form is pretty much as it has always been, serving up Rambo and martial arts and Tom Clancy novels to audiences who delight in the uncomplicated vindication of truth, justice, and the American way. The other, newer form of violence, however, reacts against this first form of canned violence and canned morality, but that is only part of the story. More important, it implicitly opposes the liberal all-inclusiveness that has become the preferred attitude of the cultural center. In tacit acceptance of Herbert Read's dictum, this form of art attacks cultural liberalism not by rediscovering conservatism but by courting extremism, the cultural equivalent of radical leftism. It perceives, quite accurately in fact, that liberalism has become embraced by the center that once opposed it, and for this reason liberalism and related attitudes are now seen as fair game.

In the case of the three novels mentioned, several themes recur. Not only is there an emphasis on violence and on what the authors themselves would characterize as sexual perversity. More-

over, the implicit theme and purpose of these novels, as of the preponderance of "advanced" art at the present time, is an ongoing
process of obsessive demarcation of the boundaries between center
and circumference, between the artist as rebel and the public at
large as conformist.

To this end, all three novels use first-person narrative—*Try*
using it only occasionally. The authors seem to be speaking directly
to us, to be taking us into their confidence, whether we wish it or
not. We are supposed to be made uncomfortable by the implicit assertion that we and the protagonist are after all essentially alike, except that, whereas he is uninhibited, we are not. Thus, shortly before
the conclusion of Homes's *The End of Alice*, the child-molesting
protagonist addresses the reader directly. "While we're having this
moment of privacy, there's something I need to talk to you about,
something that needs settling between you and me. Direct address:
I'm talking to you, Herr Reader, realizing that it's not the usual
thing, knowing I'm not supposed to disassemble the invisible scrim
that separates us. . . . I am fully aware of what you've been doing
while you've been reading this—these are my pages you're staining
with your spunky splash . . . and despite the depths to which it disturbed, you were released."[2] A little later in the book, the narrator
becomes more explicit still. "I am no better or worse than you. A
conspiracy, a social construct supported by judge, jury and tattle-
tales, has put me away because I threaten them. I implore you not
to be such a scaredy-cat."[3]

The End of Alice tells the story of a notorious pedophile and
murderer. He is recalling his past perversions in a correspondence
with a young woman who considers him something of a role
model. Just as he is interested in preadolescent girls, so she is interested in preadolescent boys. The novel recounts her interest in
the twelve-year-old Matthew, whom she successfully seduces with
impunity, while the inmate recounts his own acts, culminating in
the murder of a young girl named Alice.

Because of the narrator's "sophisticated" tone, he is meant to
resemble Humbert Humbert, the protagonist of Vladimir Nabokov's
Lolita, a connection made clear in the blurbs by the poet Richard
Howard and the novelist Oscar Hijuelos. The comparison is inter-

esting primarily because of the difference it points up between the early sixties and the present. Whereas Nabokov's protagonist is meant to be seen as an amiable misfit, the protagonist of Homes's novel is intended to have a message, and an important one, about the hypocrisy of morality and society and so forth. And, although Nabokov's book is largely humanistic and, as the age required, largely "healthy," Homes seems to delight in "unhealthy" or perverse appetites. In one scene the young woman who corresponds with the prisoner recounts that she has seen three young boys, all "at that age of supreme softness where muscles waiting to bloom are coated in a medium-thick layer of flesh, highly squeezable. They were at the point where if someone were to take such a child, to roast or bake him, he would be most flavorful."[4]

Like much contemporary culture, this work is characterized by a casual Freudianism, in which everything, from the individual consciousness to the entire social fabric, is reduced to sublimated sexuality. The child molester, in whom these impulses cannot be sublimated, says at one point, "If I could have contained my feeling, if I could have channeled my libido into my career ... if I could have given myself a more familiar and well-accepted career, as many wonderful men have done, if I could have guided my prick instead of have been guided by it, I could have been a leader of men, a molder of morals. Who do you think gives us missiles and fighter planes? Frigates? Certainly not some fur-trapped pussy, that much is clear—they have no interest. Cock and balls, that's what it's all about, everyone knows. Why don't the candidates [for political office] just go ahead and drop their shorts so we can see for ourselves what they've got, who's the bigger, better man."[5]

If anything, an escalated taste for sexual perversity—once again, as the author himself would characterize it—marks Cooper's *Try*. Like Homes's, Cooper's perversity seems to come with a message, about the dithering falsehood of the mores and standards of the center. The book is intended for two groups of readers, homosexuals, specifically pedophiles, on the one hand, and "normal" people, on the other. The invidious word "normal" is used advisedly for the simple reason that the author himself seems implicitly to draw the distinction. His work is intended at one level to shock the center, but it is also for the consumption of the center. At the heart of the novel, therefore, there is an element of bad faith, whereby the author, in relating acts of almost inexpressible abjection, pretends to be as nonchalant as possible, and whereby the reader is invited to show his contemporaneity by not being at all disgusted or surprised by what he is reading.

In the opening scene we meet the protagonist Ziggy editing his 'zine, *I Apologize*, "A Magazine for the Sexually Abused." Though there has been, in recent years, a mounting outcry against child molestation, Cooper is ambiguous on this score, if not ambivalent. He has written a fantasy of sexual license in which those whom society would consider the victims of the act, the children, either seem to be passively yet wittingly acquiescent or are themselves fully complicit. Though there are many children in the novel, and, though they interact sexually with adults, there is little or no sense of family structure. Parents are either nonexistent or ersatz, like those of Ziggy, two homosexual men who adopted him and then forgot about him. Both of these men have sex with Ziggy in the course of the novel, while a third pedophile, Ziggy's Uncle Ken, spends all his time having sex with a thirteen-year-old boy named Robin.

Not only is pedophilia presented as the most natural thing in the world, but the abjection of coprophilia is offered up for our admiration. As one character prepares to sodomize his adopted son, he explains that "I inserted two trembling thumbs in the ass-crack and parted it gently, anticipating a noseful of faint spicey steam. But a strong smell of cloistered shit filled the intermediate area, throwing my awe into limbo. For while the nature of an ass more than interests me, my son's interior foulness asked of its scholars an almost inhuman diligence. Still, desire being what it is, I managed to wedge my face into the garrulous crack."[6]

Similarly, in the intense descriptions of sex between the overweight Uncle Ken and the frail Robin, things start to go awry when the latter forgets himself, until we find "around Robin's bare hips, thighs, the very first fringe of a creeping brown stain."[7] And when Robin dies of an overdose, jovial Uncle Ken proceeds to sodomize him further and to consider filming the corpse to make a good profit on the kiddie-porn circuit. Ordinarily a novel of this sort would end with the arrest of Uncle Ken, but to the author's credit—since he is not really interested in morality— he has resisted using this ploy as a fig leaf.

Despite such outrageous writings, however, there is something in the novels of Homes and Cooper that can be assimilated to the center of society. Their excesses are excused on the vague presumption of somehow empowering women and gays, and this empowerment endows them with at least the appearance of respectability, if not virtue. It is interesting to note that nothing of the sort can be said for Ellis's *American Psycho*. Perhaps this is because the book makes fun precisely of the center's attempts to assimilate those inhabitants of the margins. It perceives an element of bad faith in contemporary liberal discourse, and it is this perception that fuels the author's anger and excess.

The murderous and affluent protagonist, Patrick Bateman, takes political incorrectness to the point of psychosis. In one scene in a video store, he fails to attract the attention of an unresponsive saleswoman at the counter. "The things I could do to this girl's body with a hammer," he muses, "the words I could carve into her with an ice pick."[8] Another woman he deems "too ugly to rape." Soon thereafter he finds "a bum lounging below the *Les Misérables* poster and holding a sign that reads: I'VE LOST MY JOB I AM HUNGRY I HAVE NO MONEY PLEASE HELP, whose eyes tear after I pull the tease-the-bum-with-a-dollar trick and tell him, 'Jesus, will you get a fucking shave, *please*."[9] He is likewise entirely unenlightened about homosexuals. "The waiter, a not-bad-looking faggot, is at a loss and helplessly lisps an excuse."[10] He is even mean to animals, tossing coins into the seal pond at the Central Park zoo.

Allied to his misanthropy is a psychotic violence, which surpasses that of *Try* or *The End of Alice* and, in its determined perversity, has few parallels in even the most gruesome of mainstream films and television shows, despite their reputation for mayhem. The protagonist often brings women up to his apartment, where he invariably tortures and murders them. "Torri awakens to find herself tied up, bent over the side of the bed, on her back, her face covered with blood because I've cut her lips off with a pair of nail scissors. Tiffany is tied up with six pairs of Paul's suspenders on the other side of the bed, moaning with fear, totally immobilized by the monster of reality."[11] A few chapters later, before introducing a rat into a woman's vagina, he explains, "I'm wearing a Joseph Abboud suit, a tie by Paul Stuart, shoes by J. Crew, a vest by someone Italian and I'm kneeling on the floor beside a corpse, eating the girl's brain, gobbling it down, spreading Grey Poupon over hunks of the pink, fleshy meat."[12]

Though *American Psycho* represents little more than a private obsession with violence and abjection, the author cannot resist grasping for loftier themes, specifically those of terminal cynicism and disenchantment. Toward the end of the novel, for instance, he reflects, "Justice is dead. Fear, recrimination, innocence, sympathy, guilt, waste, failure, grief, [were] things, emotions, that no one really felt anymore. Reflection is useless, the world is senseless, Evil is its only permanence, God is not alive. Love cannot be trusted. Surface, surface surface, was all that anyone found meaning in. . . . This was civilization as I saw it, colossal and jagged."[13] A little later on he says, "Walking down Fifth Avenue around four o'clock in the afternoon, everyone on the street looks sad, the air is full of decay, bodies lie on the cold pavement, miles of it, some are moving, most are not. History is sinking and only a very few seem dimly aware that things are getting bad."[14]

The trends that are detectable in *American Psycho*, *Try*, and *The End of Alice*, those of violence, abjection, and despair, can be found almost as vigorously in film and in the visual arts. And yet cinema tends to be mainstream in a way that fiction is not: the number of people who read a fairly difficult novel is far smaller than the audience for an upscale film like the *Silence of the Lambs*. If novels examine and confirm a general malaise in our society, we can credit films with largely disseminating that malaise, despite the persistent belief that Hollywood always insists upon a happy ending. Even such big-budget mainstream films as *Seven* or *The Usual Suspects* end on a note of profoundly unsatisfying, not to say unsettling, irresolution.

Seven is a dark, grotesque film in which a serial killer, much like the protagonist of *American Psycho*, lashes out at the moral decay of society, except that, whereas the protagonist of *American Psycho* wishes merely to have fun, the killer in *Seven* believes that each of his murders—corresponding to each of the seven deadly sins—will somehow cleanse the world of its inveterate corruption. There is little sunlight in the film. It is constantly raining, and the streets are strewn with the dirt of overflowing sewers. Through the effective use of makeup and decor, the director admits us into a netherworld of prostitutes, addicts, and the grotesquely obese. Such scenes as these graphically detail that theme of abjection that recurs in so much contemporary fiction. It is the visual equivalent of a scene in *Try* in which "Calhoun is squatting in front of a toilet, the bowl and rim marbled with urine drops, the flesh dried to scabs, some embedded with pubic hairs."[15] It is the very same mood, incidentally, that recurs in the British film *Trainspotting*, where one of the characters, after entering the most foul public men's room imaginable, relieves himself into a filthy toilet bowl and then falls in.

The moral ambiguity of a film like *Seven* recalls the dark, crepuscular mood of the conclusion of *American Psycho*. Although Brad Pitt's character shoots the villain after receiving in a box the head of his, Pitt's, pregnant wife, the conclusion is clearly meant to deny us, the viewers, that all-important sense of closure that even unhappy endings can confer. We can take no pleasure in the sense that the bad guy has been destroyed or that the good guys have won. We are implicitly invited to believe that Kevin Spacey's character represents an evil at the heart of the world, which good people like those played by Brad Pitt and Morgan Freeman can vanquish individually but against whose collectivity they are ultimately powerless. In *The Usual Suspects*, as well, Kevin Spacey, who seems to have carved a niche for himself by playing mincing, well-spoken psychopaths, is revealed in the end to have been all along the satanic villain. And yet here again he is allowed to slip through the fingers of the police, having eluded their best efforts to find him.

Just as *The End of Alice*, which can be seen as a remake of *Lolita*, points up the shifting literary taste of the past four decades, so we can see a similar transformation in Martin Scorsese's remake of *Cape Fear*. The original film from 1954 told the story of a convicted rapist who has done his time in jail and resolves to destroy the life of the district attorney who put him away. This essential plot line remains as it was, but the tone has changed completely. The original film noir version, with Robert Mitchum as the villain, was admittedly somewhat harsh by the standards of Hollywood in the fifties. But it ended not only with the undoing of the villain but also with the defusing—so to speak—of his threat. This satisfaction is not to be had from the far darker version featuring Robert De Niro. His villain, Cady, is not merely bad—a designation that Hollywood understands well enough: he is evil, the incarnation of a malign force in the world. To give him complexity he is rooted in religion—he is described at one point as a "Pentecostal cracker," and his body is tattooed with Mariological symbols, which recall Kevin Spacey's spiritual preoccupation in *Seven*. But religion itself, so far from supplying solace in a chaotic world, is the medium by which evil is played out. In every way, De Niro's version extends beyond Mitchum's realization. He is uglier, more violent, more powerful, more malignly intelligent, and more insane than was allowed or even imagined in the cinema of the 1950s.

In its resurrection of fifties film noir, with all its violence and aggravated perversity, Scorsese's movie brings to mind the works of Quentin Tarantino. This director achieved considerable fame with *Pulp Fiction*, which, although extremely violent, was essentially a comedy whose morbidity had little moral pretension to it, except of the sort that insisted that violence could be fun. But the film upon which his reputation was founded, *Reservoir Dogs*, is hardly a comedy, and it is far more disturbing. Diehard fans of Tarantino not only prefer the earlier film to *Pulp Fiction* but see the latter, because it was more light-hearted and more successful, as something of a sellout. *Reservoir Dogs* is a less pleasant movie than the one that followed it, not because it is violent, for it shares that quality with *Rambo*, but because it seems to have no point other than violence and cruelty and because it does not even bother to pretend to have one, as the Rambo movies do and as their viewers seem to require. One has seen images of torture in film many times before, but never with the unsparing, disabused point-blankness of

Reservoir Dogs. In one especially lurid scene, an ostensibly pleasant, "normal-looking" male character douses his seated, tied-up
victim with gasoline before setting him on fire. As he tortures the
victim, he sings to him and jokes with him.

It is not surprising that this same mood that is so prevalent in
contemporary cinema and fiction should also have begun to enter
painting, sculpture, and installation art. The art world has changed
in the last five years, which is to say that certain tendencies that
were always there have become more prominent, while others that
were paramount until very recently have receded once again. Only
a few years ago, political art, shrill and vociferous, could be found
in all the major galleries. Today, by contrast, politics seems largely
to have played itself out, and a more spiritualized art has taken its
place, one whose terms are violent and often grotesque. Typical of
the new trend is the prominence now given to such admittedly
older performance pieces as the one in which Mike Kelley, vaguely
alluding to dysfunctional children and adults, defecates onto
stuffed animals. His coprophiliac meditations extend to banners
that read PANTS SHITTER AND PROUD. P.S. I JERK OFF TOO. Meanwhile,
Catherine Opie, a portly lesbian performance artist, razorblades
obscenities like PERVERT onto her back, allowing the word, etched
in blood, to coagulate before the camera that immortalizes this particular act of provocation.

More often and more recently, however, this morbid impulse
takes the form of an interest in science and anatomy. A good example is the works of Damien Hirst, a British artist who has
achieved fame by cutting a whole cow into sections and exhibiting
the parts in formaldehyde-filled tanks that permit one to see the
unaltered anatomical parts. Hirst, however, is representative of a
trend in which no one has gone further than Joel-Peter Witkin. His
recent Guggenheim retrospective signaled, as strongly as one could
wish, his arrival at the forefront of contemporary visual culture.
Witkin is without question one of the most gifted and inventive of
contemporary photographers, and it is unlikely that anyone who
has looked at one of his images will soon forget the experience.
Working primarily in black-and-white gelatin prints, he creates pas-
tiches of Victorian photography. The standing joke is that, whereas

those earlier works were primly moralistic, in Witkin's case the same tone is invoked to convey subjects that are patently, aggressively obscene.

And yet, aside from the occasional image of a person fornicating with a dog, these images are not pornographic. Rather the willful obscenity of these images consists in their studied moral perversity, their desire to test all standards for no other reason, apparently, than for the sheer perverse pleasure of doing so. It is finally the antic fun of his antinomianism that revolts the more thoughtful viewer. Usually immoralists are deadly serious about their immorality. If they go to such lengths as they do, it is for weightier reasons than mere sport. That Witkin appears to be laughing at the freaks and corpses he photographs seems about as close to sacrilege as our secular society is able to come.

Witkin is a teratologist, fascinated by all the grotesque irregularities of nature. He delights in depicting Siamese twins joined at the head, dwarfs, and amputees missing the entire lower part of their bodies. In one work titled *Three Graces*, we see the familiar classical configuration, but the standing figures have both breasts and penises. In other more recent works, he has photographed corpses in a morgue in Lyon. What is so shocking about these latter works—a headless man touching his penis, the head of another man spliced in two with each half set opposite to the other so that it looks as though two identical twins are French kissing—is the absurd jocularity of it all, the willingness to make pointless, senseless fun of the corpses of those who had once been living, thinking human beings.

Though the art of Joel-Peter Witkin is of an "adults only" variety, as are the other cultural artifacts discussed in this chapter, nevertheless it shares with them an almost childish fascination with that which society at large refuses to acknowledge openly: naughtiness, freaks, corpses, sexual deviancy. And it is tempting to draw a parallel between the concerted acts of cultural rebellion that we have been discussing and the one act of rebellion of which children are really capable, drawing attention constantly to what their elders would have them conceal: feces, genitalia, bodily fluids. The desire to "gross out" their audience is a childish aim, just as the desire to

discuss sex is an adolescent aim. Surely the artists under consideration will impute a loftier purpose to what they do, but one could
probably make a good case that the difference between these artists'
rebellion and the rebellion of children is one of degree rather than
of kind.

This association with childhood or adolesence underscores a
larger societal trend in which adulthood itself is under attack. Since
the sixties, youth and its accouterments have asserted such a hold
on the imagination of centrist society that even those who are well
beyond youth elect, in their hairstyles and their lifestyles, in their
clothing and their speech, to seek the aura and prestige of youth culture. This is quite a different thing from the desire, nearly universal,
to stay young or youthful in appearance. The grandfatherly Rolling
Stones, pushing sixty but still wearing love beads and tank-tops, are
merely the preeminent example of this trend. Such prolongation of
youth is in direct contrast to, and direct rebellion against, the culture of the postwar period, in which even adolescents, as we see
them in their yearbook photographs, tried to appear prematurely
adult, even middle-aged.

Aside from this undeniably sophomoric element in much of
contemporary culture that we have been discussing, there is a further, more entrenched problem at the heart of its assault on the
center. This art differs from other forms of extremism examined in
this book because it represents, in one sense, the rebellion not of
the circumference against the center but of the center against itself.
This art has been created for the edification or at least the amuse-
ment of the center by those who are desperate to appear outside
the center. Most of the other forms of extremity detailed in this
book—neo-Nazism, anarchism, radical feminism—are carried out
by those who are situated outside of the center and are acting at
the expense of the center. Usually they are rewarded for their efforts by being reviled or ignored. In art, literature, and film, by
contrast, the extremist behavior to which we are constantly being
exposed is intended for our consumption, for the consumption of
the center.

But, at the risk of complicating things more than may seem
necessary, it should be said that the center—or part of the center—

patronizes this sort of art because the very idea of the "center," with all that it implies of conformity and compromise, has lost so much prestige since the sixties that it goes in search of rebelliousness to persuade itself that it is not really the center at all. You can tell a lot about a society from its blurbs, those little tags that publishers put on book covers in the interests of moving as much merchandise as possible. They are the voice of the center speaking to itself. They say what needs to be said if the commodity in question is to be purchased. And what would it take to sell *The End of Alice*, a tale of gratuitous murder and child molestation? This book, we learn from one blurb, "sneaks us in the back doors of our upright suburban neighborhoods to reveal the impulses that even in our frank, outspoken times we don't talk about." Another blurb tells us we will be taken, "into the veneer of middle-class convention—the tennis lessons, baby sitting, and family dinners," etc. etc. In still a third we learn that "normalcy is a charade for the suburban girl who begins a dangerous flirtation," etc., etc. In other words, the selling point of this novel is its "blowing the lid off" middle-class, mainstream, suburban convention. Which is to say that rebellion sells, not just in *The End of Alice* but in the sculptures of Damien Hirst, the morgue photographs of Joel-Peter Witkin, and the films of Quentin Tarantino. Which is also to say that rebellion against the center has become one of the fixtures of the center, and thus, in the final analysis, it is really no rebellion at all.

11

THE BENEFITS OF EXTREMISM

Ours has been by all accounts a harsh and dangerous century. And now, as it finally winds down, one suspects that very few people will be sorry to see it go. Certainly each of us will savor a decade here or there and wish to rescue it from oblivion. But mostly we will be more than happy to be done with this violent age, to make a fresh start of things.

You could almost be excused for thinking that this century had dragged on longer than any other, that its leaden years, freighted with gloom, had passed more slowly than they usually do. Of course, one can never be entirely certain just how the citizens of earlier centuries experienced the passage of the decades. But the idea is not so far-fetched when you consider, first, that our attention span has gotten far shorter than it was, so that a hundred years seems longer to us than to earlier generations; and, second, that change and innovation have occurred with a speed that has no parallel in earlier experience. Indeed, it is fair to say that this is the first time that the world, as opposed to a few cities, looked substantially different at the close of the century from the way it had at the inception.

If one had to capture the mood of the century in five images or fewer, most of them, one suspects, would be gray scenes of carnage and ecological devastation, of outraged humanity beset by merciless overlords. There would be images of bloodshed and ever-escalating wars, unrest in the First World, totalitarianism in the Second, and famine in the Third. Surely there have been some consolations in the past few years: the end of apartheid, for example, and the deliverance of Eastern Europe from the Communist yoke. Someone might also wish to include an image of Elvis or the Summer of Love. And yet, overwhelmingly, this age has been *experienced* by those who have lived through it as a difficult and inhospitable time for the human race. One could point out that the sun shone as brightly on our age as on any other—often more brightly, in fact, if we are to believe certain paleoclimatologists. But this knowledge can neither efface a tangible, lingering sense of the unpleasantness of it all nor dampen our desire finally to move on.

Whether it has been, in fact, a harsher century than any other is subject to debate. Nevertheless, here is one of those instances in which the perception is almost as important as the reality. It is unlikely that the citizens of the nineteenth century, as they bore witness to its passing away, would have been as impressed by its hardships or its brutality—though it surely had enough of both—as by the glory of its cultural achievements and the strength and prosperity it had achieved in war and commerce. The men of the eighteenth century, for their part, felt they inhabited a *siècle de lumières*, a century of lights, the sense of whose halcyon sweetness not even the violence of the French Revolution, at its close, could fundamentally disturb. We should have to go further back than that, to the seventeenth, sixteenth, and fourteenth centuries, in order to encounter an age that, in the degree of its carnage and social upheaval, can hold a candle to our own.

And yet, what really happened in the twentieth century? The question is so big that one might be astonished at how small the answer needs to be. This was the century in which technology first saturated the world. At the beginning of the century, technology played hardly any role in the lives of a race that remained almost entirely agrarian. Even city dwellers were only beginning to feel the influence of electric street lamps, telephones, and automobiles. The material appointments of existence, the clothes they wore and the houses they inhabited, had as yet little to do with technology's direct involvement in everyday life. Surely fashions had changed many times over in the course of the century. But the inhabitants of Paris in 1900 were not substantially more "electric" than the citizens of Rome under Augustus.

The entire history of the present century proceeds from this technological advance. It was technology that made possible those two world wars, compared with whose violence the most sanguinary campaigns of Alexander, Pompey, Louis the XIV, and even Napoleon—excepting, perhaps, the Russian campaign—would seem like mere skirmishes. The totalitarian regimes of Soviet Russia and Nazi Germany were the consequence, quite possibly inevitable, of such new means of communication as cinema, radio, the telephone, and loudspeakers, all presupposing a technology that had been lacking in earlier times. Urban agglomerations and the decay of agrarian society were the consequence of automobiles, mechanized farming, and revolutionary advances in engineering, such as skyscrapers. The twentieth century, then, was the century in which mechanized technology directly entered our lives.

But something else has happened in this century, something that was the consequence both of technology and of the general Enlightenment philosophy that had been in large measure responsible for technological advance in the first place. I am speaking of that increasing homogenization of peoples and cultures, that process of gathering discrete entities into a greater whole, which has been going on since the beginning of history but has been greatly accelerated in our time.

In this century such homogenization has been accomplished in several ways. First, those differences between people that had resulted from the lack of contact between them have been conquered. Before the dawn of mass communications, the Turk read the Koran, the Englishman read Shakespeare, and the Hindu read the Mahabarata. Today, they are all watching reruns of *Dallas*. Now *Dallas* has not yet abolished differences between cultures. But it has created, at very least, the context in which all people are brought into contact with the same messages. Second, homogeneity has been fostered by the vast improvement and acceleration of transportation. One sees this in the food we eat: apples from New York orchards can be purchased in New York and California, and California oranges can be purchased in California and New York. Airplanes have made travel much easier and, relatively, much less expensive than their premodern equivalents. As a result, many of us have seen far more of the world than we could in the past, when most people never ventured more than twenty miles in any direction from the place of their birth. And when we arrive where we are going, whether Oregon or Virginia, Buenos Aires or Beijing, chances are we will find waiting for us a McDonald's and a Burger King that are identical to what we know at home.

In contemporary discourse, the two things that are most often commented on and lamented are the seemingly inevitable processes of homogenization, on the one hand, and of the fracturing of society, on the other. We see this divisiveness not only at the national level, most spectacularly in the former Yugoslavia, but also in the escalating racial tensions between blacks and whites and between Arabs and Jews. We observe it in the mutual incomprehension between men and women and between conservative Christians and an increasingly secular society. More grievous, these divisions have forced into public awareness the extreme elements of each faction, and it is this sense of incessant fissure and rampant extremism that contributes directly to that malaise that afflicts our society at the present time.

That we are witnessing a proliferation of extremes, is, of course, the thesis behind the present book. And it cannot be denied that these extremes have achieved a variety and a prominence in our thoughts that are without parallel in the earlier history of our society. The constant, unrelenting threat to the center, in all its manifestations, has been debated on every talk show and news magazine, in every pulpit and op-ed page, in the supermarket tabloids, on the Internet, and in the homes of honorable citizens across America, as well as abroad. The sense that the world is coming to pieces, that it is going crazy, is surely one of the primary components of the nervousness and unease that characterize our culture at this time. From every direction we hear predictions that fill us with deep foreboding for a future that suddenly appears even more menacing than our recent past. The twenty-first century, if we can believe the pundits, will be even more dystopian than the twentieth century has been.

That at least is the received idea on the subject, the dominant conviction of the center at this time. But if we examine this notion with a clear head, we will find that *precisely the contrary is true.* We find that, in fact, *we are living at a time of greater harmony than ever before, one in which the extremes, as they are conceived, have mostly dwindled to the point of extinction before the victorious inclusiveness of an ever-expanding center.* Whereas Western society seemed far more stable and ordered in earlier ages than today, that was only an appearance, and one that several factors conspired to produce. It is not, for example, the least difference between this and earlier ages that our diversities are magnified even when they are minor, whereas in earlier ages diversity, whether at the personal or societal level, tended to be concealed under a general pall of sameness. Thus the reason there now seem to be both more homosexuals and more opposition to them than in the past is that homosexuality is no longer hidden as it once was. From the other side, as we have seen in the case of certain gay activists, it is precisely the notion of homosexual assimilation to the center, more even than the imputed intolerance of the center, that is the real object of their fear.

Likewise, the reason there appears to be so much tension between black and white Americans is emphatically not, as many civil rights leaders and many people in the media opportunistically believe, that the racial divide is greater than before. The contrary is true. The races are no longer separated as they once were, and this new proximity sometimes occasions a friction that would have been impossible in the past, only because segregation was so strictly enforced. Through an allied impulse, our sensitivity to any breath of racism is so heightened that what would have been an everyday occurrence fifty years ago—say, the use of the word "nigger"—has now become so rare and so fraught with meaning that the entire O. J. Simpson case, the Trial of the Century, may fairly be said to have turned on whether a Los Angeles police detective had or had not spoken that word even once within the previous ten years. Much the same process of assimilation can be found regarding women, Jews, and others who are seen as minorities.

The appearance of rampant extremism is greatly abetted by the media. By its very nature, the evening news, that most deceptive of enterprises, falsifies reality, whether knowingly or otherwise. If we had no other source of information, and if we implicitly believed everything we learned from it, we should imagine, given the incessant reports of violence, rape, and child molestation, that we were living in a state of murderous and amoral anarchy. The reasons for this falsification are fundamental. Reporters must cover something: aside from an event of obvious importance that demands coverage, they are certain to choose those topics that are most likely to engage the interest of their audience. More important, one obviously does not report every time a plane lands safely, only when it has crashed or been hijacked. Similarly, one recounts tales not of racial harmony, which is the rule, but rather of violent disharmony, which is relatively rare. The inevitable result is that many in the population will soon accept that planes are always crashing and that the races have never been so much at odds. And thus, without denying the existence of racism and of racist acts, we must acknowledge that they are far rarer, if more widely covered, than ever before, despite what the media would allow us to believe.

Also at play in such coverage is the almost subconscious desire of many in the center constantly to reassure themselves of their centrality. They do this by focusing on aberrations in behavior, through sensationalism and a desire to massage that part of the collective psyche that is nervous about the degree of its being normal. This is one of the essential roles played by talk television, the sort that routinely parades before the American public a motley procession of transsexuals, pedophiles, spousal abusers, and all the rest. From this perspective, the more idiotically outlandish and sensationalistic such programs are, the greater the social purpose they serve. Who would have thought that the tenth, even the fiftieth consecutive program devoted to the lurid details of incest and child molestation might, despite its manifest exploitation of human folly and frailty, have an invaluable role to play in our society?

And yet such programs as these do the unwitting work of the center, constantly reassuring the center that it is indeed the center, by bringing it into contact with those extremes, with that circumference, by whose activity alone the center can define itself. Such programs contribute greatly to a sense of rampant decadence in our society and are routinely scoffed at by high-brows for their sensationalism and immorality. In fact, for all their vulgarity, these shows are one of the most powerful moral agents in recent years. In each program and at each moment of each program, the anxieties of the center are being allayed until it emerges strengthened from this ordeal of confrontation.

But there is something else going on. Centrist society, which is the result of a long evolution, is still—in generational terms—so new that most people over the age of forty can well remember a time when things were much different, when racism was out in the open and there was nothing in the least shameful about it. Because this society is so new, we are still finding our balance in it. We presume to expect that the process of assimilation should be complete by now, and we are consistently dismayed to discover that it is not. What results is a great nervousness concerning this process of assimilation, and the logical consequence of such nervousness is a political correctness that presumes to extirpate from language and thought any tremor of contrarianism.

Indeed, the entire centrist establishment can be shaken to its foundations by the minutest inadvertence. How else can we explain such rash overreactions as the firing of Jimmy "the Greek" Snyder from network sports broadcasting because of his injudicious comments about black swimmers being more buoyant than whites? What was really happening on that occasion was that the management of ABC, whatever they really felt about his comments, had to go through the motions of outrage to satisfy their public, which itself was largely going through the motions of outrage. It is this bad faith, this sanctimonious artifice near to, but not actually at, the heart of the center, that the extremist exploits to his own advantage. The problem is not that the center is racist but that it is constantly having to act, as indeed it is, not racist. At times the result of having to maintain this appearance is an almost incapacitating loss of nerve.

Of course, to assert that the center is more powerful and more all-embracing than ever before is not to deny for a moment that extremist movements exist and will continue, in all probability, to proliferate. And yet it helps to place them in perspective, and especially to understand what has caused them to come about and flourish in the first place. As has been said, the overwhelming thrust of centrist society in the past fifty years and more has been the assimilation of those whom it once marginalized. In the United States at this time, men and women of all races work side by side. This passes without comment for the most part, and it is becoming only more prevalent with each day. And yet *the more inclusive the center becomes, the more raucous and extreme become those voices that would resist this assimilation.*

There are several reasons for this. The very process by which the center overruns the circumference and assimilates what had been left out of the center forces extreme voices, through the sheer imperative of resistance, to become still more extreme. In part, this is because all of the more moderate voices have been gathered into the greater collectivity of society, leaving only the most diehard fanatics, the lunatic fringe, behind. Those who join such a group at this point are apt to do so not because it offers some tangible and philosophical satisfaction that they need but because they wish to distinguish themselves in the most emphatic way possible from that center, which they detest for reasons that probably have more to do with their own psyches than with any political and social trends. The resulting shrillness is taken as proof that our society is falling apart. In fact it is the direct result of an ever greater cohesion.

We find this process at work at the international level as well. Globally, society is in the process of becoming more centralized, at least in the First World. On an economic front we see this in the creation of NAFTA and GATT, and politically in the European Community and the greatly enhanced role of the United Nations in world events. The joining of almost all the industrialized powers against Iraq in the Gulf War is evidence of this conflict between the center and the extreme raised to an international level.

But such growing assimilation at the international level, which has proceeded apace with the integration of the various factions within a given society and nation, is not more complete at the macrocosmic level than at the microcosmic one. Just as many extremists in our own cities are the outgrowth of earlier and unresolved conflicts, so there is still much work to be done before Europe will truly be united under a single banner and a single currency, before Serbs and Croats and Muslims will learn to live peaceably together.

Now many observers, even if they are by no means extremists, may yet take fright at this growing ascendancy of the center over the fringe. One inevitably conjures up images from Orwell and the totalitarian past. Yet all of that was the reality of the modern age rather than the postmodern age that we inhabit now. The information revolution, by bringing people together, will inevitably efface much, but not all, of the inflections and diversity of human life. At the same time, however, it will enhance, according to the bent of each person's bias, a sense of connectedness to those who share his taste or attitudes and of difference from those who do not. What is likely to result is not, as in the past, an ever greater splintering of society but rather a wealth of diversity within a context of a common interest and a common culture.

No amount of centralization, however, will ever completely extirpate from society the corrupt element that extremists represent. First of all, as has been stated, extremists today tend to oppose the center precisely because it is seen to be the center, and because they wish to stand at variance with the center. Second, if it were ever possible to accomplish such a reordering of our society—and that is highly doubtful—it would be done at far greater cost to civil liberties than postmodern societies would probably be willing to pay.

The great work of the next few generations will doubtless be to find some balance between this pull of homogeneity and the relentless fracturing of society into ever more specialized groups. What seems certain is that, as the extreme voices discussed in this book become ever more marginalized, they will also become more shrill. But it is also likely that, through its encounter with these extreme voices, the center will arrive at a stronger and more confident sense of its identity than it had before. The constant challenge that the extremes mount against the values of the center will ultimately leave the center more firmly in possession of those values that it truly prizes. But we must not expect, perhaps we should not even desire, that the voices of extremism can be silenced forever, or even briefly. For these voices, representing an ineradicable flaw in the human makeup, define for us the center of our moral and intellectual homing, all the while standing in the way of that ultimate perfection to which humanity is coming ever closer, and which it will never fully attain.

NOTES

Chapter 1 The Dismay of American Society

1. N. R. Kleinfeld, "Frosty Daffodils, Then 96 Degrees, All in the Scary Month of May," *New York Times*, May 21, 1996, Sec. A, p. 1.
2. Ibid.
3. Robert Lipsyte, "Coping: From Franco to Imus, An Activist's Long View," *New York Times*, April 28, 1996, Sec. 13, p. 1.
4. Bret Easton Ellis, *American Psycho* (New York: Vintage Books, 1991), 384.
5. Louis Uchitelle, N. R. Kleinfield, *The Downsizing of America* (New York: Times Books, 1996), 16.
6. Ibid., 5.
7. Ibid., 6.
8. Ibid., 20.
9. Jean Baudrillard, in *Selected Writings*, ed. Mark Poster (Stanford, Calif.: Stanford University Press, 1988), 171.
10. Quoted in *Commentary*, November 1995, 50.
11. Francis X. Clines, "Mrs. Clinton Calls Sessions Intellectual, Not Spiritual," *New York Times*, June 25, 1996, Sec. A, p. 13.

Chapter 2 Center and Circumference

1. Michael Winerip, "Ohio Case Triggers Tensions Between Militia Groups and Law," *New York Times*, June 23, 1996, Sec. 1, p. 1.
2. Norman Cohn, *The Pursuit of the Millenium* (New York: Oxford University Press, 1970), 148.
3. Ibid., 154.
4. Ibid., 306.

Chapter 3 The Radical Right

1. David H. Bennett, *The Party of Fear* (New York: Vintage Books, 1995), 445.

2. Ibid., 354.

3. Ibid., 355.

4. Kenneth S. Stern, *A Force Upon the Plain* (New York: Simon & Schuster, 1996), 186.

5. Bennett, op. cit., 433.

6. John George and Laird Wilcox, *American Extremists* (Amherst, N.Y.: Prometheus Books, 1996), 323.

7. Bennett, op. cit., 349.

8. Ibid., 436.

9. Mark Hamm, *American Skinheads* (London: Praeger, 1993), 42.

10. Ibid., 10.

11. Ibid., 63.

12. James William Gibson, *Warrior Dreams* (New York: Hill and Wang, 1993), 13.

13. Bennett, op. cit., 353.

14. Stern, op. cit., 26.

15. Ibid., 27.

16. Ibid.

17. Ibid., 64.

18. Ibid., 109.

19. Ibid., 111.

20. Ibid., 116.

21. Peter G. Kokalis, "Parabellum in Your Pocket," *Soldier of Fortune*, February 1996, 61.

22. Bennett, op. cit., 457.

23. Stern, op. cit., 137.

24. Paul Hockenos, *Free to Hate* (New York: Routledge, 1993), 75.

25. Ibid., 90.

26. Ibid.

27. Ibid.

28. Ibid., 87.

29. Ibid.

30. Ibid., 54.

31. Ibid., 60.

32. Ibid., 88.

33. Walter Laqueur, *Black Hundred* (New York: HarperCollins, 1993), 63.

34. Ibid., 208.

35. Ibid., 247.

218

NOTES

36. Ibid., 210.
37. Bennett, op. cit., 432.
38. Laqueur, op. cit., 208.
39. Ibid., 204.
40. Ibid., 211.
41. Ibid., 216.
42. Ibid., 255.
43. Ibid., 256.

Chapter 4 The Far Right in America and Beyond

1. James Bennet, "Candidate's Speech Is Called Code for Controversy," *New York Times*, Sunday, Feb. 25, 1996, Sec. 1, p. 22.
2. David H. Bennett, op. cit., 393.
3. Ibid., 396.
4. Ibid., 398.
5. Ibid., 394.
6. Ibid., 390.
7. Anti-Defamation League, *From Columnist to Candidate* (New York: 1992), 18.
8. Ibid.
9. William F. Buckley Jr., "In Search of Anti-Semitism," *National Review,* Dec. 30, 1991, p. 40.
10. Richard Lacayo, "The Case Against Buchanan," *Time*, March 4, 1996, p. 29.

Chapter 5 The Extremism of the Left

1. Harvey Klehr, *Far Left of Center* (New Brunswick, N.J.; Transaction Books, 1988), 93–94.
2. *Revolutionary Worker*, July 5, 1993, 5.
3. Quoted in George Woodcock, *Anarchism* (New York: Meridian Press, 1956), 87.
4. Joel Olson, "The History of Chinese Anarchism," *Love and Rage*, November–December 1995, 4.
5. Mark Dery, *Escape Velocity* (New York: Grove Press, 1996), 38.
6. Christopher Day, "Million Men," *Love and Rage*, op. cit., 17.

Chapter 6 The Extremes of Virtue

1. Dinesh D'Souza, *The End of Racism* (New York: Free Press, 1995), 387.

2. Ibid., 366.
3. Ibid., 363.
4. Ibid., 365.
5. Anti-Defamation League, *Jew-Hatred As History* (New York: 1993), 10.
6. Ibid., 7.
7. Ibid., 6.
8. Anti-Defamation League, *The Other Face of Farrakhan* (New York: 1994), 4.
9. Ibid., 3.
10. Ibid.
11. *Jew-Hatred As History*, 7.
12. Andrea Dworkin, *Intercourse* (New York: Free Press, 1988), p. 194.
13. Catharine A. MacKinnon, *Only Words* (Cambridge: Harvard University Press, 1993), 3.
14. Ibid., 28.
15. Ibid., 37.
16. MacKinnon, *Towards a Feminist Theory of the State* (Cambridge, Mass.: Harvard University Press, 1989), 127.
17. Katie Roiphie, *The Morning After* (Boston: Little, Brown, 1993), 154.
18. Ibid., 40.
19. Ibid., 41.
20. Ibid.
21. Ibid.
22. Bruce Bawer, *A Place at the Table* (New York: Simon and Schuster, 1993), 152.
23. Ibid.

Chapter 7 The Fringes of Religion

1. James Boswell, *Life of Johnson* (Oxford: Oxford University Press, 1929), vol. 1, 265.
2. Bennett, op. cit., 329.
3. Ibid., 380–81.
4. Ibid., 416.
5. Ibid., 418.
6. John L. Esposito, *The Islamic Threat* (New York: Oxford University Press), 125.
7. Ibid., 138.
8. Anti-Defamation League, *Extremism in the Name of Religion*, update (New York: 1995), 16.
9. Ibid., 2.

10. Ibid., 12.

11. Ibid., 10.

12. Anti-Defamation League, *Extremism in the Name of Religion* (New York: 1994), 11.

13. Ibid., 9.

14. Ibid., 10.

15. Ibid., 13.

16. Ibid.

17. Margot Adler, *Drawing Down the Moon* (Boston: Beacon Press, 1981), 152.

18. Marc Galanter, *Cults* (New York: Oxford University Press, 1989), 51.

19. Ibid., 52.

20. Roger A. Dean, *Moonies, A Psychological Analysis of the Unification Church* (New York: Garland Publishing, 1992), 106.

21. Galanter, op. cit., 133.

Chapter 8 The Age of Doubt

1. Allan Bloom, *The Closing of the American Mind* (New York: Simon & Schuster, 1987), 25.

2. Stanley Aronowitz, "The Politics of the Science Wars," *Social Text* 46–47, 192.

3. Ibid., 178.

4. Ruth Hubbard, "Gender and Genitals: Constructs of Sex and Gender," ibid., 158.

5. Alan D. Sokal, "Transgressing the Boundaries: Toward a Transformative Hermeneutics of Quantum Gravity," ibid., 218.

6. Ibid., 217.

7. Raymond A. Eve and Francis B. Harrold, *The Creationist Movement in Modern America* (Boston: Twayne Publishers, 1991), 31.

8. Ibid.

9. Ibid.

10. Ibid., 149.

11. Ibid.

12. Ibid., 157.

13. Mark Bourne, Lunar Lunacy (website), http://www.sff.net/people/mbourne/weirdnessideas1.htp

14. Ibid.

15. Arthur Schlesinger Jr., "History As Therapy: A Dangerous Idea," *New York Times*, May 3, 1996, Sec. A, p. 31.

16. Ibid.

17. Deborah Lipstadt, *Denying the Holocaust* (New York: Free Press, 1993).

18. Anti-Defamation League, *Anger on the Right*, (New York: 1991), 5.
19. Lipstadt, op. cit., 179.
20. Ibid., 81.
21. Jean Baudrillard, *The Gulf War Did Not Take Place,* trans. Paul Patton (Indiana University Press, 1995), 23.
22. Ibid., 24.
23. Ibid., 27.
24. Ibid., 61.

Chapter 9 The Remains of the Counterculture

1. Adam Parfrey, ed., *Apocalypse Culture* (New York: Feral Press, 1990), 358.
2. Michelle Handelman and Monte Cazazza, "The Cereal Box Conspiracy Against the Developing Mind," in Parfrey, ibid., 197.
3. V. Vale and Andrea Juno, eds., *Modern Primitives* (San Francisco: Re/Search Publications, 1989), 95.
4. Anton Szandor LaVey, *The Satanic Bible* (New York: Avon, 1969), 25.
5. Ibid., 12.
6. V. Vale and Andrea Juno, op. cit., 6.
7. Ibid., 38.
8. Ibid., 48.
9. Jack Sargeant, *Deathtripping: The Cinema of Transgression* (London: Creation Books, 1995), 111.

Chapter 10 Extremist Culture

1. Herbert Read, *Art and Alienation* (New York: Viking Press, 1967), 24.
2. A. M. Homes, *The End of Alice* (New York: Scribner, 1996), 186.
3. Ibid., 188.
4. Ibid., 22.
5. Ibid., 53.
6. Dennis Cooper, *Try* (New York: Grove Press, 1994), 112.
7. Ibid., 88.
8. Bret Easton Ellis, *American Psycho* (New York: Vintage Books, 1991), 112.
9. Ibid., 113.
10. Ibid., 215.
11. Ibid., 304.
12. Ibid., 328.
13. Ibid., 375.
14. Ibid., 384.
15. Cooper, op. cit., 49.

ACKNOWLEDGMENTS

Though many people have helped me in the course of my writing this book, I would like first and foremost to thank my editor, Hillel Black, for suggesting to me in the first place that I write it, and then for reading it with such care and good judgment. I'd also like to thank Carrie Nichols Cantor, India Cooper, and Karen Drew for their care in reading the finished manuscript. Thanks as well to my agent Jake Elwell, and also to his colleague George Weiser. Finally, I'd like to thank the Anti-Defamation League of B'nai B'rith for placing their incomparable library at my disposal, and I'd like specifically to thank Alan M. Schwartz and Marc Caplan for all the help they gave me.

INDEX